Landmark Vi

French Al

Paul Scola

Dedications

To my wife, Angela, for her assistance and note taking.
To my children, Clare, Anne-Marie and Thomas for their interest and encouragement.
To Sister Louis Bertrand O.P. for her help and support in getting to know this fascinating region.

Acknowledgements

Richard Brocklehurst for use of his photographs.
The officials of French Tourist Offices for their advice.

Published by

Landmark Publishing
Ashbourne Hall, Cokayne Ave, Ashbourne,
Derbyshire DE6 1EJ England

Copyright Code for the Photographs

A - Paul Scola

B - Richard Brocklehurst

C - Comité Départemental du Tourisme, Isére

D - 123 Savoie

E - Comité Régional du Tourisme, Franche Comté

F - Comité Dolin, Chambéry, France

G - Maison Dolin, Chambéry, France

H - Musée Opinel, Saint Jean de Maurienne, France

The corresponding code is clearly marked at the end of each caption.

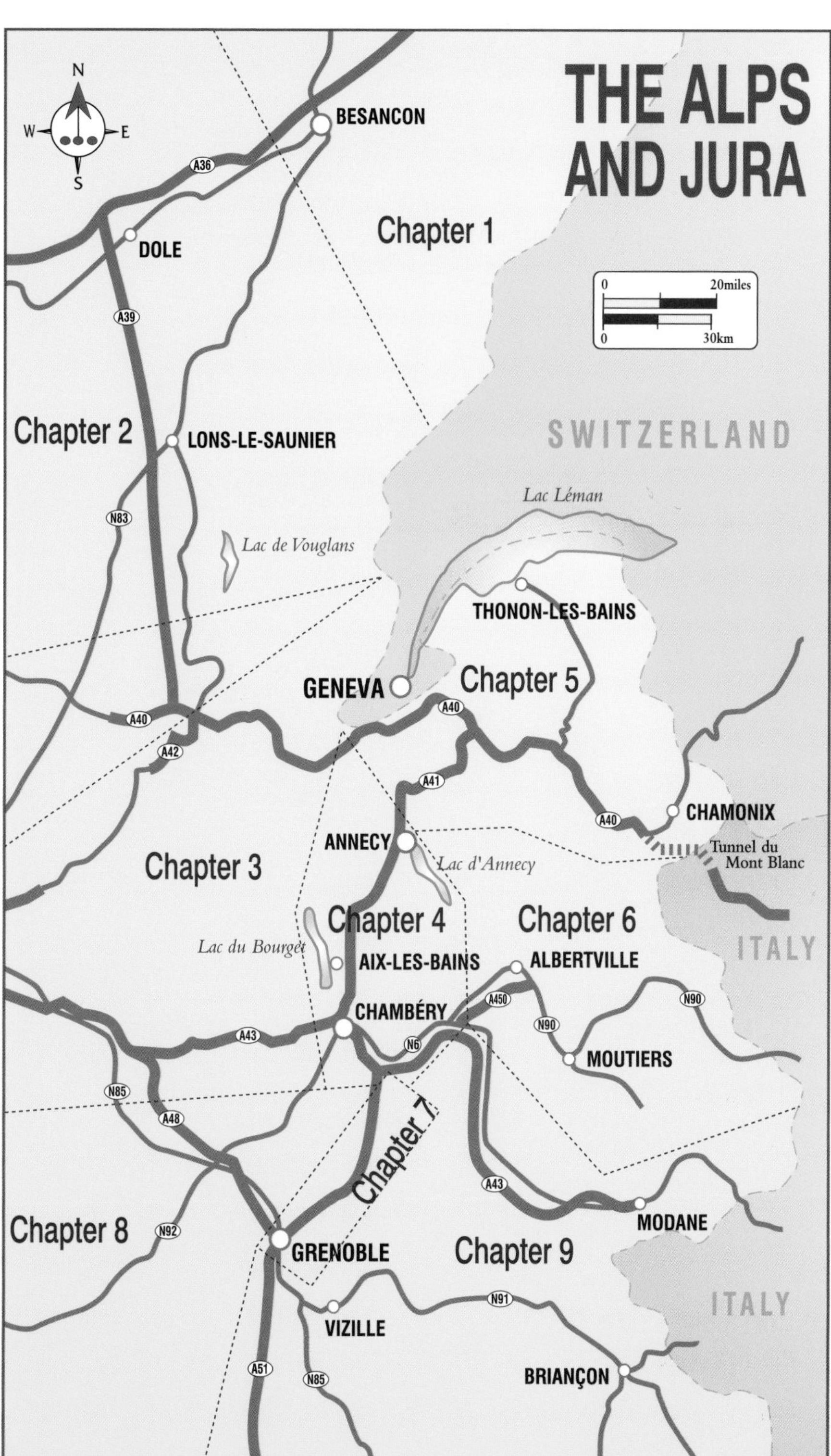
THE ALPS
AND JURA
N
S
W
E
0
20miles
0
30km
BESANCON
A36
DOLE
A39
Chapter 1
Chapter 2
LONS-LE-SAUNIER
N83
SWITZERLAND
Lac Léman
Lac de Vouglans
THONON-LES-BAINS
GENEVA
Chapter 5
A40
A42
A41
A40
CHAMONIX
Tunnel du
Mont Blanc
ANNECY
Lac d'Annecy
Chapter 3
Chapter 4
Chapter 6
Lac du Bourget
AIX-LES-BAINS
ALBERTVILLE
ITALY
A450
N90
CHAMBÉRY
A43
N6
N90
MOUTIERS
N85
A48
Chapter 7
A43
MODANE
Chapter 8
N92
GRENOBLE
Chapter 9
ITALY
VIZILLE
N91
A51
N85
BRIANÇON

Contents

Welcome to the

French Alps & Jura

*Opposite page: Houses at Annecy reflected in the Canal du Thiou. *A*
*Left: Chartreuse, Cross-country skiing. *C*

This most mountainous region of France falls into three quite distinct areas, the Jura (from the Celtic, meaning 'forest') to the north, the Savoie region (or Savoy as it is known to English-speakers) around Mont Blanc, and the mountains to the south of Savoie, the Hautes Alpes (High Alps).

Top Tips

Aiguille du Midi, Chamonix

Take this highest cable car in Europe and travel 2500 vertical metres in 25 minutes. Wear warm clothes, it is a lot colder at 3,842 metres. Complete the journey by taking the spectacular cable car across the glaciers to the Pointe Helbronner.

Grenoble Museums

It would be easy to spend the day in the Musée des Beaux Arts, built in 1994 and housing wonderful works of art, but a short walk across the river or a ride in the Cable Car takes you to another excellent museum, the Musée Dauphinois.

Besançon Citadel

Within the walls of the citadel there are several places of interest from museums about daily life in the Franche-Comté region to a very interesting small zoo. On the way up to the citadel you could call into the Cathedral to see the Astronomical clock with its 30,000 working parts.

Beaufort Cheese Making Cooperative

Beaufort is a beautiful Alpine town, set in its own valley, the Beaufortain. In the centre of the town, surrounded by mountains on all sides is the Cheese Cooperative. You can see how the cheese is made and part of the exhibit is a lovely film of life in the valley. Finally you get a chance to taste this "Prince des Gruyères".

Couvent de la Grande Chartreuse

Although the monastery and church are reserved for the monks, the exhibition centre gives visitors have a very good opportunity to understand what has led people over the centuries to devote themselves to the contemplative life in this delightful spot, set in its own "Zone du silence".

The mountains continue on to the Mediterranean coast of France as Les Alpes Maritimes (Maritime Alps), but these are rather different in nature and fall outside the scope of this guide.

The French Alps and the Jura have become a favourite area for visitors to France. In winter they provide sports of the very highest quality and variety for every type of skier and snowboarder, but in many ways this is not the most interesting of the many facilities that the area offers. The region has a fascinating history and is full of indications of how people have lived there throughout the ages. It is of especial interest to the nature lover — it has the largest National Park in France as well as others of equal reputation in addition to many regional parks. The walker has a great variety of terrain to explore and scenery unparalleled anywhere else in Europe. For the sports-minded, every activity is catered for from mountain-biking to playing tennis in clear, unpolluted air at 6,560ft (2,000m). At lower altitude there are beautiful lakes where sailing is available, which also have beaches for those who simply wish to relax.

The region is 175 miles (280km) from north to south and 80 miles (129km) wide. To the east Switzerland and Italy can be reached very easily in places. The Jura actually spills over into Switzerland where it is known as 'Le Jura Suisse'. As well as the land-frontier, the Lake of Geneva (Lac Léman) also acts as a border with Switzerland. The region then borders on Italy. There are fewer crossing points into Italy, but two dramatic tunnels, the Mont Blanc and further south the Fréjus, lead into Italy. The mountain passes, the Petit St Bernard, the Mont Cenis and the Montgenèvre are only certain to be open in the summer.

Regions, Provinces and Departments

The region covered in this guide is not one single administrative unit. Before the revolution, mainland France used to be made up of provinces but it was then divided into departments. In recent times, in an attempt to update and streamline administration within France, the country is being divided once again into *régions*. These regions tend to be very large, and the area covered by this guide covers the southern part of the region of Franche-Comté in the north, and about half of the region of Rhône-Alpes in the south. Franche Comté, one of the smaller French regions, is centred on Besançon, the northernmost town in this guide. Rhône-Alpes, one of the largest and most dynamic regions, is administered from Lyon which lies to the west, but the Alpine section of the region is very important economically and has Grenoble as its capital.

Certain of the pre-revolutionary provinces still figure in people's minds very strongly, and there are three in the region which create a sense of identity for those who live in them. These are the èèè Comté in the north, and Savoie and the Dauphiné in the south. Savoie was one of the last regions to become a part of France and many people who live there would still say that they are Savoyard first and French second.

Wildlife

The region is noted for the extent and variety of wildlife in all its forms. It is a paradise for nature lovers whatever their level of knowledge and expertise. Because of this heritage the movement in France to conserve wildlife began in this area and has gained enormously in impetus recently. The region now boasts one of the most developed national parks in Europe, the Parc National de la Vanoise, as well as the Parc National des Écrins. Besides these two parks, there are the Parc Régional du Vercors south-west of Grenoble and the Réserve Nationale des Bauges to the east of Chambéry. There is an ever-increasing number of smaller parks, such as the Parc du Haut Jura.

Within the parks, hunting is strictly forbidden, as are overnight bivouacking, walking dogs and picking flowers. However, walkers are positively encouraged. Accommodation is well organized with numerous mountain huts, run by the parks or the Club Alpin Français. One of the reasons for the setting up of the park was the effect that uncontrolled access to the area was having on wild animals such as the chamois and the ibex, which were almost threatened with extinction. Now there are ever-increasing numbers of both.

The parks are all of interest, often for different reasons. The Réserve Nationale des Bauges, despite its proximity to large towns such as Chambéry, Aix-les-Bains and Annecy is noted for its wild sheep with their spiral-shaped horns. Further north in the Jura region there are many parks and reserves set up to protect plants and trees. For example in the Forét de la Joux, near Champagnole, there is the Réserve de la Glacière where the trees are officially protected.

In the Jura about 40 per cent of the land surface is covered by trees although this rises to over 60 per cent in the Valserine Valley. Seventy per cent of the Chartreuse region is forest. The Alps are not so thickly covered because the valleys are heavily cultivated and trees do not generally grow above 5,900ft (1,800m).

Although the direction in which the slope faces is important in mountain areas with regard to the trees that grow there, it is mainly the height that determines which type will grow. Generally it is found that trees which grow on the plain, such as oaks, sycamore and chestnut will grow freely up to about 2,620ft (800m). Above this height, although there are deciduous trees in favourable conditions, the forests are mainly composed of conifers. The main exception is the beech tree that grows up to about 4,920ft (1,500m). This makes a very colourful picture in the autumn as the leaves change colour. Above 4,920ft (1,500m) it is rare to find any trees other than conifers. There are many varieties of conifer in the region, but the three main ones are the fir, the spruce and the larch. Some of these conifers can grow to an immense size. Perhaps the most famous single one is the Sapin Président in the Forêt de la Joux at over 148ft (45m) high and 13ft (4m) around the circumference.

Many of the birds and animals in the Jura and the Alps rely on the trees and forests to provide cover and food, but a surprisingly large number exist above the tree line. Many of these, such as the mountain hare and the ptarmigan are related to similar species found in the Arctic and are recognised to be a direct throwback to the Ice Age. For them the Alpine terrain is a sort of Arctic island in the middle of the temperate zone.

The most well-known wild animals found at high altitude are the ibex, the chamois and the marmot. The male and female ibex move around in groups with their young often numbering as many as thirty or forty. In winter they have a light brown coat which changes to pale yellow in summer. The males have huge ringed horns that can measure as much as a metre long. The chamois are smaller than the ibex and have small curved horns. Their coat also depends upon the season. In winter it is long, shaggy and dark brown and in summer smooth and dark yellow. Although they do not live exclusively in the national parks, it would be quite difficult for the non-specialist visitor to get a sighting outside them. The same could be said about the marmot. These are rodents about the same size as a rabbit, with a long brown coat. They hibernate, and in the autumn they can be seen at the entrance to their burrows sitting on their hind legs all fattened up for a long winter underground. They have a very characteristic cry which echoes round the mountains.

There are many other animals typical of the region, such as mountain hare and ermine, both of which adopt a white coat in the winter. They are very difficult to spot, as are the Alpine shrew, vole and field mouse, which live above the treeline up to 9,840fft (3,000m). Other wild animals such as foxes, martens, weasels and polecats range over the whole region and increasingly wolves have been known to visit the area, particularly in the Belledonne range of mountains. The forests also protect many other lowland wild animals, as different as the boars, which are especially numerous in the Bauges and the red squirrels that can be seen in the High Jura above St Claude.

Birds are important contributors to the food chain in the Jura and the Alps, and in the lower regions many varieties common throughout Northern Europe can be seen. The nuthatch with its long straight bill and orange underbelly, the pied woodpecker with its vivid red plumage and short sharp drilling sound, and the crossbill with its crossed beak and sharp 'jip', 'jip', 'jip' call are all to be found in the forest area up to 5,900ft (1,800m). Predatory birds such as kestrels, hawks and buzzards are much in evidence at the lower levels. Just below the snowline is the habitat of the most famous Alpine birds. The Alpine chough with its long yellow beak, its black plumage and its shrill 'chirrish' cry that echoes round the hillsides is one of the most common. The ptarmigan, which changes colour from grey with a white underbelly to pure white in winter and the golden eagle live in the High Alps and can be spotted in the Parc National des Écrins.

The flora of the region is especially interesting for the visitor, because it is possible to see with in a matter of hours a variety of plants that would need a journey of thousands of miles on level ground. This is how markedly the climate and the soil change as one rises from the valleys to the high mountains.

Lowland plants are similar to species throughout Northern Europe, but often grow very vigorously in this area because of the high rainfall, the frequent protection afforded by the mountains and the intensity of the sun in the spring. Although plant life in this band is controlled by man's activities to a great extent, there is still much of interest, from wild strawberries in the hedgerows to poppies in the cornfields. In the fields a tall yellow flower might be seen. This is the yellow gentian, very different from its small blue Alpine namesake. This is considered poisonous by grazing cattle and is left well alone by them, but its long roots are used to make Genepi, a powerful alcoholic drink.

The forest area harbours a rich variety of bushes and plants. Bilberries are numerous throughout the region, as are primrose, violets, lily of the valley and cyclamen. Many bushes grow in the undergrowth such as wild cherries, hazel and box. The forests also encourage the growth of mushrooms. Many of these are edible and some such as the morille mushroom, found especially under ash trees are very sought after and consequently very expensive.

Above the tree line is the habitat of the true Alpine plants. They are very accessible nowadays and are at their best in the spring and summer. There are cultivated gardens of Alpine flowers such as at the Col de Lauteret or Samoëns, but the real pleasure is coming upon the different species almost by accident, while exploring the high mountains by car or on foot. In the Jura there are many species in the area of Mont Rond above the Col de la Faucille and in the Alps any of the high passes such as the Col de la Croix de Fer will give the visitor an opportunity to see Alpine plants at close quarters. But these areas must be treated with care. This is illustrated by the case of the edelweiss, which became the symbol of the High Alps. It suffered from its popularity and although still in existence in the Jura and the Alps is hard to find. The picking of flowers is absolutely forbidden in the national parks.

The upland meadows are full of flowers such as the dark blue spring gentian and trumpet gentian, the brilliant yellow 'Boules d'or', and pink-coloured wild orchids. Above the meadows, plants such as the Alpine asters, purple saxifrage and campanula seem to thrive on the rocky soil and the high altitude.

Food and Drink

There are two main wine-growing areas which produce wine of the very highest quality. These are in the Jura between Lons Le Saunier and Arbois and in Savoie between Chambéry and Montmélian. But there are many other areas that produce good wine, notably in the Bugey and in the hills south of Lac Léman.

Although there are many wines grouped under the title Côtes du Jura, the two most famous *crus* or types of wine are Arbois and Château-Chalon. Most of the wine produced is of good enough quality to have an Appellation d'Origine Contrôlée. Arbois was the first to get this in 1936. The Jura produces red and white as well as rosé and sparkling wines. In addition, there are two other Jura wines that are well known and certainly worth trying. These are the Vin Jaune, Yellow Wine, and the Vin de Paille, Straw Wine.

Red and rosé wines, the best of which come from the Arbois area, are becoming more popular, although at one time they were less appreciated than the white or yellow wines. They are obtained either using Poulsard grapes on their own or mixing them with Trousseau or Pinot. They have a delicate bouquet and are often drunk with the *entrée*. The white wines of the area are made from the Chardonnay grape and tend to be very dry. The famous Vin de Paille is more an apéritif or a digestive than a wine, it is often up to 17 per cent proof.

The hills at the entrance to the Combe de Savoie in the Alps southeast of Chambéry are covered in vineyards. These grow mainly Mondeuse and Gamay grapes. From these come the Vins de Savoie, both red and white. Montmélian and St Jean-de-la-Porte are the most appreciated red wines, both made from Mondeuse grapes. Generally, the white wines of this region and the area to the south of Lac Léman are better regarded than the red. Aprémont and Chignin are among the best from Savoie, while Crépy or Frangy from the lakeside region go very well with fish.

Cheese-making has been a tradition for many centuries, especially in mountain regions. Every area within the region has developed its own cheese with its particular characteristics. In the Jura the most common cheese is the Comté, but there are many others such as Morbier, Bleu de Gex and Mont d'Or. In the Alps the two cheeses most widely sold and eaten are Tomme and Reblochon, but amongst the others are goats' cheeses, blue-veined cheeses, such as Sassenage as well as the "Prince Des Gruyères", the incomparable Beaufort.

Many traditional dishes have cheese as their basic ingredient. One basic cheese dish is the raclette. The name comes from the French word for 'to scrape'. A large cheese is halved and the edge is suspended over a flame. As the cheese becomes runny, it is scraped oft and put on to the guests' plates one at a time to be eaten with salad. Another much better known dish is the Fondue Savoyarde. There are many recipes for this, but it is a mixture of cheese, wine, garlic and other ingredients, such as Kirsch and nutmeg, melted in a bowl. To get the cheese, guests dip chunks of bread into the mixture on the end of a long fork. It is often said that white wine should be drunk with a fondue, but traditionally a Marc de Savoie or a Kirsch is preferred, because it is claimed that it assists in the digestion of the cheese. Another cheese dish, seen on the menus of most restaurants, is the Tartiflette, which uses a whole Reblochon. This is presented as a traditional mountain recipe but was only invented relatively recently. It is a dish of slices of cheese, diced potato, cream and bacon, topped off with half a Reblochon cheese. If pasta is used instead of potato, it is called a croziflette.

Apart from its wines and cheeses, the region has many other specialties obtained from the lakes, rivers and fields, or based on locally-grown ingredients. The area is well-served with fish, which is a popular starter throughout the Jura and the Alps, but especially on the shores of Lac Léman. The rivers and lakes provide trout, pike, lavaret and char. They are cooked in a variety of ways according to traditional recipes. Cooked meats are another regional speciality. The Jura is well known for its smoked ham and its delicious saucisse de Morteau. These are smoked in a huge open chimney called a *tuyé*. The distinguishing feature of the sausage is the wooden peg used to fold the skin at one end. The Alps have many varieties of cooked meats and sausages, but there are also sausages made from a mixture of meat and vegetables, called pormoniers.

The region provides many ingredients that have become important parts of local dishes, from mushrooms and maize to wild strawberries and bilberries. The region is famous for its fruit tarts, using the locally-picked fruit. Bilberry tarts are particularly delicious in Savoie. Every sort of mushroom is found in the woods of the Jura and the Alps, but one of the most sought-after is the morille, which is a sort of truffle, a speciality of the Jura.

Maize, for many years considered to be the food of the very poor has come back into fashion as a regional speciality. It can be found in many dishes, in the form of a soup called *gaude* in the Jura, or as a cake called *polenta* in the Alps.

A local dish that is now known throughout the world is the *gratin Dauphinois,* based on diced potatoes and milk. There are many different recipes for both *gratin Dauphinois* and *gratin Savoyard,* each one claiming that it is the original. Some say that eggs should be added to the basic potatoes and milk, others that grated cheese should be added to the top before browning, while certain experts say that a real *gratin Dauphinois* has neither eggs or cheese.

There has been a tradition in the mountains of brewing every kind of alcoholic drink from every kind of available fruit, berry or plant. This tradition was certainly helped by the monks in the great number of monasteries that dotted the region. It is seen nowadays in the production of Chartreuse, although this does not take place in the monastery any more, but in the neighbouring town of Voiron. The drink is based on a secret sixteenth-century recipe that uses over a hundred plants as well as wine and honey. Green Chartreuse, the most widely drunk, is 55 per cent proof. The other types of Chartreuse tend to be less strong.

A very popular Vermouth is made in Chambéry that many people prefer to its North Italian equivalent. In the region of Pontarlier in the Jura there are many types of liqueur, using raspberries, strawberries and bilberries. Absinthe is still produced in Pontarlier. Further south in the Alps many liqueurs are made from Pear Brandy to Walnut Liqueur. Finally, a drink not to be missed is the Marc de Savoie, a strong white eau-de-vie, distilled from pressed grape skins. It is as smooth as cognac, but has a more earthy flavour and tastes less sweet.

1. Besançon & the Doubs

The northern part of the French Jura takes up most of department No 25, the Doubs. The name is hardly surprising since most of the region lies within the huge loop of the River Doubs as it flows northeast from its source and then back through Besançon towards Central France.

The highest point of the area, the Mont d'Or at 4,788ft (1,460m), is in the southern part of the region close to the source of the Doubs, which gets its name from the Latin word, Dubitatus - doubtful about where it is going. What is particularly striking about the countryside here is the way that in places the rivers have cut their way deep into the limestone, creating gorges of great depth. Although the countryside is very pleasant with upland farms and villages, the main interest lies in the rivers and the towns and villages that are to be

Opposite: Vue de Besançon. *E

BESANÇON AND THE DOUBS

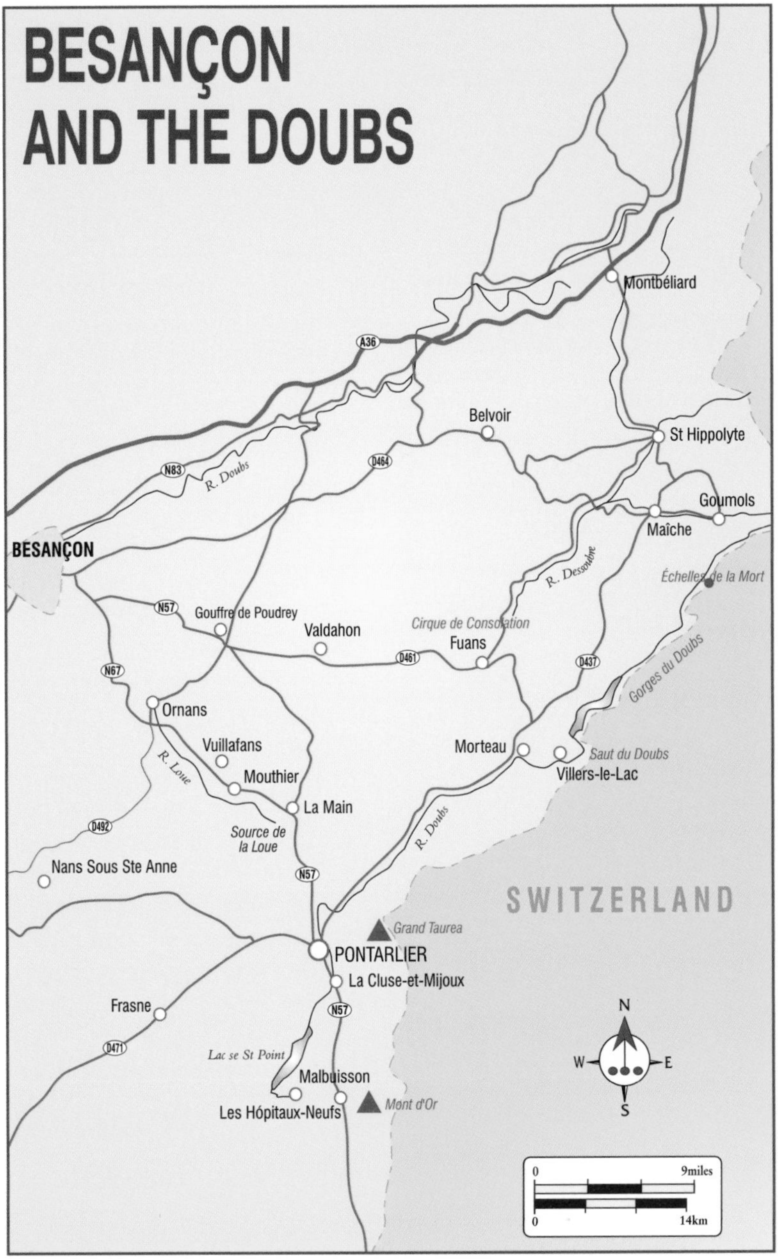

A36
N83
R. Doubs
D464
Montbéliard
Belvoir
St Hippolyte
Goumols
Maîche
BESANÇON
Échelles de la Mort
R. Dessoubre
N57
Gouffre de Poudrey
Valdahon
Cirque de Consolation
Fuans
D461
D437
Gorges du Doubs
N67
Ornans
Vuillafans
Mouthier
R. Loue
La Main
Morteau
Villers-le-Lac
Saut du Doubs
Source de la Loue
R. Doubs
D492
Nans Sous Ste Anne
N57
SWITZERLAND
Grand Taurea
PONTARLIER
La Cluse-et-Mijoux
Frasne
N57
D471
Lac se St Point
Malbuisson
Les Hôpitaux-Neufs
Mont d'Or
N
W
E
S
0
9miles
0
14km

found on their banks.

A good way to explore the region and its rivers is to use Besançon as a base and then make excursions in different directions to take in all the major points of interest. An excursion east of Besançon would go towards the Swiss border and could include the Dessoubre, a delightful tributary of the Doubs, as well as the Gorges du Doubs where the river cuts deepest into the limestone mountains. An excursion south could take in the valley of the Loue and with a short journey across country could meet up with the early part of the Doubs, passing the Lac de St Point and Lac de Remoray. This could then be a starting point for visiting the central section of the Jura to the west, although this could also be done by following the Doubs as it flows calmly and peacefully through countryside west from Besançon.

Besançon

Before visiting Besançon, the bustling and busy Capital of the Franche Comté, it is best to see the town and its layout from one of the nearby forts. The river makes the most extraordinary loop almost coming back on itself. At the narrowest point of the loop, the two stretches of water are prevented from joining up by a high rocky outcrop, on top of which in a near impregnable position overlooking the town is the Citadelle. In fact a subterranean canal does connect the two parts of the river, which helps to create the idea that the centre of the city is on an island. The map shows the middle of the city in the shape of a lyre or ancient harp and the streets stretch up the middle like strings. The central one is the Grande Rue, a pedestrianised thoroughfare that goes from the river almost in a straight line to the cathedral and the gates of the Citadelle.

Of the two forts that are outside the loop of the river, the Fort de Chaudanne gives a better view of the town. However if you are entering Besançon by the N57 from the direction of the motorway, the Fort de Brégille is easier to reach. Bear left, skirt the river through the trees of the Promenade Micaud and turning left again, cross the railway by a level-crossing. The steep winding road leads up to a vantage point on a shaded, grassy area in front of the forbidding walls of the fort. The Citadelle is straight opposite on its rocky base with the wood-covered hills behind and the town away to the right. The multi-coloured tiles of the buildings in the centre and the red tiles of the other buildings within the loop give an indication of the development of the town.

It is a good idea to park near the Pont de la République, because it will be possible to visit the excellent information office, a modern building at the end of the Promenade Micaud. This is the starting point for Le Petit Train. The itinerary takes in the Citadelle where it is possible to break the journey, as well as all the major tourist attractions within the town. For those who have the time, usually over 2 hours, this is an excellent way to get to know the town.

While crossing the bridge, it is possible to look down and see the embarcation point for the pleasure boats that provide another and even more original way of seeing the town. They follow the Doubs downstream, go through a lock and then pass through the underground canal beneath the Citadelle before joining the river upstream and completing the circle. The journey takes about an hour-and-a-quarter, but there are not many sailings, so it is best to check the times and plan accordingly while crossing the Pont de La République. The Rue de la République goes directly to the centre of the town, where it meets the Grande Rue at the animated Place St Pierre with its modern fountains and café terraces taking over one corner of the square. It is an ideal place for a rest before visiting the many interesting attractions of the town.

Facing on to the square is the Hôtel de Ville, the sixteenth century town hall. To the right of the main door is a large niche that used to house a bronze fountain representing Emperor Charles V astride a double-headed eagle. This disappeared during the Revolution, leaving only the eagle of Besançon above the main doorway. The other building looking on to the square facing the Hôtel de Ville is the Church of St Pierre. This neo-classical building with its wrought-iron cross is an eighteenth-century reconstruction of an earlier church.

The temptation is to turn immediately towards the Citadelle to visit Besançon's most obvious attractions. However, it is worth turning right towards the river and crossing over the Pont Battant. The Church of Ste Madeleine, built between 1746 and 1766 with the two towers added a century later, is on the left just over the river. It faces on to the Place Jouffrey, named after the Marquis de Jouffrey d'Abbans, who used the Doubs to test out his new invention, the steam-driven boat. Besançon is proud of its inventors. The cinema pioneers, the Lumière brothers were born in the town, as was the Comte de Chardonnet, who invented the first ever artificial textile, Chardonnet Silk based on nitrocellulose.

Returning back across the bridge, the eye is caught by the long regular terraces of houses overlooking the river. These were designed and built by Vauban, more famous for the forts and defence works that he constructed throughout eastern France and especially round Besançon. Hardly surprisingly the road in front of them is called the Quai Vauban.

On entering the Grande Rue, a left turn goes towards the Place de La Révolution, a bustling market area in the mornings. At the end of the market buildings is a fountain, surmounted by a huge ornamental vase. On the far side of the square is the Musée des Beaux Arts, the Art Gallery, housed in what

The Vouivre

The calm and shady ource of the River Loue is associated with the legend of the Vouivre, a winged serpent, that only came out of its cave once a year. This was between the first and last stroke of midnight on Christmas Day, giving just enough time for the bravest to slip into his cave and steal some of his treasure. This legendary serpent has an English equivalent in the Wyvern.

The Citadelle in Besançon

The road up to the Citadelle begins to rise steeply behind the cathedral, with glimpses of the lovely tiled roof of the cathedral tower through the trees, and on the final bend, as the road turns back on itself by one of the outer walls, an impression is gained of the Citadelle's solidity and strength. The building of the Citadelle took from 1674 to 1711 and was so costly that Louis XIV was heard to sigh, 'If only the walls of Besançon were made of gold...'. As an institution it has had a chequered career, first it was a barracks, then a Cadet School and a prison before becoming a fortress again in 1870. Sadly, during World War II it was a place of execution for the many Resistance fighters captured in the area. There is so much to see at the Citadelle that a visit could take at least half a day. It is possible to drive up and park outside the Citadelle for the duration of a visit. However the main attractions of the Citadelle are the museums, but a word of warning - these are all closed on Tuesdays.

To enter, the visitor passes into the outer area of the fort through the Front St Etienne. Within this building to the left are the restaurant, the bar and the toilets. The restaurant has a terrace with very good views of the town. Behind the Front St Etienne there is a child's playground in the open ground to the left, while to the right in the corner the low building is the Musée Agraire. This houses a collection of agricultural implements and vehicles, mainly from Franche Comté.

The path leads through some defence works and crosses over a bridge to enter the main part of the fort through the Front Royal. The tower to the left of the Front Royal is the Tour du Roi, and to the right the Tour de La Reine. Both provide different, but excellent viewpoints over the town and the River

was once the Hay Market. The interior courtyard was entirely rebuilt in a most imaginative way by the architect L. Miquel. He was a pupil of Le Corbusier, whose most famous construction, the church at Ronchamp, is 50 miles (80km) north-east of Besançon.

After returning to the Grande Rue and going towards the Citadelle, it is worth taking a right turn just before reaching the Place St Pierre to see the Palais de Justice, which is behind the town hall. It has very beautiful wrought-iron gates, with the date 1861 highlighted in gold. For the visitor who wants to go direct to the Citadelle from the Place St Pierre, it is possible to catch 'Le Petit Train' that passes every 45 minutes on its way up to the fort.

In the Grande Rue on the right is the magnificent Palais de Granvelle, a town house built for Nicolas de Granvelle in 1540, where the courtyard is often filled by a stage and chairs since it is a favourite venue for concerts and other musical events. This is especially the case during Besançon's music festivals in September, when evening jazz concerts

Doubs below. The long building down the centre of the fort is the old Cadets' Barracks. It now holds the Musée de la Résistance et de la Déportation as well as the Local Archaeological Records. Entry to the Resistance Museum is not allowed to young children. To the left of this long building, the most obvious construction is the well. This is 433ft (132m) deep and had to be driven down through the rock. The human treadmill, used to haul up the water buckets is an interesting feature. Beside the well is a memorial to Resistance fighters executed in the Citadelle and next to that is the Chapelle St Etienne on the site of the original church. The Musée Comtois is to the right of the Front Royal, and on the left is an interesting museum of dairy production. Notice the one-legged milking stools, used throughout the Jura and the Alps at one time.

To the right of the Cadets' Barracks, facing across the Cour des Cadets is the Musée d'Histoire Naturelle containing an excellent exhibition of world and local wildlife. At the back of the courtyard is the Front de Secours and beyond this, the zoo. It is worth going through the zoo and to the right to reach the Tarragnoz look-out post, with its impressive views of the valley and the river below. In a break in the trees towards the south the statue of Notre-Dame-de-la-Libération can be seen.

More regional wild life, such as fish and snakes, is on show in the Aquarium between the Natural History Museum and the zoo. The little zoo behind the Front de Secours has animals such as lions, Siberian tigers and primates as well as birds like flamingo and the stork. It is pleasantly laid out and uses the original defensive works to the best advantage.

are given in the open air. The Palais now houses the excellent Musée du Temps, which concentrates on the region's clockmaking history with many outstanding examples of the craft.

As the Grande Rue continues towards the Citadelle, it passes through what was the original Roman settlement. The first evidence is on the left in the Square Castan, named after the archaeologist who unearthed the remains of a huge Roman theatre and temple complex. The four pillars, which give some idea of the scale of the buildings, were part of a raised water tank fed by an aqueduct. The road then goes through the most striking Roman relic, the Porte Noire. Despite its name, this was not a gateway, but rather a Triumphal Arch, probably built in the second century and dedicated to Marcus Aurelius. It has a more detailed decoration than any other known Roman arch.

Immediately behind the Porte Noire is the Cathédrale St Jean. This can be entered through the side door that can be seen from the Porte Noire. The cathedral was one of two in the city,

The Château de Joux

The Château de Joux, is one of the most well known castles in Franche Comté. It can be seen from a long way off as it is approached from Pontarlier, since it towers over the valley acting as an obvious guardian over the lines of communication south. It began life as a robber baron's castle in the ninth century, built in order to exact tolls from passing merchants, and later became a prison. Nowadays it is a museum of arms and military uniform. Even for those not interested in the museum, the building is very interesting and impressive. It is quite easy to get to by road, which is one way, up from the Pontarlier side and down on the far side, and there is a very large car park at the top. Between 15 and 19 August, the castle is the setting for the Festival des Nuits de Joux.

the other stood on the site of the Citadelle but was demolished in 1675 by Vauban to make way for his new plans. The cathedral has a lovely round altar, called "La Rose St Jean" and a number of good paintings. The Astronomical Clock in the cathedral is certainly worth a visit. This wonderful mechanism, built in 1857 and restored in 1900, has 30,000 moving parts, 70 dials and a parade of 21 mechanical figures. It can give 122 different indications of time and astronomical positions. Visit it if possible on the hour to see the movements in action.

Just to the east towards the river are the only city gates still in existence, the Porte Rivotte, dating back to the sixteenth century. The gates have two fine towers with beautiful circular tiled roofs. These are seen to better advantage if you walk through and look back from near the railway bridge. When Besançon became French, Louis XIV had the royal sun emblem put onto the front on the pediment. Returning to the centre of town along the Rue Rivotte and the Rue de Pontarlier via the Place J. Cornet, there are a number of fine town houses, such as No 2 Place J. Cornet, the birthplace of De Chardonnet, the inventor of artificial silk.

East of Besançon

The villages in the countryside to the east of Besançon are quite isolated and are authentic agricultural communities centred round working farms. Many of these farms, where cheese is produced, have begun to sell direct to the public and provide the visitor with a good opportunity to taste the produce. For example in the village of Épenouse, 6 miles ($9^1/_2$km) north of Valdahon, the Fromagerie Artisanale Liechti welcomes visitors and encourages them to taste the wide range of cheeses in the 'Cave de Dégustation'.

The visitor will find most visual interest in the area round the Gorges du Doubs, where the river forms the border with Switzerland. To reach this area, take the N57, the road to Pontarlier and Lausanne, but be prepared to take a left turn along the D461 towards Valdahon and Morteau about a mile after the Gouffre de Poudrey. This huge cave is on the left of the N57 about 14 miles ($22^1/_2$km) from Besançon, it is the largest cave in France and claims to be one of the largest in Europe and its dimensions are certainly impressive. It is 197ft (60m) high, 360ft (110m) deep and 1,968ft (600m) across. There are guided visits every half hour in the summer, except during a lunch period from 12 noon until 1.3Opm. The most remarkable aspect of this cave is the number and size of stalagmites and stalactites. Some of them are over 23ft (7m) in height and date back many hundreds of thousands of years. The illumination in the cave shows them up to very good effect.

There is a sign to the left in Fuans to the Cirque de Consolation, but for a good view of the Cirque, the amphitheatre, it is best to go straight on past this turn. About 2 miles (3km) further on, turn left by a café and then turn left immediately down a rough track past the TV mast. Affer a short drive along this track, there is an obvious parking spot. A short walk will lead to the Roche du Prêtre, a look-out point over the Cirque de Consolation, the natural amphitheatre formed originally by the River Dessoubre. The valley of the Dessoubre stretches away ahead. Down in the valley bottom below are the buildings of a monastery. After viewing the valley from this vantage point, return to the village of Fuans and take a right turn following the sign to the Cirque de Consolation. The road continues down through the trees, at one time through a tunnel, until the valley bottom is reached. Drive into the car park of the monastery— now used as a seminary. This is a good point from which to explore the park and visit the chapel. There is a covered area next to the car park, as well as a huge covered building outside the gates, either of which can be used as a picnic site. The park makes a delightful walk through the woods in this beautiful, unspoiled spot.

A right turn on leaving the monastery car park leads down the valley of the Dessoubre towards St Hippolyte. This river has the reputation of being the prettiest in the area and can be appreciated since the road follows it very closely along the whole of its length with many opportunities to stop and admire.

At Le Pont Neuf just over half-way to St Hippolyte, a left turn leads towards the village of Belvoir, 12 miles away (19km), where there is an excellent castle, dating from the twelfth century but restored in the 1950s by the French artist Pierre Jouffroy. Many of the artist's works are on view, but the chief exhibits are the furniture and the armour.

There is a centre of regional produce in nearby Provenchère. Here there is a museum, Aux Produits du Terroir Comtois, showing how cheese was produced over the ages, as well as a shop selling every kind of regional produce, cheese, smoked ham, Jura wine etc. From Belvoir, many roads lead east towards the Doubs and St Hippolyte.

Further upstream, the Doubs has been dammed both naturally and artificially to create long lakes. The first of these dams is the man made Barrage du Chatelot. This can be reached by taking the road to Le Pissoux to the left of the Le Russey-Morteau road. There are very steep roads into and out

*Palais Granvelle et son Musée du Temps. *I*

*The Château de Joux. *E*

*The 'Sant du Doubs'. *E*

Drives

The Goumois Corniche

St Hippolyte is at the confluence of the Dessoubre and the Doubs. Although a road follows the River Doubs, it is better to take the D437 towards Maîche. After about 5 miles (8km), a left turn goes towards the Goumois Corniche, the high-level road that overlooks the Doubs. There is a roadside map explaining the route. The road is not very well made up and needs care. At the beginning of the actual corniche, there is a seat on top of an old gun emplacement that gives a very good view of the valley below. From the road the woods and meadows on the Swiss side of the river look very neat and attractive as they come down the valley side. The frontier village of Goumois can be seen far below and can be reached by taking a left turn. Towards the end of the corniche, there is an excellent view down the length of the Gorges du Doubs, with cliffs pressing in on each side of the river leaving no room for a road or track on either bank.

Les Échelles de La Mort

Since the Doubs was the frontier, it was inevitably used for smuggling in times gone by and one of the remnants of this is a site further upstream, the Échelles de La Mort. This series of ladders up the cliffside, the 'Ladder of Death', was originally used by smugglers. It is certainly a site worth visiting but the way of reaching it by car needs a passport. Four miles ($6^1/_2$km) beyond the village of Charquemont, there is a border point into Switzerland. Visitors are usually waved through, but a passport is needed to get back into France. Immediately after the solid white frontier building, there is a sharp and difficult turn left, leading down to the power station of Le Refrain deep in the valley with the cliffs towering above. Park beside the power station and walk up the path towards the stairway. There are several series of steel ladders and although unlike the original wooden ones, they have been made safe and solid with handrails, they certainly demand a head for heights as they reach the belvedere at the top.

La République du Saugeais

Montbenoît near Pontarlier is of the capital the strangely named République Saugeais. There is a signpost at the roadside to this effect beside the road. It is not in fact an independent country of course, but the name (from a Swiss tribe called the Saugets) shows that the valley has a history of independence. In 1947 the local Prefet made the hoteler, M. Pourchet, President as a sort of joke, but it was built upon so that now the Republic has a President, a Prime Minister, an anthem and a flag.

of Le Pissoux.

The next dam upstream is entirely natural and has created above it a lake that stretches back 2½ miles (4km) to the town of Villers-le-Lac. It is an impressive stretch of water, at times hemmed in by cliffs well over a hundred feet (30m) high, but the main point of interest is where the river breaks through the natural dam and falls 75ft (23m) to its natural level, the famous Saut du Doubs. The most satisfying way to visit this site is to get a boat from Villers-le-Lac. It will take a good half an hour to go down the lake, at first open and light, then dark and dominated by the overhanging cliffs, until the end of the lake is reached. On the French side, there is a path past the souvenir stalls alongside the river until in about 10 minutes the waterfall is reached. It is a lovely walk through the trees next to the river that seems very peaceful and not very fast-flowing at this point, in contrast to the sound of the waterfall ahead. There is a protected viewpoint to look over the waterfall that is as impressive for the sheer quantity of water as for its height. Before returning to the lake, follow the signs to the right to the higher belvedere, giving good views of the waterfall and of the lower lake, the Lac de Moron, leading to the Barrage du Chatelot. There are paths from this point down to the water's edge, but they are very steep and not really to be recommended.

The Saut du Doubs can be reached by car, avoiding the need to catch a boat. From the centre of Villers, drive towards Le Pissoux. Just after the Restaurant du Belvédère, on the right-hand side going towards Le Pissoux, there is a sign to the hamlet of Les Vions. Follow the road for about half-a-mile and park. The road continues down, but it is forbidden to ordinary traffic, there are no-entry signs on each side. This extremely steep road is to supply the cafés and shops at the end of the lake. Follow the road on foot, it is a quarter of an hour's steep walk down to the lake. To return to Villers-le-Lac, there is a corniche road that turns through the trees just past the car park. It threads its way through the trees and gives very impressive views of the Doubs over a hundred feet below. This road is not well made up and drops away very steeply in places. It needs great care, and in fact could be more satisfactory as a walk than a drive back to Villers-le-Lac. The river between Villers-le-Lac and Morteau is very calm and peaceful, running in a wide open valley. The town of Morteau got its name from the slowness of the river at this point — *matte eau* — dead water. A typical Jura upland town, Morteau has a long tradition of agriculture with the added interest of clock-making over the last 100 years. Besides the cheese and other dairy produce, Morteau is particularly famous for its smoked meats, and especially its cooked sausage. The most well-known is nicknamed the 'Jésus de Morteau'. Clock-making is represented by the Musée de l'Horlogerie du Haut Doubs. This lovely building, recently renovated, is a good example of a country house of the period, with huge open fire places and wooden floors. There is a particularly fine tiled stove in what was the kitchen downstairs. All around the salon on the left of the entrance are pictures relating episodes during the Spanish occupation of the

La Franche Comté

Once part of the County of Burgundy, the Franche Comté was set up as a free County in 1384 when it was given an element of independence with its capital in Dole. In 1493 it became part of the Habsburg Empire and was ruled from Spain. There are a number of Spanish influences, mainly architectural, throughout the region. The period of Spanish rule, particularly under Emperor Charles V, was seen as a golden age. Franche Comté was often invaded by the French. Louis X1V conquered the region in 1665. He was forced to return it, but not for long! In 1674 he revisited the region and finally annexed it. This was formalised in the treaty of Nijmegen in 1678. This period had two major effects that are seen to this day. Dole was deprived of its role as capital in revenge for its strong opposition and Besançon became the new capital. The second and more obvious effect was that Vauban, the King's fortification expert, created his famous forts in the region to house permanent garrisons and prevent any further attempts by the population or others to re-create the free County. The old County was divided into departments in 1790 and the name lost its resonance until in 1982 it was brought back to life when Franche Comté was formally recognised as one of the new administrative regions of France with Besançon as its capital. The Franche Comté lion lives on in the emblem of the Peugeot car company which was initially set up in the region.

Franche-Comté. The museum shows how the clock-making in the area was based in workshops rather than in large factories. Besides its agriculture and industry, Morteau is nowadays a tourist centre. It has an excellent three-star campsite on the banks of the river and many organised activities such as canoeing. Fishing is also extremely popular along the banks of the Doubs at this point. In the winter, under the title of Le Val de Morteau, all the villages around unite together to create a very well-organised centre for cross-country skiing - *le ski de fond.*

From Morteau, the D437 and D461 return to Besançon 40 miles (64km) to the north. Alternatively, the D437 going west joins the area to the south of Besançon at Pontarlier. The road to Pontarlier follows the line of the Doubs for the whole of its length. The Doubs, the railway and the road are all pushed together as they pass through the Défilé du Coin de la Roche. This valley, at no time particularly steep, runs into the Défilé d'Entre Roches, equally open and accessible. Just by the hamlet of Colombière between the two "defiles", next to an hotel on the right, are the very ornate doors of the Grotte-Chapelle de Notre-Dame de Remonot. This chapel is a place of pilgrimage since the water is said to be good for the eyes. A short walk away above the road there is another cave

Military Architecture

The whole region has been subject since Roman times to Military intervention, whether for territorial expansion or to protect trade routes. For this reason castles, forts and gun emplacements abound. The most famous of the builders is undoubtedly Sebastien de Vauban, Louis XIV's military architect. He developed the great forts throughout Eastern France. All are still standing and most can be visited. Vauban's were built to protect French territory but there are many others whose purpose was to keep out the French. These are the forts and fortifications found throughout Savoy, the most well known being the great line of forts at Esseillon in the Maurienne valley, built between 1817 and 1830, but not needed since Savoy became part of France in 1860. The next period of fort building came after France's defeat in 1870 and many were built on the border with Italy as a sort of high altitude Maginot line.

in the limestone cliff-face, the Grotte du Trésor.

The abbey church of Montbenoît nearby has cloisters dating from the fifteenth century with well-preserved vaulting. The interior of the church, especially the stalls built in the early sixteenth century, owes its richness to the gift of one man, Ferry Carondelet, one of Charles V's ministers. He had been Charles' ambassador in Rome and when he returned to Franche-Comté, he brought back many ideas from Renaissance Italy that he put into practice in churches such as Montbenoît and the Cathédrale St Jean in Besançon, where

*Citadel. *E*

*A farm on the Swiss border near Morteau. *E*

he is buried. There is no signpost to say that you are leaving the République Saugeais, but the outskirts of Pontarlier indicate its end. Pontarlier is one of the main towns on the N57 and is an important link in any excursion south from Besançon.

South of Besançon

South of Besançon is the valley of the River Loue and beyond it the upper reaches of the River Doubs. The quickest way to reach the Loue Valley is to take the N57 out of Besançon and 6 miles (10km) later take the D67 off to the right in the direction of Ornans. As the N57 leaves Besançon, it passes through a short rock tunnel. This is the Porte Taillée, the Cut Gate. It was cut by the Romans to take into the city the aqueduct that was to feed the elevated reservoir in the present-day Square Castan. Immediately after this tunnel, a steep little road to the right leads up to the statue of Notre-Dame de la Libération, the city's war memorial. From this statue, minor roads through the village of La Vèze meet the D67 at its junction with the N57. Instead of taking the D67 at this point, it is possible to continue along the N57 until the village of Mamirolle. A right turn here goes through Trépot

Absinthe, the Green Fairy

The Val de Travers near Pontarlier is the traditional home of La Fée Verte, 'The Green Fairy', the absinthe drink made by Pernod. According to legend this famous liqueur was created by Docteur Ordinaire, a French doctor in exile in Switzerland. In 1805 the Pernod company from Pontarlier began distilling this absinthe based drink using a secret formula. Absinthe was banned in France in 1915 and this led to the temporary demise of the company, whose premises were taken over by Nestlé. But Pernod did not completely disappear, it opened new distilleries in Spain where absinthe was not banned and later began to produce its famous pastis, which is similar to absinthe but without the health damaging wormwood. Although Pernod no longer exists in Pontarlier, artisinal clear absinthe is now produced in the town and premises where it is made can be visited. In 1901 the Pernod factory was struck by lightning and all the stored absinthe poured into the River Doubs. When this appeared later in the waters of the River Loue to the delight of the locals, it finally solved the question of whether there was an underground link between the two rivers.

and Foucherans in the direction of the D67. In Trépot there is an old fruitière, which is now a museum where all the processes of making Comté cheese are explained.

About a mile before Ornans on the D67, there is a right turn to the villages of Scey and Cléron. In the village of Cléron, 4 miles ($6^1/_2$km) away, there is a castle on the banks of the River Loue that was built in the fourteenth century to protect the salt route from Salins-les-Bains. It is a beautiful example of a fortified castle of this region with its square red-tiled central tower and circular donjons. The gardens are open during the summer months. A particularly good view of the exterior of the castle is obtained from the bridge over the Loue, looking upstream.

After visiting the castle it is best to return direct to the D67 and turn right into Ornans. This lovely little town occupies both banks of the River Loue, set in an obvious valley with cliffs overlooking it. The bridges over the river offer some of the best views. Just before the centre of the town, there is a shaded square to the right of the road. It is normally possible to park here and it is best to do so. This is the Place Gustave Courbet named after the artist who was born here and whose body now rests in the village cemetery. His house is now a museum. To reach it, cross the footbridge in the far corner of the square that gives delightful views of the houses that back on to the river, walk up and turn left by the Post Office with the traditional Comtois grilles over the windows. The Musée Natal de Gustave Courbet in the actual house, where the artist was born and brought up, is on the same side of the river beyond the bridge. Courbet's work is also celebrated in a 20 mile (32 kms) Route Courbet which can be followed showing seven of the sites he actually painted with reproductions of his work. Returning from the museum, cross over the Grand Pont for more excellent views of the river and the houses

Gustave Courbet

Gustave Courbet's masterpiece, 'A Burial at Ornans' is one of the stars of the Musée d'Orsay in Paris. Born in Ornans in 1819, Courbet was relatively unknown when this painting was exhibited at the Paris Salon in 1851. It celebrated the lives of ordinary people from his home town which remained close to his heart throughout his life. He embraced Realism and emphasised the nobility of everyday life. He was seen in official circles as a rebel for his support of the poor and art critics called him 'The Master of Ornans' not without irony. Courbet was however very proud of his roots and returned frequently to his home town. His support of the poor led him in 1871 to become a member of the Paris Commune, which was put down with some savagery. Courbet's life was spared but he was faced with such a huge fine that he fled to self-imposed exile in Switzerland, where he died in 1877. His body was returned to Ornans. Later, his sister donated 'A Burial at Ornans' to the French Ministry of Fine Arts.

reflected in it. Turn left along the main street. The Town Hall on the left dates from the fifteenth century and was the administrative centre of the whole valley for many years. This road leads back to the Place Gustave Courbet.

On leaving the square earlier and crossing the footbridge, a sign will have been seen to the Miroir de la Loue. This is a point a little below the centre of the town where the river widens out and acts as a sort of mirror giving a reflection of the houses, the church and the cliffs. In fact to reach this, it is less confusing to stay on the road past the square and continue down the Avenue Président Wilson past the hospital. Just after a beautiful example of a nineteenth-century French town house on the right-hand side, take a left turn towards the river. The Miroir de la Loue is beside the bridge over the Loue at this point.

The road to Pontarlier goes for about 10 miles (16km) alongside the river giving very good views of the river, especially at Vuillafans and Lods, where there is a good little museum of wine and vines. The source of the river Loue, a beautiful spot and well worth visiting, is not far beyond. It comes out of the Gorges de Nouailles beyond the picturesque village of Mouthier-Haute-Pierre. In spring the cherry trees here are particularly lovely. The dark Marsotte cherries are used to make a local Kirsch which has a very good reputation. There are excellent view-points into the Gorges from the D67, the Pontarlier road, beyond Mouthier, and there are various ways of reaching the source of the River Loue as it cascades out of the limestone cliff which towers above. Nearby, there are two caves high up, the source of the Pontet and higher up the Counterfeiters' Cave, La Caverne des Faux-Monnayeurs. This was actually used by counterfeiters during the Revolution, and for a long time afterwards entry to it **was** barred for fear that a lot of the money they created had been left hidden there. They can be reached by means of the fixed ladders, but are not a recommended part of the walk.

From La Main, the N57 leads towards Pontarlier, 10 miles (16km) away. As the town is approached, it has a very industrial appearance and seems to be not much more than a crossroads. In fact it is an important centre for the area with particular importance for tourism. Statistically the area around Pontarlier has more hotels, more gîtes, more camping and caravan sites and more second homes than any other in the Northern Jura. The reason is that it is so well placed for visiting many different parts of the Haut Doubs, the mountainous part of the region.

Pontarlier

The town, like so many constructed largely of wood, was almost totally burned down in the eighteenth century, and when it was rebuilt the commemorative arch, the Porte St Pierre that stands at the end of the Rue de la République was erected. It was built in 1771 as a plain arch, but the clock tower was added in the nineteenth century.

The centre of Pontarlier is the Place d'Arcon with the Town Hall, the Tourist Office and the library. The most striking building in the Place is also the oldest,

*Looking down on Besançon and the River Doubs from the Citadel. *E*

the Chapelle des Annonciades. This building with its original Renaissance front is now an art gallery, the Salon des Annonciades. This is now run by the "Friends of the Museum", who also organize a series of events each year under the name of "Les Absinthiades" to celebrate Pontarlier's position as the capital of the making of absinthe, the Green Fairy.

Directly east of Pontarlier is one of the highest hills in the Northern Jura, the Grand Taureau at 4,340ft (1,323m). It is signposted to the left after the bridge over the Doubs. The road in fact goes almost to the summit and only a short 30 minute walk is needed. It is the perfect viewpoint not only of the Jura hills but of the Swiss mountains and Mont Blanc.

Further south of Pontarlier on the N57 is one of the most obvious *cluses* in the Jura. This deep valley cutting across the hills is La Cluse-et-Mijoux, with a fort on one side and a castle on the other. The castle is the imposing Château de Joux

Using Pontarlier as a base, there are two good excursions into the High Jura, south to the top of Mont d'Or and west to the Lac de St Point and Lac de Remoray and the source of the Doubs. Eight miles (13km) south of Pontarlier on the N57 after passing through the valley of Cluse-et-Mijoux, the little village Les Hôpitaux-Neufs is reached. To the right is the ski resort of Métabief. There is a walk from the village to the top of the Mont d'Or which takes about 2 hours to the summit and back. This can be shortened by driving above Métabief on the D385 to the long ski-lift. The walk goes under the line of the ski-lift to the top of Petit-Morond and then follows the crest of the hill up to the summit of Mont d'Or. There is a local cheese Le Vacherin Mont d'Or, a soft creamy cheese, produced between autumn and spring from the milk of cows fed on hay. There are various legends about the name of the mountain, the most popular being that a young shepherd found a cache of gold on the mountain which allowed him to marry the daughter of the local lord. Many others tried to repeat his success but after many years' mining only ore or 'fool's gold' was discovered.

The source of the Doubs is 10 miles (16km) away upstream near the village of Mouthe. The signposted road past the war memorial leads up to a car park with the source a very steep 5-minute walk beyond. The water rising from the rock at this point 3,115ft (950m) high has over the centuries cut its way through the limestone of the Northern Jura, creating the Gorges du Doubs and dramatic loops through the hills as in Besançon, 150 miles (240km) downstream.

*Fisherman on the Lake of St Point. *E*

Places to Visit: Besançon & th

Besançon

Citadelle de Besançon W

99, rue des Fusillés
25042 Besançon
☎ 03 81 87 83 33
www.citadelle.com
The times of opening apply to all the museums within the Citadel. In Jul and Aug the Citadel opens at 9.00 and closes at 19.00. In other months it closes an hour earlier. It is recommended that a minimum of half a day is needed to get full advantage of all that there is to see.

Boat trips on the Doubs

Les Vedettes Bisontines
Embarcadère Pont de la République
25000 Besançon
bateau "Le Vauban"
☎ 03.81.68.13.25
www.sautdudoubs.fr
This cruise which takes about one and a half hours is available every day in Jul and Aug. It goes through the tunnel under the Citadel and circles the town.

Musée des Beaux Arts W

1 place de la Révolution
25000 Besançon
☎ 03 81 87.80.49
www.besancon.fr
This Art Gallery, reputed to be the oldest in France, is open every day of the year except Tue and National Holidays 9.30–12.00 and 14.00–18.00. On Sat and Sun it is open from 9.30–18.00 and is free on Sun.

Astronomical Clock

Horloge astronomique de Besançon
Rue de la Convention
Cathédrale St Jean
25000 Besançon
It is open every day except Tue from Apr to Sept 9.50–17.50.
In other months it is closed on Wed as well as Tue. It is fully closed in Jan.

East of Besançon

Fromagerie Artisanale Liechti

Epenouse 25530 VERCEL
☎ 03 81 58 32 43
This cheese cooperative, so typical of the region, is open to visitors every day from 10.00–11.30 and 14.00–19.00. In Jul and Aug it is open from 9.00.

Gouffre de Poudrey W

Maison des Guides
25580 Etalans
☎ 03 81 59 22 57
www.dino-zoo.com
There are guided tours lasting one hour, starting at 9.30 in Jul and Aug. At other times they are in the afternoon. Included in the price is a Son et Lumière show. There is a detailed leaflet in English.

Doubs

Musée de l'Horlogerie du Haut Doubs **W**

Château Pertusier
25500 MORTEAU
☎ 03 81 67 40 88
www.musee-horlogerie.com
Open from May to Sept 10.00–12.00 and 14.00–18.00. The guided tour takes about an hour.

South of Besançon

Musée Natal de Gustave Courbet **W**

Musée Départemental
Maison Natale du peintre
1, place Robert Fernier
25290 Ornans
☎ 03 81 62 23 30
www.musee-courbet.com
Open every day except Tue from 10.00–12.00 and 14.00–18.00. In Jul and Aug open 10.00–12.30 and 13.30–18.00.

Pontarlier

Chapelle des Annonciades

69 rue de la République
25300 Pontarlier
This is now an exhibition and houses interesting temporary exhibitions.

Absinthe Distillery

Sarl Distillerie Pierre GUY
49 rue des Lavaux
25300 Pontarlier
This Absinthe distillery is open to visitors from 8.00–12.00 and 14.00–18.00 from Tue to Sat throughout the year.

Le Musée Municipal de Pontarlier **W**

2 place d'Arçon
25300 Pontarlier
☎ 03 81 38 82 14
www.musees-franchecomte.com
Open every week 10.00–12.00 and 14.00–18.00 on Mon, Wed, Thur and Fri. On Sat, Sun and National Holidays 14.00–18.00.

Le Château de joux **W**

25300 La Cluse-et-Mijoux
☎ 03 81 69 47 95
www.chateaudejoux.com
The castle is open in Jul and Aug from 9.00–18.00. From Feb to Jun and during Sept it is open from 10.00–11.30 and 14.00–16.30.

2. Central Jura

Opposite: Waterfall at Baume-les-Messieurs. *F

The department of the Jura, department No 39, is the centrepiece of the geographical region of the Jura, and it includes three distinct types of terrain.

The plain occupies the upper section starting at Dole in the north and stretching south-east. The plateau takes up most of the rest of the department and rises above the plain behind towns such as Arbois, Poligny and Lons-le-Saunier. In the southwest of the region the plateau begins to rise and this culminates in a long range of mountains that then drop abruptly into Switzerland and Lac Léman.

Dole

In the north, the town of Dole, the one-time capital of the region of Comté until replaced by Besançon in 1676, had a parliament, law courts and even a university. It was systematically destroyed by fire by Louis XI in 1479 and was rebuilt early in the sixteenth century around the Basilique Notre-Dame. The church itself, built over a period of 80 years, is most impressive with a very broad nave and some superb nineteenth-century stained-glass windows. In the right-hand corner there is a holy chapel and the stained-glass window tells the story of how the Communion Bread was the only thing not burned in a fire at Faverney, and, after this miraculous event, was brought to Dole. Outside the church, the old Town Hall is on the right of the market square and ahead is the covered market, built in 1882. To the right and behind this up the steep slope, the pedestrian precinct stretches to the Rue des Arènes. This leads to the delightful Place aux Flours with its fountain and modem sculpture, *Les Trois Commères*. This was made for the town by the German sculptor Boetcher, who originates from Lahr, Dole's twin town in Germany.

Go past the back of the church along the Rue Carondelet. This street goes down to the Rue Granvelle. A slight left turn leads on to the Rue Pasteur, named after perhaps Dole's greatest son, Louis Pasteur. It used to be called Rue des Tanneurs because it was the local centre of the tanning industry and as a leather worker Pasteur's father lived at No 43, the Maison Natale de Pasteur. His son Louis was born there in 1822, but the family moved in 1825 to Arbois. The house is now classed as a historic monument and on the first floor there is a museum devoted to Louis Pasteur's work and scientific discoveries, as well as many of the pictures painted by his family. Quite as interesting is the reconstruction of Louis' father's tanning workshop on the lower floors with all the tools of the period.

Dole is surrounded by parks and waterways that provide both relaxation and activity. The Cours St Mauris and the Promenade du Pasquier are the closest open spaces to the town centre on either side of the Canal du Rhône au Rhin and connected by the Pont du Pasquier.

A visit to Dole can be given a new dimension by taking a boat trip on the Doubs or the Canal du Rhône au Rhin, or even hiring a boat, which can be done for the week or a weekend. The organizers will provide an itinerary as well as a guide to get past the first lock. A few days on the Doubs would be the ideal way to explore the countryside of the northern part of the Jura. Since bikes can be hired as well, it is a perfect way of quickly getting off the beaten track.

The Forêt de Chaux, to the west of Dole, is France's third largest forest and has been important through the years for providing fuel for metal forging and glass-making. This huge area of 20,000 hectares (49,400 acres) has only narrow forestry roads crossing it. On the southern side are some hamlets around La Vielle-Loys. These were a centre for glass making, producing a million bottles a year at one time.

A longer way back to Dole would be to turn left at Montbarrey and continue west for about 10 miles (16km). This leads to one of the region's most remarkable sites, the ancient royal salt works of Arc et Senans.

Salins-les-Bains

Salins-les-Bains for many centuries rivalled Besançon in terms of its population, its wealth and its position. In the Middle Ages salt was needed for preserving food and its importance conferred great wealth on the owner of the salt mine. In the thirteenth century, the Chalon family from Nozeroy took over the town, and the money from the salt enabled them to become the most influential feudal family in Franche Comté. The town was also important as a staging point on the route from Burgundy to Switzerland via Pontarlier. This accounts for the presence of forts overlooking the town from both sides of the valley, the Fort St André to the west and the Fort Bélin to the east. Both can be reached by car and give a very good view of Salins-les-Bains stretched along the River Furieuse at the bottom of the valley. The towers of the four churches indicate that the town was at one time four parishes. The church immediately beneath Fort Bélin, the Église St Antoine, has the most impressive site and is the most interesting to visit, especially for its wooden pulpit and stalls.

There are many impressive buildings to admire, such as the Town Hall built in 1718, and there are good walks, such as the Promenade des Cordeliers on the other side of the river, but there are two essential visits both connected with the town's major industry, Les Salines and the Thermal Baths.

In 1843 one of the de Grimaldi family later of Monte Carlo fame bought up the salt works, but his intention was not simply to extract salt. He saw the arrival of the railway in the town as an ideal way to profit from the new craze for 'taking the waters'. In 1854 he built the Thermal Baths and followed this soon after with the Grand Hôtel des Bains, concert halls and finally the Casino.

Arbois

A visitor to Arbois arriving from Salins or Dole will see on the right as he approaches the Grande Rue a little garden with a statue of Louis Pasteur, who lived here for most of his life. His house is now an excellent museum, well worth a visit. Arbois is a charming little town with evidence everywhere that it is the capital of wine producing in the Jura, with a museum of wine making, "le Vigneron Arboisien, 200 ans de vie" in the Tour Gloriette and the Musée de la Vigne at du Vin. One of the main charms of Arbois is its setting on the edge of the Jura plateau. The edge of the plateau to the east of the town offers two quite extraordinary sights. The plateau has been eroded away in many places to form a *reculée,* an amphitheatre, which takes the form in some places of a cliff as high as 750ft (230m). It is one of the best examples of a *reculée,* and because of its shape is called the Cirque du Fer à Cheval, the Horse Shoe. At the base of the cliff is a very interesting cave system, Les Planches. It is best to take the D107 out of Arbois alongside the River Cuisance. After about 2 miles (3km) pass through the very pretty hamlet of Les Planches and park at the end of the valley. A short walk in the shadow of the immense, slightly overhanging limestone cliff goes to the entrance. The lower entrance of the cave was used as an emergency hide-out by Bronze Age man and there have been many discoveries of habitation, including two human skeletons. Deeper into the cave it is possible to see the wonderful effect of erosion on the limestone as it creates weird shapes such as giants' pots, organ pipes and chimneys, formed from the bottom upwards by the pressure of water. The whole system is very imaginatively lit and has safe concrete walkways. Even more important for most foreign visitors, it has a short but clearly expressed guide book written in English.

After visiting the cave, take a left turn just in front of the church in the village

Arc et Senans

This wonderful collection of buildings is a perfect combination of classical architecture and eighteenth-century industrial idealism. The plan was to bring the brine some 15 miles (24km) from Salins-les-Bains in wooden pipes and to use wood from the forest as a fuel source to extract the salt. Claude-Nicolas Ledoux, an inspector of salt works and a recognised architect, was given the job in 1793 of constructing the works. He intended to build an entire town in concentric circles around the salt works (the Salines) and the director's house. This town would cater for every need with a church, a market, public baths and gymnasium. Unfortunately the works never made as much money as had been predicted, and although salt was produced for a number of years, Ledoux' scheme was never fully realised. The buildings now house an International Centre for Studies of the Future as well as a salt museum and other exhibitions. The Coopers' (Tonneliers) Building to the left of the entrance has a permanent exhibition showing Ledoux' original plans and ideas.

and drive up the D339 as it threads its way through the trees. Turn left on to the D469 which continues the climb up the side of the *reculée* and is cut through the rock near the top. As the road levels out, there is a car park and a café. A 2-minute walk through the trees leads to a belvedere that gives a superb view of the amphitheatre.

Poligny

Poligny can be reached by returning to Arbois and turning left on the N83. A slightly longer way, but one providing a more impressive first view of Poligny is to continue driving away from Arbois on the D469 and turning right on the N5. Whichever way Poligny

Captain Lacuzon

Every summer in Château Chalon there is a *Son et Lumière* for thirteen nights depicting life in the village from 1630 to 1670, when Franche Comté was resisting the armies of the King of France. The show centres round the exploits of Claude Prost, a local Resistance leader who took the name of Captain Lacuzon during the wars against Louis XIV. Exiled when Louis finally succeeded, Lacuzon continued to represent the independent spirit of the Comtois and does so to this day.

*Dole under the snow. *F*

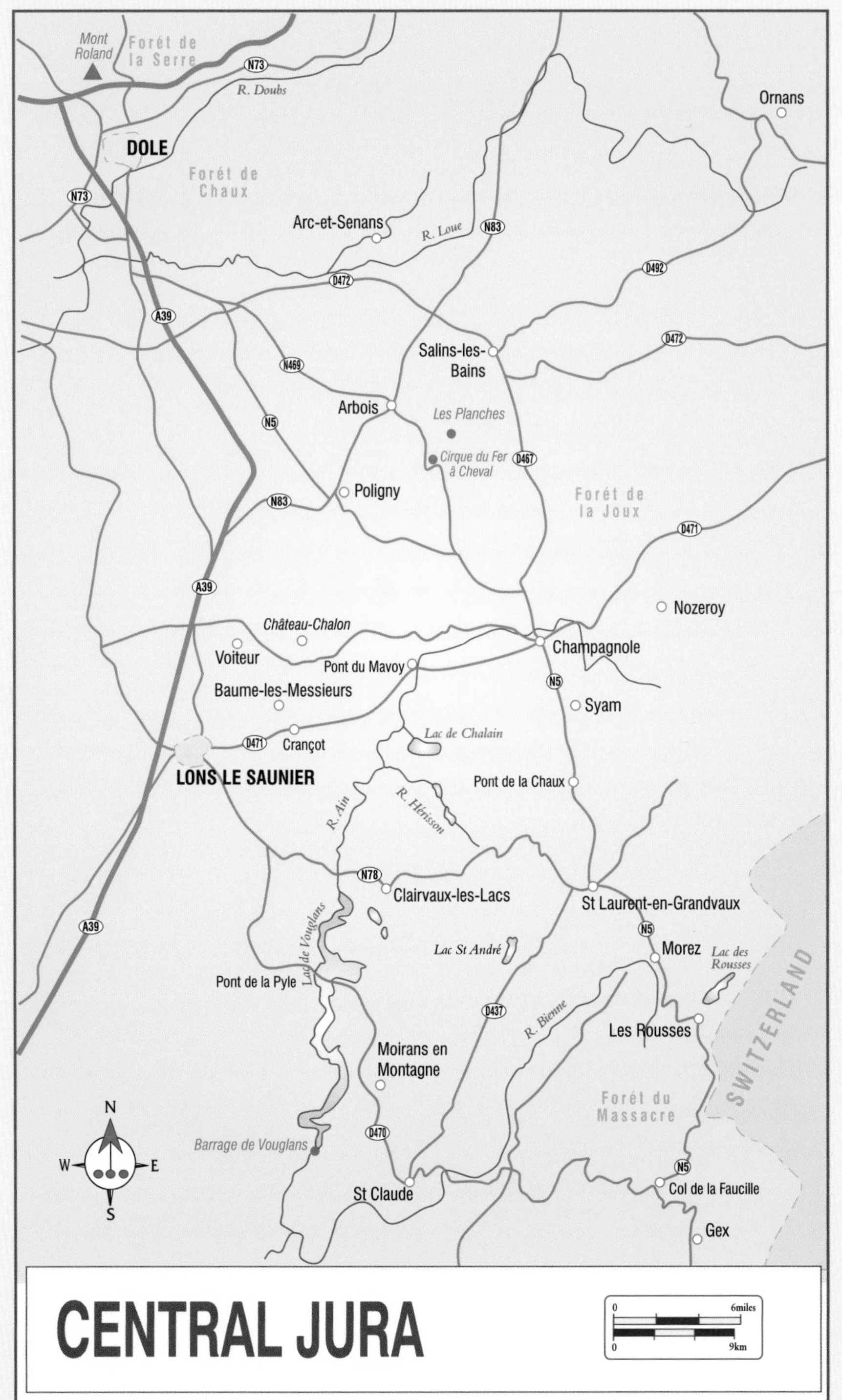
Mont Roland
Forêt de la Serre
N73
R. Doubs
Ornans
DOLE
Forêt de Chaux
N73
Arc-et-Senans
R. Loue
N83
D492
D472
A39
D472
Salins-les-Bains
N469
Arbois
Les Planches
N5
Cirque du Fer à Cheval
D467
Poligny
Forêt de la Joux
N83
D471
A39
Nozeroy
Château-Chalon
Voiteur
Champagnole
Pont du Mavoy
N5
Baume-les-Messieurs
Syam
Lac de Chalain
D471
Crançot
LONS LE SAUNIER
Pont de la Chaux
R. Ain
R. Hérisson
N78
Clairvaux-les-Lacs
St Laurent-en-Grandvaux
Lac de Vouglans
A39
N5
Lac St André
Morez
Lac des Rousses
Pont de la Pyle
D437
R. Bienne
Les Rousses
Moirans en Montagne
SWITZERLAND
Forêt du Massacre
N
W
E
S
Barrage de Vouglans
D470
N5
St Claude
Col de la Faucille
Gex
CENTRAL JURA
0
6miles
0
9km

The Salines

The Salines, the salt works, have been a museum since 1966. The underground galleries, 1,315ft (400m) long and constructed in the thirteenth century to protect the salt springs, are very impressive. The salt is very deep (820ft, 250m) and cannot be mined as such, it has to be extracted in the form of brine. This was done by an ingenious system of pumping water down to dissolve the salt and then extracting the salt-laden water. The mechanism for this is still in place. When it came to the surface it had to be heated for the water to evaporate, leaving only grains of salt. Two of the original boilers can still be seen. It needed anything from 12 to 18 hours to evaporate away all the water from the pan.

is approached, it is best to park in the Place called both Place Nationale and Place des Déportés with its impressive fountain. This will give good access to Poligny's main areas of interest. The Croix du Dan can be seen on a hill to the south overlooking the town. A walk down the Rue du Collège and back up the Grande Rue passes a number of ancient buildings. The Information Office, which can be found in the Place de Déportés, provides a very good leaflet with detailed walks and cycle rides in the area.

Returning up the Grande Rue, there are many interesting old town houses. A fine example is the Hôtel de Ville with its courtyard and external stairway leading upstairs to the old courtroom. Beyond the Place Nationale is the ancient hospital, the Hôtel Dieu, which also has a beautiful interior courtyard and cloister. It houses an interesting pharmacy section with its many *faïence,* earthenware jars, a lot of which were made in the town.

Lons-le-Saunier

From Poligny the N83 goes directly round the edge of the plateau to Lons-le-Saunier, the Departmental town and the entrance point to another fascinating section of the plateau. Lons has grown greatly in recent years and this is obvious from all the flats and factories on the outskirts of the town. Besides its importance as an administrative centre, it has many of the traditional Jura industries, such as spectacle- and toy-making. It is also a centre of transport, but its most well-known firm is perhaps Bel, the makers of *La Vache Qui Rit,* the 'Laughing Cow' cheeses.

In the Place de Liberté there is a statue of Général Lecourbe, which faces down towards the theatre. On the left is the belfry and clock tower, which was paid for by public subscription after the devastating fire of 1637. As a result of this fire, the buildings date from the seventeenth century or later, with very few exceptions. To the left is the Rue du Commerce, notable for its beautiful arcades. Although the houses all date from the same period, each was built in an individual style. This gives the street a certain charm. A lot of the houses have very impressive interior courtyards in the style of the region. No 24 is the house where Rouget de Lisle, the writer of the *Marseillaise,* was born in 1760. On the hour, listen for the theatre clock which chimes the six notes of the line *Aux armes citoyens* in honour of Lons' most famous son.

Further into the Place Perraud, is the Puits Salé, the Salted Well. Near the Puits Salé, at 25 Rue Richebourg is the Museum of Archaeology. The building was the original Bel factory but the firm has long since outgrown it. The museum has many temporary exhibitions, but is especially proud of the items including the dug-out canoe discovered in 1904 on the banks of Lac de Chalain. There is also an exhibition of how a Neolithic family would have lived 6,000 years ago. The street continues on down to the Promenade de la Chevalerie, where there is a magnificent statue of Rouget de Lisle. This is the work of the famous sculptor Frederic Bartholdi, who was to go on to build the American *Statue of Liberty* in 1886. The rather odd-looking rococo-styled Thermal Baths are straight ahead. They were built in 1892 to capitalise on the salt springs under the town.

Among the many things to see in the area, there are two, Château-Chalon and Baume-les-Messieurs, which are really exceptional and should not be missed. Although they merit separate visits, they can be combined into a 25-mile (40km) round trip. Going north on the N83, take a right turn along the D70 to Voiteur. This road goes between the foothills on the left and the plateau on the right. Two miles (3km) further down this road on the left-hand side is the very solid-looking Château du Pin rising above the woods and the vineyard. The road continues into wine-producing country with vineyards occupying most of the hillsides, which look at their very best in autumn. At Voiteur follow the D5 to Château-Chalon as it winds its way upwards through the fields of vines. The village is worth exploring on foot. It was originally a fortified castle on the rocky spur overlooking the foothills and the plain of Bresse beyond, and the village was built up around it. The present castle cannot be visited, but the fortified eleventh-century church with its massive stone tiles can be. The huge pillars and very early vaulting inside are of interest. An impression of the strategic importance of the village can be gained by looking down from the Belvédère de la Rochette near the church. Before leaving the village, take an opportunity to taste the local wine, especially the Vin Jaune de Château-Chalon.

For another view of the village go back down the D5, turn left at Voiteur along the D70 in the direction of Baume-les-Messieurs. Château-Chalon can be seen along the top of the ridge on the left. As the road follows the River Seille, the cliffs start to rise up on the left and the overhanging cliff on the right gives the impression of drawing the visitor into a secret valley as the square-towered church on the left is passed. It was to this valley in the sixth century that the Irish monk St Colomba came and established a monastery. Baume later declined in religious

*Bridges taking the railway past Morez. *F*

importance but gained in social prestige to such an extent that the name was changed in the sixteenth century from Baume-les-Moines to Baume-les-Messieurs to reflect the social position of the monks. The abbey was disbanded in 1792 and its huge estates reverted to the newly-formed republic. The church houses the tomb of Jean de Watteville as well as many members of the Chalon family. In the old storehouse, there is a folk museum which concentrates on local crafts.

After visiting the monastery, cross the bridge and turn left up the D70. This impressive route with the cliffs rising high on each side goes to the very end of the valley with its cave on the right and the staircase, the Échelle de Crançot, cut in the rock on the left. The cave is entered along a gangplank that takes the visitor above the normal level of the River Dard as it issues from the rock. After heavy rain the river comes out of this upper cave as a waterfall. The caves inside are notable for their height. The system has now been developed nearly a mile into the limestone cliffs, but this can only be visited by expert cavers.

There is a superb viewpoint overlooking the whole valley. This is the Belvédère de Crançot that can be reached by scrambling up the Échelle de Crançot. This stairway is cut into the rock and can be very intimidating, especially in the wet. If it is too risky, drive back down the valley and pass the village before turning right behind the abbey. The road climbs up out of the valley. Turn right towards Crançot, go through the village and turn right about a mile later. Park opposite the café and walk down beside the café to the belvedere. The view is considered to be the most breathtaking in the Jura.

*Above: The Old Town Hall at Poligny. *A*

*Left: The entrance to the valley of Baume-les-Messieurs. *A*

There are other excursions in the Lons area, such as to the Château de Frontenay standing among the vineyards to the north of Château-Chalon and the Cirque de Ladoye, an amphitheatre 4 miles (6km) to the east of the same village. The area to the south of Lons, the Revermont, deserves a visit,

The Forêt de la Joux

The Forêt de la Joux is a huge forest, mainly of pine with many hamlets and villages in and around it. To help visitors appreciate it, a special road has been marked out as 'La Route des Sapins'. This goes through the important areas and gives access to the most interesting and impressive sections of the forest. Although it is well hidden, the railway also threads its way through the forest. Just before reaching the Gare de la Joux in the very centre of the forest the 'Maison Forestière du Chevreuil' can be seen to the right. This Information Centre and the Arboretum nearby give a very clear idea of the importance of the forest and the forester's work and both certainly deserve a visit.

While in the forest, there are two other areas not to be missed. About a mile before the Information Centre, on the right of the road, is the entrance to a walk through the woods called 'La Glacière'. It gets this name because it is the coldest part of the forest in winter, but this has not prevented the growth of the quite marvellous-looking fir trees. The other area to visit is beyond the Information Centre about 2 miles ($3^1/_4$km) down the very windy road. On the left there is a viewpoint looking north over the rolling wooded hills, while on the right about 20yds into the forest is the 'King of the Forest', the Sapin Président de la Joux. This fir tree stands at 148ft (45m) high, measures nearly 13ft (4m) in circumference and is reckoned to be over 200 years old.

especially for visitors who like walking and riding. The best way to see this area known as La Petite Montagne is to leave Lons by the N83 south and turn off on to the D117 in the direction of St Julien.

La Région des Lacs (The Lake District)

The natural lakes of the Jura are mainly situated in a group to the east of Lons-le-Saunier, but the area known as La Région des Lacs is extended south by man-made lakes created by damming the River Ain. The most convenient base for exploring La Région des Lacs is Clairvaux-les-Lacs, reached from Lons on the N78. Except for the Clairvaux lakes, the natural lakes lie to the north of the town, while Lac de Vouglans, the largest of the man-made lakes, is to the south.

Lac de Vouglans

This lake was created in 1968 by the building of the Vouglans Dam. The steep, tree-covered banks have been left in their original state and there is only access to the lake in a few places. To visit these and to see the area around the lake, it is best to start at Pont-de-Poitte on the N78, where there is a bridge over the Ain. When the river is in spate, it is a most impressive sight and can be seen to best advantage by taking a road to the left just after the bridge.

This leads to the Saut de la Saisse. The river is also worth seeing at this point during a period of drought for the strange shapes in the river bed. There have been many factories through the years built to take advantage of the water power and the buildings of the iron works, the Forges de la Saisse, are still there.

From Pont-de-Poitte take the D49 towards La Tour-du-Meix, passing by St Christophe on a hill-top with its twelfth-century church. At La Tour-du-Meix turn left and the road crosses the lake by the impressive Pont de la Pyle, which was built at the same time as the dam.The old bridge is now many metres under water. One of the main points of access to the lake is to the left of the bridge. This tourist village, Surchauffant, has a camp site, a beach and a port, where boats can be hired. It is also the only base on the lake that has cruise boats. After crossing the Pont de la Pyle, there is a very small road that goes back on itself to the right and leads down to a small bit of beach below the bridge. This road is normally only used by photographers! To reach the other beach area, take the D301 for 3 miles (5km) towards Maisod and follow the signs to 'Plage de la Mercantine'. This has facilities for hiring wind-surfers, boats and pedal boats, as well as a large sloping field and beach, but is less commercial than Surchauffant. The road continues towards Moirans-en-Montagne, but about 2 miles ($3^1/_4$km) before the town there is a car park and a signpost to the right to the 'Belvédère Regardoir'. This can be reached in about 10 minutes on foot and provides one of the best views of the lake. The Vouglans Dam can be reached by taking the D299 out of Moiransen-Montagne, an important wood-working and toy-making town.

Lac de Chalain

The Lac de Chalain, is similar to the Lac de Vouglans in that it provides facilities for water sports of all kinds, but it has a very much more dramatic appearance, enclosed by hills on three sides. The best base for visiting the northern lakes is the very pretty village of Doucier. This is 10 miles (16km) to the north of Clairvaux on the D27. The eastern end of the lake is entirely surrounded by a camp site, set in the grounds of a castle, the Domaine de Chalain.

Hérisson Falls

The river Hérisson drops down from the plateau in a very impressive series of waterfalls that can be reached by continuing on the D326 past the lakes. Park in the large car park beside the café/restaurant at the end of this road. A short well-signposted walk through the trees leads to the foot of the final but most impressive of the waterfalls, the Éventail, the Fan. The path zigzags up through the trees to the left of the waterfall and it is worth taking it to see at least the first of the other waterfalls above. The path is well laid out and quite safe. At the top take a short path to the right and look over the edge of the Éventail before continuing on upwards for about 10 minutes to an entirely different type of waterfall.

This is the Grand Saut, the Great Leap, where the water drops 197ft (60m) directly from the top of an

Louis Pasteur (1822 – 1895)

Louis Pasteur was born in Dole, but his family brought him to Arbois at the age of three. Although his work took him away, he constantly returned and kept a house at No 81 Rue de Courcelles until his death in 1895. This is now a simple and rather lovely museum full of his everyday objects, completely renovated in 1994. It also has the laboratory and many of the test tubes and instruments that he actually used for his many studies. His work covered an enormous range from discovering the secret of vaccination to purifying liquids by what is now called "pasteurization". This was first done to prevent wine deteriorating. This made him a hero in his home town.

overhanging cliff to the rocks at the bottom. It is quite easy, safe and almost dry to walk behind the Grand Saut. This path winds round to a wide but not very deep cave, the Grotte de Lacuzon, where the Resistance hero used to stay while planning his next move against the French. There is in fact a bridge over to the cave lower down if you want to avoid getting splashed.

The Central Plateau

Champagnole lying on the N5 and the D471 is an important crossroads in the centre of the plateau. It is essentially a modern town, since it completely burned down on five occasions, the

*The bridge over the Lac du Vouglans. *A*

Cheeses from the Jura

The farms in the Jura were traditionally too small to produce a cheese with every milking in so from the 18th century on they adopted the idea of cooperatives, using the 'fructus commun', the combined fruit of their labours to make cheeses. This is the basis of the word 'fruitières', the small cheese making cooperatives which are to be seen throughout the region.

The three cheeses with their own Appellation d'Orgine Controlée (A.O.C.) are Comté, Bleu de Gex and Morbier.

Each 'round' of Comté, a traditional gruyère, made from 500 litres of milk from Montbéliard cattle, weighs up to 50 kgs. The milk is gently heated to 54 degrees for half an hour, during which time the curd is broken down in to small grains with a special cutting paddle. The cheese is lifted from the vat in an open weave cloth and placed in a mould. The remaining whey is then slowly pressed out. The finished 'round' is kept to mature for a minimum of three months, acquiring a light brown crust and a delicious nutty flavour.

The Bleu de Gex traces its origins to the monks of the Abbey of Saint Claude. Much more mild than blue cheeses from other areas of France, it has a slightly perfumed taste, said to come from the Alpine flowers eaten by the Montbéliard cattle which produce the milk. The blue mould comes from the Penicllium Glaucum introduced during the creation process.

The main characteristic of the Morbier cheese is a layer of wood ash in its centre. It is a rich, creamy cheese. There are several versions of why the ash is there. Some say it was a naïve attempt to create a blue cheese, but one of the most likely versions is that the farmer did not have enough milk from one milking and left a layer of ash to seal in the morning's output before adding the evening's production.

There are numerous goats' cheeses and one real local speciality, the Concoillotte du Jura. This is a mixture of skimmed milk, butter, water and salt plus any ingredient such as garlic to give it a distinct taste. It is eaten with a spoon like yoghurt.

final time being 1798. It has developed as an industrial and commercial centre since the nineteenth century, although its tradition of metalworking goes back several centuries. Champagnole is a thriving market town with its main market on Saturday, often spilling over from the market place down the sides of the main streets. In the Town Hall there is a very good Archaeological Museum with many Roman and Gallic artefacts, such as combs, brooches and coins. There is also an excellent Information Office is very well stocked and keen walkers are well served by a variety of walking guides. On one of the walks (easy 6 mile 11 kms) it is possible to visit the source of the river Ain. The "source de l'Ain" is set in a lovely wooded amphitheatre, is not far away and is reached by driving through Sirod and Conte and following the marked road to the end. A short walk of about 10 minutes through the trees leads to this delightful spot. Another natural phenomenon well worth the visit is where the River Same has cut a gorge 13ft (4m) wide but 130ft (40m) deep in the limestone. Although a little way from the road, the path to this Gorge de la Langouette on the left just before the bridge, is very well signposted. The D127 on the way back to Champagnole passes through the village of Syam, where there is a beautiful country house built in 1818 by Jean-Emmanuel Jobez who set up a small ironworks, which still operate as "Les Forges de Syam" The house which is open in the summer makes a very interesting visit.

East of Champagnole, the D471 climbs on to the plateau through a gorge, the Défilé d'Entreportes. Once on the plateau, there is a choice. To the left is the start of the Forêt de la Joux, and straight on is the open plateau with Nozeroy on the right. Nozeroy was the home of the Chalons, the most powerful family in the Jura in the Middle Ages. It used to be encircled by ramparts, with a magnificent fortified gateway. This still exists as the Porte de l'Horloge. It is as well to park in front of it in the Place Henri IV, since the town is best seen on foot. Pass through the gateway and go down the Grande Rue, which maintains an atmosphere of the Middle Ages, with its ancient houses of warm golden-coloured sandstone.

Two Distinct Wines From the Jura

Vin Jaune, yellow wine, one of the most celebrated wines of the Jura, is made from Savagnin grapes which are picked as late as possible. After fermentation, the wine is poured into oak casks and is not touched for six months. During this period it can lose up to 40% of its volume and the finished product can reach 14.5% proof. It is sold in special bottles of 62cl, called 'clavelins'.

Vin de Paille, straw wine, gets it name from the fact that the grapes are left on beds of straw for up to three months before being pressed. The wine is then left in casks for a minimum of three years. It is drunk as a liqueur rather than a wine, it can be up to 18.5% proof. It is sold in 37.5cl bottles.

The Mountains of the Jura

The N5, as it goes from Champagnole to the Col de la Faucille and on down to Gex and Geneva, cuts through the mountains of the Jura, an international centre of cross-country skiing (Le ski de fond). The N5 then goes through Morbier and Morez before making a long slow climb to Les Rousses, which is the most popular tourist centre in the summer and is a very good base from which to explore the surrounding mountains.

Morez, the industrial centre of the area, is famous for metalworking, spectacle-making *(la lunetterie)* and clock-making. There is a very interesting museum in the Place Jean-Jaurès that highlights the development of the local industry. Morez is also the home of a cheese named after a village 2 miles ($3^1/_4$km) to the north, Morbier, the cheese with a layer of ash in the centre! The most memorable sight in Morez, especially for someone passing through on the N5, is the series of viaducts that had to be built to get the railway through such difficult terrain.

One of Les Rousses' main attractions in summer is the lake that has facilities for watersports and the hiring of pedalo boats and sailboards. It is well signposted from the village. The surrounding ground is very peaty and this peat used to be a great source of fuel. In the winter the temperature is so low that the ice can be up to a foot thick in places. The water from the lake flows north-east along the River Orbe, contrary to the other rivers in the Jura that flow west or south-west. Down the valley is the village of Bois d'Amont, famous for its manufacture of the thin circular wooden tops and bottoms of cheese boxes. There is a little museum about this activity, called La Boissellerie, in restored woodworking barns. From Les Rousses, the N5 passes on the right the Forêt de la Massacre, so named from a sad episode in 1535 during a war between France and Savoy. It reaches Le Col de la Faucille. The many hotels and gift shops mark

Cross-country skiing (Le ski de fond)

In winter, this section of the Jura is an international centre of cross-country skiing. There are many skiing areas, usually with interlinking cross-country tracks. Every year in February more than 4,000 competitors take part in a 40-mile (65km) skiing race, the Transjurassienne, using a lot of these tracks from Lamoura to Mouthe. More resorts are now getting equipped for downhill skiing, but cross-country skiers outnumber downhill skiers by two to one. The reason for its popularity is the relatively level ground that can be found at over 3,280ft (1000m) and the thick snow on the ground from December to April in certain areas. The first skiing resort that the N5 reaches is St Laurent-en-Grandvaux, which boasts 140 miles (230km) of prepared tracks.

A clocktower in the village of Byans sur Doubs. *E

it out as an important international crossroads, but in fact Switzerland is not reached by road for another 15 miles (24km). There is a large car park in front of the cable car station at the Col. It is very worthwhile taking the 5-minute cable car ride to the summit of Mont Rond for its unforgettable view of Lac Léman and the French Alps to the south. Mont Blanc can be seen 50 miles (80km) away straight ahead and many other mountains can be made out on a clear day up to a hundred miles away. Although the café and cable car terminus is modern, the chimney is fashioned in the traditional style used in the Jura for smoking meat. This is called the *tuyé*. For the more active, there is a concrete *luge* track near the lower cable car station that uses a short chair-lift to reach the top. If returning to Les Rousses, it is worth making a detour via La Cure to the village of Prémanon. This pretty village, or rather collection of hamlets dominated by Mont Fier to the west, is an important tourist resort in winter and summer. Besides facilities such as its synthetic ice rink it has become well known because of the Paul Emile Victor Polar Museum, an essential visit for information on polar expeditions.

Places to Visit: Central Jura

Northern Jura

Dole

Maison Natale de Pasteur W

43, rue Pasteur
39100 DOLE
☎ 03 84 72 20 61
www.musee-pasteur.co
In Jul and Aug open from Mon to Sat 10.00–18.00 and 14.00–18.00 on Sun. In Apr, May, Sept and Oct open 10.00–12.00 and 14.00–18.00.

Boat trips on the River Doubs

Société Nicols,
Port de Dole
☎ 03 84 82 65 57
In Jul and Aug excursions leave Dole every day from 9.00–19.00 and in Sept on Sat and Sun at the same time.

Saline Royale

25610 Arc et Senans
☎ 03 81 54 45 45
www.salineroyale.com
This UNESCO World Heritage Centre is open in Jul and Aug from 9.00–19.00. During the other months open from 10.00–12.00 and 10.00–17.00.

Salins Les Bains W

Les Salines à Salins les Bains
Place des salines
39110 Salins-les-Bains
☎ 03 84 73 10 92
www.salinesdesalins.fr
Guided visits, which take about an hour, set out at 10.00, 11.30. 14.30, 15.30 and 16.30 throughout the summer months with additional times as necessary in Jul and Aug.

Thermal Baths W

Centre Thermal et de Remise en Forme
Place des Alliés
39 110 Salins-les-Bains
☎ 03 84 73 04 63
www.thermes-salins.com
The Thermal Baths welcome daily visitors to the "SEL a vie" treatments. These take place from Feb to Dec 14.30–18.30

Arbois

Musée de la Vigne at du Vin W

Château Pécauld
39600 Arbois
☎ 03 84 66 40 45
www.musees-franchecomte.com
Open in Jul and Aug from 10.00–12.30 and 14.00–18.00 except for Tuesdays. During the other months open from 14.00–18.00 except for Tue.

Le Vigneron Arboisien, 200 ans de vie

Tour Gloriette
Office de Tourisme d'Arbois
39600 Arbois
☎ 03 84 66 55 50
www.arbois.com

Cont'd overleaf

Cont'd from previous page

W = Perfect for Wet days

Places to Visit: Central Jura

Open every day in Jul and Aug. Free entry.

Pasteur Museum W

Maison de Louis Pasteur
83, rue de Courcelles
39600 ARBOIS
☎ 03 84 66 11 72
Pasteur called this house his "Château de la Cuisance" and it was his family home when he returned to Arbois. All visits are with guides. From Jun to Sept they are every hour from 9.45 to 11.45 and from 14.00 to 18.00. In Apr, May and Oct they are in the afternoon every hour from 14.15 to 17.15.

Grotte des Planches W

39600 Arbois
In July and August the caves are open ever day from 9.30–18.00. During other months 10.00–12.00 and 14.00–17.00. Closed Nov to Mar.

Poligny

Ancien Hôtel Dieu

20 place des déportés,
39800 Poligny
☎ 03.84.37.24.21
www.ville-poligny.fr
This one-time hospital houses an excellent apothecary museum and a collection of "Faience" pottery. It is open daily in July and August.

Maison du Comté

Avenue de la résistance
39800 Poligny
☎ 03 84 37 23 51
www.vente-comte.com
This exhibition of the way in which Comté cheese is made is open in Jul and Aug from Tue to Sun 10.00–11.30 and 14.00–18.00.

Lons-le-Saunier

Musée d'Archéologie W

7 rue des Cordeliers
39000 Lons-le-Saunier
☎ 03 84 47 88
Open throughout the year every weekday except Tuesday 10.00–12.00 and 14.00–18.00. On Sat and Sun open only in the afternoon.

Musée des Beaux Arts W

Place Philibert de Chalon
39000 Lons-le-Saunier
☎ 03 84 47 64 30
Open throughout the year every weekday except Tue 10.00–12.00 and 14.00–18.00. On Sat and Sun open only in the afternoon.

Musée Rouget de Lisle W

24, rue du Commerce
39000 LONS-LE-SAUNIER
☎ 03 84 47 29 16
Open from mid-Jun to mid-Sept from Mon to Fri 10.00–12.00 and 14.00–18.00. Weekends and public holidays 14.00–17.00.

Château-Chalon

Domaine Berthet-Bondet
39210 Château-Chalon
☎ 03 84 44 60 48
www.berthet-bondet.net
The cave is open for visits and

tastings from Mon to Sat 10.00–12.00 and 14.00–19.00.

Abbaye de Baume-les-Messieurs

Mairie
39210 Baume-les-Messieurs
☎ 03 84 44 61 41
There is free entry to the exhibitions which tend to be temporary.

La Région des Lacs

Boating on Lac de Vouglans

Plage de la Mercantine
Maisod
☎ 03 84 25 45 97

Boats can be hired here, but there are also excursion available from:

Bateaux "Le Louisiane"

Bateaux-croisière
pont de la pyle
☎ 03 84 25 46 78
There are excursions daily and an evening dinner cruise lasting two and a half hours.

Hérisson Falls

Maison des Cascades du Hérisson
Lieu-dit Val Dessus
39130 Ménétrux-en-Joux
www.cascades-du-herisson.fr
The museum is open every day from Apr to Sept. A visit can be combined with the cost of a parking ticket for the falls.

The Central Plateau

Musée Archéologique
26, rue Baronne-Delort,
Champagnole
☎ 03 84 52 49 32
www.tourisme.champagnole.com
Open ever day in Jul and Aug except Tue 14.00–18.00

Forges de Syam W

Route de Champagnole
39300 Syam
☎ 03 84 51 61 00
www.forgesyam.fr
Open in only at weekends in May, Jun and Sept. Open throughout Jul a and Aug except Tue 10.00–18.00

The Mountains of the Jura

Le Hameau du Fromage

7 Zone Artisanale
25330 Cléron
☎ 03 81 62 41 51
Because this is attached to a restaurant it is open from 9.00 until 24.00 every day.

Centre Polaire

Prémanon W

Centre Polaire Paul-Emile Victor
1, rue de la Sambine
39220 Prémanon
☎ 03 84 60 77 71
www.centrepev.co
This interesting centre, set up by the Polar Explorer Paul-Emile Victor (1907–1995), is open every day except Tue 10.00–12.00 and 14.00–18.00. Closed from ,mid-Nov to mid-Dec.

3. Southern Jura & the Bugey

The great curve of the Jura ends in a line of mountains that carry on towards the south. This range links with the small massif of the Bugey and runs into the Chartreuse and beyond that the Vercors. Together these limestone ranges act as a kind of western defence, an outer wall protecting the Higher Alps within the Prealpine enclosure.

The busiest route through these Prealpine ranges follows the valley from Nantua to Bellegarde. The valley is followed by the road, the railway and recently by the A40 motorway, using a stunning combination of tunnels and viaducts, as can be most clearly seen just outside Nantua. Another

Opposite: Sunset above Lac d' Aiguebelette. *D
Below: La Borne au Lion-the old boundary of Franche Comté. *F

motorway, the A43 from Lyon to Chambéry (see Chapter 4) finds a line at the southernmost point of this region, where its route is shortened by a long tunnel through the spine of the range (L'Épine), although the old road detours to pass round the end of the most southerly mountain. Beyond this are the mountains of the Chartreuse and the Vercors.

There is a low-level route where the Jura ends and the Bugey begins. This was the original one chosen by the railway and it made the little village of Culoz an important name on international railway timetables. The road and the railway follow the 12-mile long (19km) Cluse des Hôpitaux, with its limestone walls before turning towards the Grand Colombier, the Jura's southernmost peak and skirting round south of it to meet the Rhône Valley. There is a turning off this road that goes right after the Cluse des Hôpitaux, passes through Belley, crosses the Rhône and makes its way towards the mountains. It is possible to continue on this road, using the Col du Chat, but in 1932 a mile-long tunnel was driven through the mountains at a height of nearly 1,500ft (390m). On a sunny day this little-known route is the most dramatic and impressive way of entering the Alpine region. As the visitor emerges from the darkness of the tunnel, Aix-les-Bains and the Lac du Bourget (see Chapter 4) glisten below, with the Bauges mountains behind and the Belledonne range stretching away to the south.

The major routes tend to cross the Southern Jura and the Bugey from west to east, but there are many smaller roads that thread their way between the ranges from north to south. It is these minor roads and the quiet unexplored areas which they open up that gives this region its charm. Although the north is quite heavily populated around St Claude and Oyonnax, as well as round Nantua and Bellegarde, the south of the region is delightfully agricultural with farms and small villages dotting the hillsides.

St Claude

One of the most eye-catching features in St Claude is the Grand Pont, the high-level bridge spanning the River Tacon. St Claude was chosen 1,500 years ago by two hermits, Romain and Lupicin, as an ideal spot to set up a monastic retreat far from the world. The two original monks attracted many others until a large community of 1500 monks was formed. In the seventh century the Bishop of Besançon, later known as St Claude, gave up his post to come and rule the monastery as abbot. In the eleventh century the monastery and the town that had grown up around it took on the name of St Claude, whose body was preserved in the church.

In the centre of the town opposite the Cathedral there is a good museum, the Musée de la Pipe et du Diamant, bringing together St Claude's past and present skills in the making of pipes and the working of precious stones, the other major industry in the town. It has tools and machines as well as many examples of the finished articles. There is also a 40-minute film, showing the skills involved in the different processes. Perhaps the most interesting room for the non-specialist visitor is the pipe room with every type and size of pipe on show.

Mijoux and the Valserine Valley

The D436 from St Claude in the direction of Septmoncel and Mijoux enters the Gorges du Flumen. This most impressive gorge, cut deep into the mountain by the River Flumen, stretches for 4 miles (6$^1/_2$km) and the road climbs up the side giving more and more impressive views until the top is reached at the Belvédère du Saut du Chien. The road is narrow and goes through two tunnels. Parking is not possible until the belvedere is reached. From this point there are good views into the gorge, and the river can be seen descending in a series of waterfalls. The next parking spot is by the extraordinary shaped Chapeau de Gendarme. This is where the strata of rock were under such intense pressure in the Tertiary Era that they folded into a shape not unlike a policeman's hat.

For a final sight of St Claude and the Gorges du Flumen, there is a right turn in the hamlet of L'Evalide that takes the D25 for 2 miles (3$^1/_4$km) to a look-out point, the Belvédère de la Cernaise. This road also goes towards the hamlet of Le

Coulou, where there is a little known but good little toy museum, Le Musée du Coulou.

The D25 continues south towards the village of La Pesse, which is the starting point to reach the summit of the Crêt de Chalame. This is one of the highest points in the Jura at 5,067ft (1,545m) but is not difficult to climb. Turn left opposite the church in the village of La Pesse. The Crêt de Chalame is indicated. Park near the memorial to the Maquis. This spot used to be the frontier point between France, Switzerland and the Franche-Comté. The frontier indicator, a small stone post with a Fleur-de-Lys on the French side, an 'S' on the Swiss side and a lion on the Franche-Comté side, is called 'La Borne au Lion'. It is about an hour's walk on a well-marked path to the summit. The final section is quite steep. The whole of the Valserine Valley is laid out below, with the Alps and on a clear day the Mont Blanc massif to the south. It does not take much longer to descend by continuing south and following the path down through the trees to meet a track that returns to 'La Borne au Lion' along a forestry road.

From the Chapeau de Gendarme, the road to Mijoux continues through Septmoncel, known for its cheese and its stone-cutting. There are workshops in Septmoncel and surrounding villages such as Lamoura, which welcome visitors. The scenery is almost Alpine with its high-altitude pastures, forests, villages and, increasingly, ski-runs and ski-lifts. A road off left to Lamoura goes into the area that is most well-known for skiing and called by the collective name of Les Rousses Haut Jura. In the summer it is very good high-altitude walking country with laid-out paths, such as the GR9, the long-distance track that goes from the Jura to the Côte d'Azur. While walking, the visitor may come across posts marked GTJ. These mark the Grande Traversée du Jura, a cross-country skiing route that goes the length of the mountain range.

The village of Lajoux is the highest in the Jura and is now the centre of the Parc Naturel Régional du Haut Jura. It is the northernmost village in the skiing area now called Jura Sud and is becoming increasingly popular as a centre for winter and summer visitors. From Lajoux the road drops down in a series of bends to the village of Mijoux at the head of the Valserine Valley, once the border between France and Savoy. The Col de la Faucille, described in Chapter 2, is easily reached from Mijoux by following the signs.

La Fête des Soufflaculs

La Fête des Soufflaculs is held at the beginning of April and is wonderfully light-hearted affair with a procession and carnival characters. However it harks back to darker days when the monks would invade the town to blow out the devil with bellows *(soufflets).* Unfortunately for the ladies of the town, the monks thought that the devil resided on their person, which is why even today skirts have to be held very tightly round the knees during the festivities.

Pipemaking in St Claude

*Pipes madein St Claude. *F*

The monastery of St Claude became a very popular centre of pilgrimage and the town's craftsmen served the pilgrims by making statues, rosaries and other holy objects. It was this work with wood that was at a later date to make the craftsmen of the town world-famous when they transferred these skills to making pipes.

The wood-carvers and turners had been making pipes, usually porcelain or metal bows with a wooden or horn stem, when in the 1850s briar imported from the Mediterranean area began to be used with great success. The process was patented and St Claude became the world centre for the manufacture of briar pipes. Many of the workshops in town encourage visits. For example Pipes Genod, 13 Faubourg Marcel is a working factory, but visitors are allowed to see the pipes being made. In order to encourage pipe-smoking and promote the making of pipes, there is a Confrérie des Maîtres Pipiers de St Claude, a brotherhood of pipe-makers, based at No 45 Rue du Pré, the town's main street. The brotherhood wear blue and gold robes and meet regularly in the manner of a medieval guild.

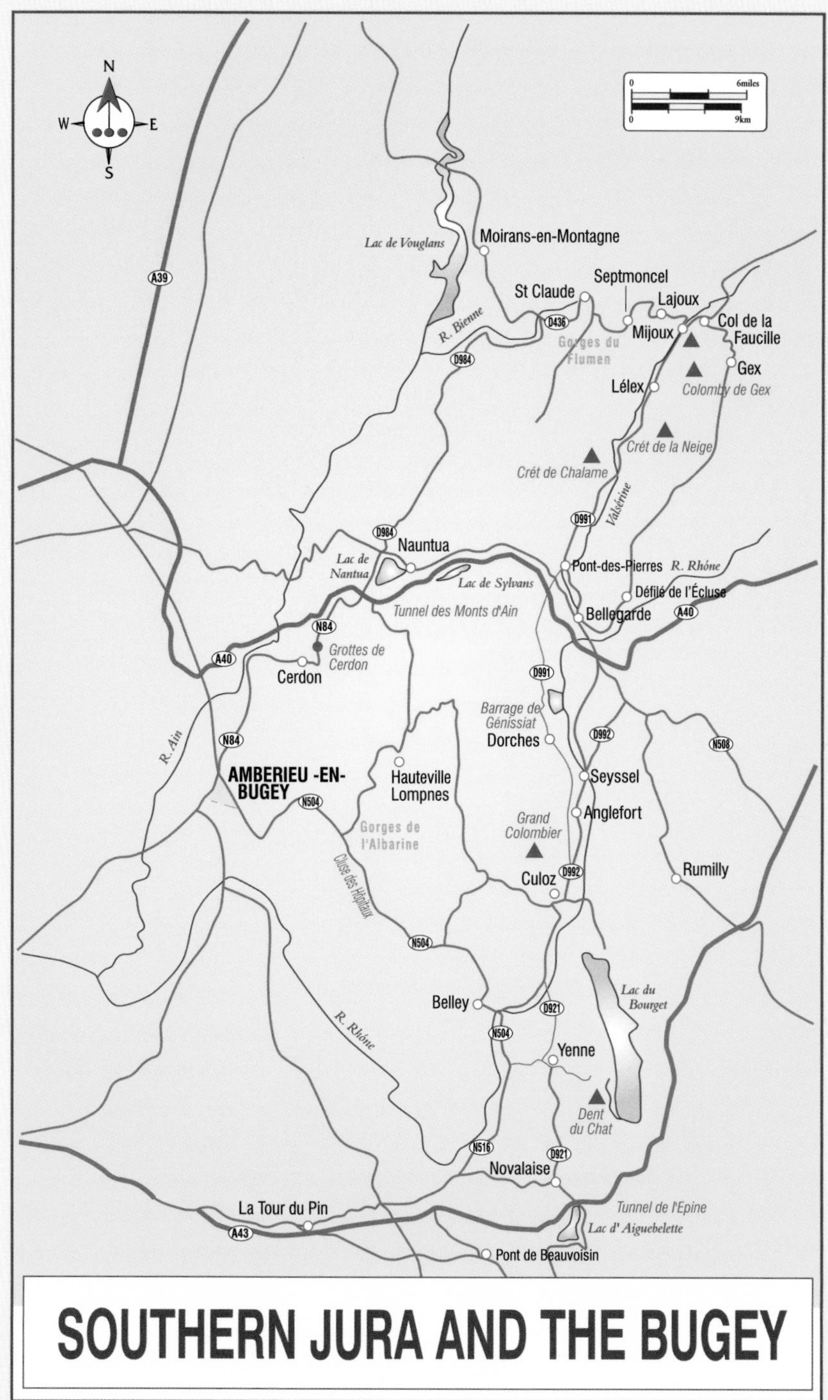

SOUTHERN JURA AND THE BUGEY

A Walk in the Parc Naturel Régional du Haut Jura

From the village of Lélex in the Valserine Valley, it is possible to get high into the mountains using the Télécabine La Catheline. This leaves only a short walk on well marked paths to reach any of the summits. From the upper station, the GR9 goes north-east to Mont Colomby de Gex. It is not necessary to go as far as that, a 2-hour walk, to reach the ridge and look south over Geneva and its lake towards the Alps. The upland pastures here, protected by the rules of the Parc, are famous for their Alpine flowers, especially the pinks, the gentians and the orchids, including the celebrated *sabot de Vénus,* the ladies slipper orchid. There are many varieties of lily, particularly the lovely Turk's Cap lily with its swept-back purple petals. Since it is a conservation area, visitors are asked not to pick the flowers. The soil is also very good for bushes, such as cotoneaster, juniper, bilberry and bearberry, with its dark green leaves and red berries. Botanists find this mountain range very interesting because a lot of the vegetation seems to be a 'throwback' to the glacial period. The pine trees and the rhododendrons are normally found either higher in the Alps or much further north in Scandinavia

Nantua

Before visiting the town of Nantua, it is worth making the trip south for 12 miles (19km) along the wide, relatively deserted N84 towards Cerdon to see the Grottes de Cerdon and to visit the village in its impressively deep valley beyond. The huge sign to the Grottes du Cerdon is easily seen on the right of the road. A roadway leads down towards the cave system. The central cavern, the Fromagère, is very imaginatively lit to get the maximum effect from its size. It gets its name because for centuries it was used by local cheesemakers to store their produce. In 1981 the further galleries were cleared so that it is possible to continue through the system and come out at the far end, where there is a very good view of the amphitheatre (la reculée) of Cerdon. The accompanied visit takes about an hour.

Although the village is quite close, the N84 winds round the mountainside, passing a dramatic memorial to the Maquis. The rebirth of France is symbolised by the figure of a woman emerging from the rock which has enscribed on it the words 'Where I die, the Motherland is reborn'. The village beyond is famous for its nineteen fountains and its brass and copper workshop and museum, La Cuivrerie de Cerdon. The waterwheels, old forge, mechanical hammers and presses make this a worthwhile visit.There is also an opportunity to see the sort of products that have been made since the workshops opened in 1854.

The return to Nantua has to be on the N84. The road to the south of the lake would make an attractive short cut, but it is 'one-way' from Nantua. In the centre of Nantua, there is a memorial to the local MP, Jean-Baptiste Baudin, who died on the barricades in Paris defending the Constitution against the Coup d'État that was to bring Napoléon III to power. Visitors with an interest in the local life and Resistance during World War II will find the little museum next to the church interesting. The lakeside, where it is possible to hire boats and sailboards, is dominated by a memorial to the deportees in the war, that perhaps intentionally by its macabre nature is a constant warning and witness to the sufferings of the persecuted. It shows a skeletal figure laid out and apparently about to be crushed under the weight of a very thick lintel.

The viaduct, carrying the A40 towards Bellegarde towers over the eastern end of the town. In order to appreciate the vision and the skill of the engineers who built it, it is worth stopping to watch the flow of traffic as it moves on to the viaduct after emerging from an apparently tiny hole in the mountain above.

The Bugey

The main part of Le Bugey is the area caught in the huge loop made by the River Rhône after it passes through Bellegarde. To the south of the Rhône the hills continue towards the Chartreuse and are bounded by the Lac du Bourget and the River Guiers. This area, once known as Le Petit Bugey, has been remaned the Avant Pays Savoyard. The River Rhône has been dammed in many places as it flows south, in order to generate power. The most impressive dam is at Génissiat 10 miles (16km) south of Bellegarde. A good approach is to use the N508, the Annecy road, out of the town and turn right after 5 miles (8km). This drops down towards the dam and across it. It is usually possible to park on the road next to the office building, although the official car park is 200yd beyond. The best view of the dam is from the viewpoint that has been constructed at the end of the buildings. There is a permanent exhibition there and a commentary in several languages. Running parallel to the river is the quite enormous evacuation canal. This is usually empty, but is necessary, especially in the spring, to run off the spate caused by melting snow in the mountains. When it is in use, the water flows out of the canal into the river below in a great arc. This is known as

The Father of Gastronomy

A famous son of the town of Le Belley is Jean Brillat Savarin who studied gastronomy in the late eighteenth century and whose book *The Physiology of Taste* became world-famous. He was born at No 62 Grande Rue. His statue is at the end of the park Le Promenoir and has on it the lovely inscription 'Inviting someone to eat means taking responsibility for his happiness for the time that he is under our roof'.

Mandrin – Savoy's Robin Hood

The Château de Rochefort was used by the notorious bandit and smuggler, Louis Mandrin, as his base in Savoy, from which he raided over the border into France. This Robin Hood-like character is celebrated in many hotels in the area which claim to have his boots, 'Les Bottes de Mandrin', supposedly left behind when he had to escape in a hurry. The cave where he and his gang of up to 75 followers holed up, "La Grotte de Mandrin", can be visited. He was betrayed by a mistress and captured by French soldiers who crossed the border illegally. His execution by being broken on the wheel in Valence caused a diplomatic crisis between France and Savoy.

the ski jump, Le Saut de Ski.

Seyssel, once a frontier point between France and Savoy but now the border town between the departments of L'Ain and Haute Savoie, can be visited with a short detour. Before reaching the famous bridge suspended from a single pillar surmounted by a statue of the Virgin in the centre of the Rhône, there is a park between the road and the river. In the centre is a 16-ton, 3,000-year-old tree. This was discovered buried in peat when the Chataugne Dam was being built. It has been sculpted and inserted upside down to create a focal point for the park. Across the river there is a lovely little covered market place on the left with sculpted wooden eaves. After visiting the town, a right turn leads back across the river over a new bridge, built with a central pillar to mirror the old. Ahead is the Grand Colombier which can be very easily climbed and is well worth the effort. The road, which leads up from Anglefort, goes almost to the top, leaving only a 20-minute walk either to the north summit or the south summit. It is possible to see the three lakes of Léman, Annecy and Bourget as well as the line of the Alps to the east and the Massif Central to the west with the Jura to the north.

Belley, 10 miles (16km) to the south, was the capital of Le Bugey. This town is a very good base from which to explore the surrounding area. Its one-time importance can be seen by the presence of the Cathédrale St Jean, the Bishop's Palace next door and its many administrative buildings. The Romantic poet Lamartine went to school in the town and has given his name to the college on the Rue Girerd. His statue opposite the school is a reminder of this. From the information centre by the Place de la Victoire it is possible to obtain information about the many walks in the Bugey hills to the west with their many little lakes and streams.

The N504 south from Belley goes east through the Défilé de Pierre Châtel before continuing through two tunnels and crossing the Rhône over the Pont de la Balme. It then skirts the limestone cliffs on the way to Yenne. This little market town is in a wide valley with the mountain of the Dent du Chat rising to the east. It was the home of a famous figure of the modern French theatre,

The Old Sardinian Road

These steps of Les Échelles were taken away by King Charles Emmanuel II, who had the roadway up-graded for carts and carriages. This was commemorated by his statue in the cave and gave the name 'La Route Sarde', the Sardinian Road, to the new passageway. The ravine had been used since Roman times and in the Grande Galerie (Grand Goulet) there are the remains of a wall erected by the Romans to try to prevent the water flooding the ravine.

*The Old Sardinian Road. *D*

Charles Dullin. The house where he was born in 1885 is now a museum. The road through Yenne leads up and through the tunnel under the Dent du Chat mountain to provide one of the most impressive entrance into the French Alps. A good excursion from nearby Novalaise is to turn right to the Col de la Crusille, where a signpost shows the way to walk to the Col du Barchet. Down below in the plain to the west, on an isolated hill, can be seen the Château de Mandrin,

The most popular attraction of the Avant Pays Savoyard is the beautiful Lac d'Aiguebelette set further south in the shadow of the Montagne de l'Épine. It is 10 miles (16km) around, almost crescent-shaped and surrounded by villages and vantage points. It is a good base for camping and caravanning, because besides the attractions of the lake and the surrounding area, the nearby motorway, the A43, brings many other areas very close.

The N6 forms the southern boundary of the Bugey region as it goes south from Le Pont-de-Beauvoisin following the line of the River Guiers through the Gorges de Chaille to Les Échelles and then north to Chambéry. Just north of Les Échelles, the road rises steeply and then goes through a tunnel. This tunnel was built by Napoléon in 1804 to avoid the very difficult part of the road above. Just after the tunnel, on the right, are the celebrated Grottes des Échelles. The caves are off a deep ravine, the Défilé des Échelles, once used as a road. It was steps (échelles) up the side of the ravine that gave the place and the town its name. These were once used by travellers as a way of reaching the Alps.

Places to Visit: Southern Jura

St Claude

Musée de la Pipe, du Diamant et du lapidaire W

1, place Jacques Faizant
39200 Saint-Claude
☎ 03 84 45 17 00
www.musee-pipe-diamant.com
Open from May to Sept every day 9.30–12.00 and 14.00–18.30.

Pipes Genod W

13 Faubourg Marcel
39200 Saint-Claude
☎ 03 84 45 00 47
Visits to the workshops and demonstrations take place from Mon to Thur 9.00–11.30 and 14.00–18.00 as well as Fri mornings.

Valserine

Lélex

Télécabine de la Catheline
The cable car is open on Sat, Sun and Mon from mid-July to the end of Aug as well as 14 Jul and 15 Aug.

Grande Traversée du Jura

Association Grande Traversée du Jura
15-17 Grande rue
39150 Les Planches en Montagne
☎ 03 84 51 51 51
www.gtj.asso.fr
For anyone wishing to follow the route on foot, on bicycle or on skis, this is an excellent centre for detailed information.

Nantua

Grottes du Cerdon W

01450 Labalme sur Cerdon
☎ 04.74.37.36.79
www.grotte-cerdon.com
The caves are open in Jul and Aug from 10.00–18.00. From mid-Apr to end of Jun and from Sept to mid-Oct 12.30–17.30.

Cuivrerie de Cerdon W

01450 Cerdon
☎ 04 74 39 96 34
www.cuivreriedecerdon.com
Guided tours take place morning and afternoon from May to Sept and in the afternoon from Oct to Apr.

Musée départemental d'Histoire de la Résistance et de la Déportation

3 montée de l'Abbaye,
01130 Nantua
☎ 04 74 75 07 50
Open from May to Sept, but closed on Mon.

& the Bugey

*Summit of the Dent Du Chat with Mont Blanc in the background. *D*

The Bugey

Lac d'Aiguebelette

Musée Lac & Nature
Place de la Gare
73610 Lépin-le-lac
☎ 04 79 36 08 45

Visits to this little museum, which is open mid-Jul to the end of Aug from 15.00–20.00, are free. It is also possible to hire boats from the same place.

Grottes des Échelles W

Site de St Christophe la Grotte
73360 Saint Christophe La Grotte
☎ 04 79 65 75 08

There are guided visits to the caves, once the hideout of Mandrin, throughout the day in Jul and Augfrom 10.30–16.45. At other times of the year they are at weekends, at 11.30, 13.45, 15.15 and 16.45 on Sun and at 14.45 and 16.30 on Sat.

4. Towns & Lakes in the Pre-Alps

*Below: Château de Menthon above Lac d'Annecy. *A*

Annecy and Le Lac d'Annecy

Annecy is a town that has everything. It has charm, character, history, and it is set in a beautiful site surrounded by mountains at the head of what is claimed to be the cleanest lake in Europe. More than just a beautiful town, it is an important commercial and industrial centre with a lot of light engineering and research. It seems to be bursting with activity and growth. The water in the lake has been completely purified, and this has obviously increased its attraction as a holiday area. All the villages surrounding the lake are geared up to receive visitors and provide activities, such as boating, fishing and walking. This tends to mean that Annecy and its lake are quite overcrowded at certain times of the year, notably in late July and August. To see the town at its most beautiful, it is highly recommended to visit it in spring, when the flowers are beginning to bloom, or in autumn, when the trees in the town and surrounding hills are on the turn.

Annecy is often called the 'Venice of the Alps' because the River Thiou, that takes the water from the lake, has been canalised and runs through the old town with footpaths alongside it. Other waterways such as the Canal du Vassé also run through the town and add to its charm. Since many parts of the town are not accessible by car, it is best to park near the Town Hall, built in 1847 to an Italian-inspired design, and proceed on foot from there. To get the full flavour of the old town, go down to the River Thiou. The pleasure boats will be lined up on the left, ready to take passengers on a tour of the lake. This is the Quai Napoleon Ill. There is a monument remembering the fact that the Emperor marked the first anniversary of Savoie's annexation by giving the town a steam boat, La Couronne de Savoie. Turn towards the town and walk between the river and the Church of St François. This church, perhaps a little sombre now, belies a brilliant past. It was a centre of international interest in the seventeenth and eighteenth centuries, because it housed the remains of two local saints, St François de Sales and St Jeanne de Chantal for a number of

Excursions on Le Lac d'Annecy

There are many different types of boats offering cruises on the lake. Information and tickets can be obtained from the Tourist Office or from the booths on the Quai Napoléon III. The main cruise boats provide tickets so that passengers can join and leave the boats at any point and they are an excellent way of seeing the lakeside villages. A wonderful way of experiencing the lake is to go on an evening's cruise which includes dinner. An increasingly popular way of being taken round the lake is by a small 1930's wooden boat, seating about six or seven people, called "Un canot automobile". They also provide a taxi service to different lake-side restaurants.

years before and after their canonisation, and it became a place of international pilgrimage. After passing the church, there is a two-arched footbridge over the river. This bridge provides an excellent view of the Palais de l'Isle, which forms an island. The triangular end of the building is shaped like the prow of a ship. Dating from the twelfth century, it was the Count of Geneva's base in Annecy and through the years has been High Court, a mint, a prison and is now a museum. The bridge also provides a view of the pathway alongside the Thiou, Le Quai de l'Isle, with its restaurants and its flowers. The view of the Palais de l'Isle and the Quai de l'Isle from the bridge is one of the most photogenic in the area, the texture and shape of the Palais contrasting with the colour of the flowers and the reflection of the buildings in the river. Annecy won first prize for its floral displays so often that it has been declared 'hors concours', a category that puts it above comparison.

On the other side of the bridge is a maze of narrow streets, dominated by the castle. This area is always animated and busy, but especially so on Sundays when there is a market that takes over most of the narrow streets on both sides of the river. The main street is the Rue Ste Claire that runs parallel to the river. Although there are many streets to the left going up to the castle, it is worth going right down the Rue Ste Claire in order to reach the Porte Ste Claire. This would have been the way out of town in medieval times for the road to Chambéry and Aix-les-Bains. Since it is in such good condition, even down to the old hinges, it gives a good

St François de Sales

The plaque on the façade of the church of Notre Dame in Annecy tells how the childless Madame de Sales came to pray for a son. Her prayer was answered and the son was later to become St François de Sales. The other plaque says that on the 8 September 1614, when St François was preaching in this church, a white dove came down and settled on him. St François, born in the Château de Sales, came from a noble family. He received the classic aristocratic education and his father had a career in law lined up for him – as well as a suitable wife. Much against his father's wishes, he trained for the priesthood and was ordained in 1593. He then joined in the immense task of restoring Catholicism to the area between Annecy and Geneva, specifically the Chablais. He did this by a combination of charismatic preaching and writing leaflets, pamphlets and books. His most famous book, still read today, is "An Introduction to the Devout Life". St François was made Bishop of Geneva in 1602, but remained in Annecy, where he set up a company of nuns, the Order of Visitation, under St Jeanne de Chantal and the Académie Florimontane. He died in Lyon on 28th December, 1622. Now the patron Saint of writers and journalists, he left many papers and sayings. One of his best known is "Nothing is so strong as gentleness, nothing as gentle as real strength", which in a way summed up his life.

*Le Pont des Amours at Annecy. *A*

impression of medieval Annecy huddling for protection around the base of the castle.

The houses and shops in the Place Ste Claire have been completely renovated, but great care has been taken to preserve the character of the square. There is a pathway, the Chemin des Remparts, from the Porte Ste Claire up to the château. This contains the Musée Régional, which concentrates on regional popular art, such as pottery, woodwork and furniture, as well as archaeology and natural history. The building itself is also of interest, it was built over many years and in many styles. To the right of the gateway into the inner courtyard, there is the solid windowless block of the Tour de la Reine, which dates back to the twelfth century and is the oldest part of the castle. The most obvious feature in the inner courtyard is the arcade that covers the well, said to be over 100ft (30m) deep. To the left of this is the Logis Nemours, built in 1545,

*Le Château de Montrottier. *A*

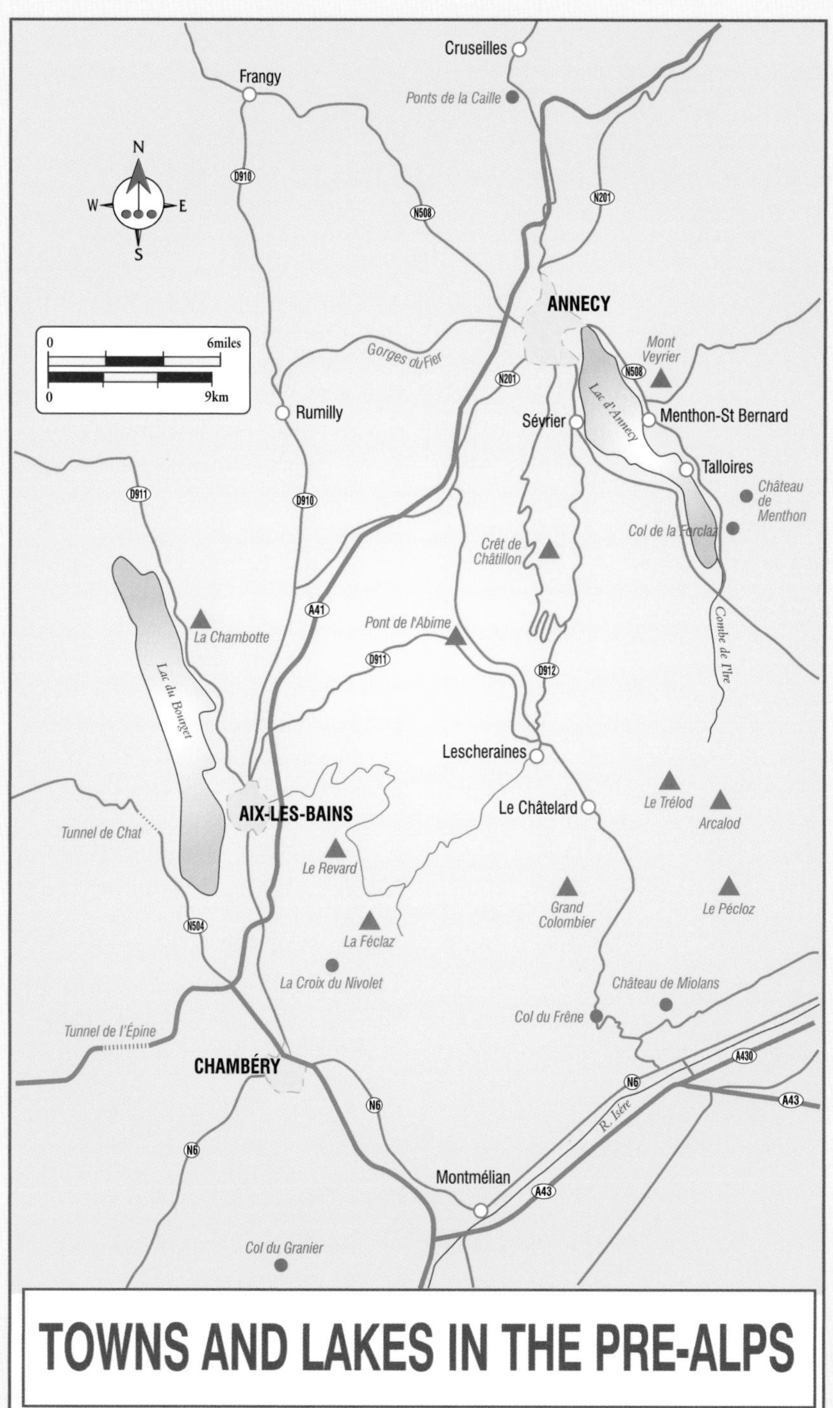

TOWNS AND LAKES IN THE PRE-ALPS

while to the right is the Logis Neuf, built in 1571. At the extreme right is the Tour Perrière and the Logis Perrière, built on the instruction of Amadeus VIII, the first Duc de Savoie, in 1445. This part overlooks the town, and from the terrace in front of it there is a very good view of the old town tightly packed together with its red tile roofs and narrow streets, while the newer parts of the town stretch away filling up the valley. It also gives a wonderful view of the lake.

A pedestrianised street leads down from the castle to the river Thiou. Before going into the town, it is worth crossing the Thiou and following it to the left. About 200yd downriver, there is a delightful riverside walk, the Promenade Lachenal dedicated to one of France's most influential mountaineers, who lived in Annecy. Turning back towards the town centre on the other side of the Thiou and crossing the main road, there is a small road which leads into the Rue Jean-Jacques Rousseau. The most imposing building in this street is the Ancien Evéché (the Old Bishop's Palace) with the Cathédrale St Pierre next to it on the left. The Palace, a rather severe eighteenth-century building, that towers over the narrow street, was built by Monseigneur Biord, the tenth Bishop of Geneva, by that time permanently resident in Annecy. He elevated the little Franciscan Chapel of St Pierre and turned it into a cathedral, next to which he had his palace built. The Palace now houses the National School of Music as can be heard when passing. The Cathédrale St Pierre is interesting for its architecture and its associations. From the outside it looks like a typical Renaissance church with its arches and its high rose window. However inside it is very obviously Gothic with its vaulting and the layout of the naves. The façade has obviously been grafted on, perhaps with the intention of improving its appearance in line with its new status. By association, the cathedral brings together two of the greatest men that the region produced. When St François was made Bishop of Geneva in 1602, he was based in the cathedral. One hundred-and-fifty years later, the young Jean-Jacques Rousseau was expelled from Geneva, and while resident in Annecy, was persuaded to become a Catholic by a Madame de Warens whom he first met in the Cathedral garden . One of the great free-thinkers of the eighteenth century, he was to stay in Annecy for another 2 years before moving to Chambéry. Round behind the cathedral there is a little path between the houses, so typical of the old town, that leads through to the beautifully arcaded Rue Filaterie. Take this and turn left towards the Place de Notre-Dame.

When the Victorian art critic John Ruskin was staying in Annecy, he was very impressed by the first building on the left, the old Town Hall, with its ornate steps leading up to the front door. He was most struck by the very beautiful cast-iron balustrade, a detail that is carried through to the two balconies above. It is still in a state of excellent preservation. Although it has had a long and interesting history, at one time the Headquarters of the Revolutionary Council in Annecy, it is now the presbytery for the Church of Notre-Dame-de-Liesse. The present church, built in 1845, is a rather ugly copy of the original one. The spire, which is not characteristic of the region, leans slightly. The main claim to fame of this church is that for a number of years it was the home of the Holy Shroud, which was later taken to Turin. The plaque on the façade tells how the childless Madame de Sales came to pray for a son.

The Rue Royale, which becomes a pedestrian precinct and leads into the Rue Paquier, shows all the charm of the old town, with its arcades set on very solid pillars. Giving onto the Rue Paquier is the fine Hôtel de Sales. It can be distinguished by its wrought-iron balcony and the busts set in the wall above the archways. These represent the four seasons. This town house, built by the de Sales family in the sixteenth century, served as the residence of the Ducs de Savoie when they stayed in Annecy. Just after the region became part of France in 1860, it was the Head Office of the Banque de Savoie for a number of years. Most towns in the area have a branch of this bank, but its Head Office is now in Chambéry.

At the end of the Rue Paquier, the Town Hall and the beautiful school next to it can be seen to the right, but there are many more places to be seen, not included in this brief introductory tour. Among these is the church opposite the Town Hall, the Église St Maurice. Its size is very impressive, but most interesting are the frescoes that were uncovered when the church was being restored in 1953. One represents Cardinal Martignes of Luxembourg at prayer, and the other the death of Noble Philibert of Monthoux, dating from 1458.

Further up the hill beyond the castle is the modern Basilique de la Visitation. It is, in fact, far enough away to warrant driving, since it is a good 20 minutes' walk. It was started in 1922, but not completed and consecrated until 1949. The mortal remains of Annecy's famous saints, St François de Sales and St Jeanne are conserved and venerated in the church. One reward for going to the basilica is the very good view of the town, the lake and the lakeside gardens.

The main lakeside garden, the Jardin Public behind the Town Hall, the Theatre and the Casino, is bound on one side by the Thiou and on the other by the Canal du Vassé. The trees are particularly interesting. There is a great variety of different types, each tree being marked with the name of its species. In the park there is a statue of Berthollet, the famous French chemist, who was born at Talloires. The bronze basreliefs depict scenes from his life, for example when he accompanied Napoleon to the Egyptian pyramids. The beautiful artificial Island of Swans, 'Isle des Cygnes', created in 1854, can be seen nearby in the lake. The swans that inhabit the island symbolise the grace and beauty of the setting. To continue walking round the lake, cross the Canal du Vassé by the Lovers' Bridge (Le Pont des Amours). The canal seen to the left almost covered by an archway of plane trees is particularly beautiful with all the boats drawn up at the water's edge. The park beyond the bridge, the Champ de Mars, stretches towards the Avenue d'Albigny, but if you keep to the lakeside, you come to an orientation point. The view from here shows

Palaos de l'Île, Annecy. *B

Lac d'Annecy. *A

the full beauty of the setting of the lake with villages down to the water's edge against a backdrop of mountains. Many of the beaches can be seen, such as the Parc à l'Impériale to the left, where an entrance fee is charged, and the Plage des Marquisats on the right-hand side of the lake, which is free, as well as many ports, where boats and sailboards can be hired. Further along the lake on the left are the villages of Veyrier and Talloires, and on the right Sévrier and Duingt. The lake almost seems to join between Duingt and Talloires, but in fact opens out beyond for another 2 miles (3km). The mountains above are quite accessible and give some wonderful views, not only of Annecy and its lake, but over a much wider area to Mont Blanc and beyond.

Tour of Lac d'Annecy

This 20-mile (32km) tour is best done by car down the eastern left-hand side out of Annecy. Almost before leaving

Annecy's Bell Foundry

In Sévrier there is a Bell Foundry and Museum of Bell-Making (Musée de la Cloche). This famous bell foundry made, among many others, the 26-ton bell of the Basilique du Sacré-Coeur which overlooks Paris from Montmartre, as well as the twenty-seven individual bells of the Carillon Savoyard in Chambéry. The museum is housed in a purpose-built building on the N508 that runs beside the lake. The foundry is behind the museum.

*Musée de la Cloche, Sévrier near Annecy. *A*

town, a left turn leads to Annecy-le-Vieux.

Three miles (5km) further on is the village of Menthon-St-Bernard. A left turn along the D269 goes up to the Château de Menthon. This magnificent castle with its strong walls, turrets and high-pitched roofs replaced the original, where St Bernard, the founder of the Great St Bernard Monastery in Switzerland, was born. It has a fine collection of Louis XIV furniture. There is a very good view of the lake from the terrace.

After returning to the village, continue the road south, but to get to Talloires turn right down the D909. This little village in its perfect setting has become famous for its hotels and restaurants, many of which have a world-wide reputation. The Hôtel l'Abbaye was in fact a monastery, originally founded in the ninth century. The bay of Talloires is enclosed on its northern side by the

Les Bauges

The area between Chambéry, Aix-les-Bains and Annecy is the Parc Naturel Régional du Massif des Bauges, set up in 1995. It has recently become better equipped for holidaymakers in villages such as Aillon-le-Jeune and Lescheraines, but it still maintains a very unspoilt and even rugged air with its little villages and high Alpine pastures. It is pure Prealpine scenery, dominated by the limestone peaks of Le Trélod (7,170ft, 2,186m), L'Arcalod (7,270ft, 2,217m) and Le Pecloz (7,412ft, 2,260m). It has a long history of agriculture with its own cheese, the Tome des Bauges.

large Roc de Chore projecting into the lake and providing protection from the north. There is a beach to the south and all kinds of boats can be hired. The tour of the lake can continue on the road that skirts very close to the edge of the lake, until it meets the N508 back to Annecy. But it is much better to return to the D42, turn right and go up to the Col de la Forclaz. This presents a dramatic view of the lake, a little spoilt by the quarry on the end of Mont Taillefer on the other side. To the right of it, a wide and quite heavily populated valley comes down to the lakeside. This is the end of the Massif des Bauges, which separates Annecy from Aix-les-Bains. Behind the populated valley is the Montagne de Semnoz, the summit of which can be almost reached by road. From the Col de la Forclaz the road gently descends to Montmin, set in its rather isolated-looking Alpine scenery. More of the mountains of the Bauges can be seen, the most obvious being the pyramid-shaped Sambuy. Five miles (8km) further, the road to Annecy, the N508, is reached.

Two miles (31/4km) further, at Doussard, a small road to the left leads off into the Combe de l'Ire. This has always been strangely wild and unvisited and is now part of the Bauges Nature Reserve, where deer, chamois, ibex and marmots are protected. The road to Annecy from Doussard is of less interest, although the castle at Duingt looks impressive and villages such as St Jorioz and Sévrier have delightful beaches, and the bell-making museum is worth a visit.

Excursions from Annecy

From Annecy there are several excursions to be made. One of these is on the road to Geneva for those going north, while two others are between Annecy and Aix-les-Bains. Either could be included on a journey between the two towns.

Ten miles (16km) to the north, the N20, the road to Geneva, crosses the gorge of the River Usses, which is 450ft (137m) deep at this point. The present road bridge, 482ft (148m) long, was built in 1925. It has one of the largest single-span arches in Europe. Next to it is the original bridge, which was built in 1839 on the instructions of the King of Sardinia, Charles Albert, and is named after him. For its time it was a marvel of engineering with its castellated towers 60ft (18m) high and supported by twenty-four cables, each 600ft (1 83m) long. For those going north on the motorway the towers are just visible over to the left after the Ponts de la Caille sign.

To the west of Annecy are the Gorges du Fier. A visit to this quite remarkable natural phenomenon can be linked to a visit to the Château de Montrottier nearby. Take the N508 out of Annecy towards Frangy and Bellegarde, and then after 3 miles (5km) the D14 left and the Gorges are signposted. The walk through the trees is on the other side of the rail tracks. These are crossed over a narrow footbridge. Look down from the bridge to see the shapes that the water has created in the rock 120ft (74m) below. As the path goes alongside the Fier, the Château de Montrottier can be seen on the hill on the right. The castle can be visited later by returning to the car and driving. However it is possible to make a visit part of a circular 3-mile (5km) walk, although it is quite steep in places.

If continuing to Aix-les-Bains, turn right along the D912 and 5 miles (8km) later the D911 goes northwest to Aix-les-Bains, although a stop is recommended on the way to see the Pont de l'Abîme. This is to the right about 5 miles (8km) along the D911. It takes the road to Gruffy over the River Chéran, 300ft (483m) below.

The point where the D911 turns off the D912 is at the very centre of the Bauges mountains, and they certainly deserve a closer look.

The main town of the Bauges is Le Châtelard on the south-bound D911, and beyond this, the road becomes more Alpine with the Dent de Pleuven and the Arcalod to the east. At École there is a choice. Continue straight on for 6 miles (9km) to the Col du Frêne. From here, and especially from the hotel just below the Col, there is a wonderful view of the Savoie Valley - the Combe de Savoie with the River Isère flowing down its length. Beyond the valley, the mountains stretch from the Beaufortain to the left, right round to the Chartreuse on the right. A left turn at École, along a forestry road goes high into the Vallon de Bellevaux, the Bellevaux Valley, an integral part of the Bauges National Park. After about 3 miles (5km), a track to the right leads up to a small oratory and the Chapel of Notre-Dame-de-Bellevaux. This is the site of a medieval monastery, and it gives more than any other a real impression of the isolation and serenity that medieval monks were seeking. This valley is particularly worth visiting in the autumn, because the forest has a high proportion of beech trees and the colours of their leaves give a special quality of light as they turn.

Aix-les-Bains

Aix-les-Bains has been a spa since Roman times and gets its name from the Latin Vicus Aquensis, the Town of the Waters. As a spa it ranks with the finest in Europe, from Vichy to Baden-Baden. In the Thermes Nationaux which treat 50,000 patients a year, are the headquarters of spa water treatment in France. Although the presence of the spa has affected the history of the town, it is as well known and appreciated nowadays for its lake.

A visit to Aix-les-Bains should start

in the very centre, in the Place des Thermes in front of the Thermes Nationaux. All around is evidence of the town's existence throughout history as a spa. The most dominant feature is the Arc de Campanus. This Roman archway was erected by Lucius Campanus as a family memorial at the end of the first century AD. It is 30ft (9m) high and the archway measures 11 1/2ft (3m) across. The niches were made to contain busts of various members of the Campanus family. The building of the Thermes Nationaux has been constantly renovated. In the basement, the remains of the original Roman baths can still be seen. The present building is mainly eighteenth and nineteenth century, completed in 1857, and was opened by Victor Emmanuel II, soon to be King of United Italy. The newer building was added in 1929, but was completely modernised in 1972. A visit can be made to the vast caves behind

*The Abbaye de Hautecombe overlooking the Lac du Bourget. *D*

the Thermes Nationaux building, from which the aluminium spring used to issue. The effect of the chemicals in the water has made very interesting shapes on the sides of the cave.

The Hôtel de Ville opposite the Thermes Nationaux was sold to the town in 1865 by the Seyssel family. It is a fine example of a sixteenth-

*Proud of her new bell! *A*

A drive from Aix-les-Bains

Mont Revard, which overlooks the town from the east, is very easy to visit by car by taking the D913 that rises up the hillside behind the Thermes Nationaux. It is a 15-mile (24km) journey that seems to take the 3000ft (915m) climb in its stride. Above Travignin, on the approach to the Col de la Cluse, there are widening views over the Sierroz Valley and the Albanais with the regular line of the Jura mountains some way in the background. The view from Mont Revard is exceptional because of its central position. To the east, the Mont Blanc massif is clearly visible across the intervening mountain ranges, while to the west the Dent du Chat rises above the lake, the Petit Bugey, and the Rhône can just be seen as it flows down the Pierre Chatel gorge, to the right of the Dent du Chat. In the winter, Mont Revard is a favourite resort both for downhill and cross-country skiing. The marked cross-country ski-runs join up with those of La Féclaz and St François to form the great 'Nordic Plateau'. In the summer, these make wonderful walks, where the smell of pine, mixed with the purity of the air enhances the beauty of the surroundings.

century French château, and inside it has a beautiful Renaissance staircase. Nearby is the Temple of Diana, another fine monument that houses the Musée d'Archéologie et de Préhistoire. There are many exhibits of the Roman occupation of the area, including part of the statue of a Roman emperor, thought to be Constantine.

To the right of the Thermes is the park. This animated and lively spot is central to the town's function as a spa. It provides an area to walk and relax, as well as to 'take the waters' in the building at the rear of the park. In the corner of the park, there is a bust of H.R.W. Hudson, a benefactor of the town, who died in 1936. This is the first evidence of the important presence of the English in the town. There is a Boulevard des Anglais, an Avenue Lord Revelstoke, and in the Place du Revard a bust of Queen Victoria who formally visited the town, but also came incognito on other occasions using one of her titles, the Countess of Balmoral, to look for a property to buy – apparently unsuccessfully.

Near the Place du Revard can be found the Casino, the Palais de Savoie. This was built originally in 1848, but was completely modernised in 1936. Standing in its park with an open-air theatre capable of holding 3,500, it gives some idea of the sumptuous lifestyle that used to be enjoyed by the visitors to Aix, when it was one of the international European social centres. This can also be seen in the many hotels such as the Bernascon above the Chambéry road, the Avenue de Marloz. About half a mile down this road there is an interesting house high up on the left. This was built by a well known local business man, Léon Grosse in 1900, but is now the property of the town and undergoing restoration.

Alphonse de Lamartine

Lamartine was one of the first of the Romantic Poets and he made Aix famous with his poem "Le Lac". During a stay in Aix for health reasons in 1816 he met a fellow invalid, Madame Charles and fell deeply in love. When he returned the following year he heard that Madame Charles had been too ill to travel and had just died. His poem, a desperate reaction to this news, became the classic Romantic poem. On the spot where he wrote Le Lac, there is a monument to commemorate the event. This is between the town and the lake, but slightly to the south at Tresserve. The house in which Lamartine stayed no longer exists since it was on a site needed by the Thermes Nationaux when it expanded. However in the Musée Faure many items of furniture and personal objects have been brought together to give an idea of the sort of life that he would have led when he visited Aix in 1816 and 1817.

Before going down to the lake, there is a visit not to be missed. This is the Musée du Docteur Faure in the Boulevard des Côtes. It has a superb collection of Impressionist paintings. It also has the finest collection of Rodin sculptures outside the Rodin Museum in Paris, as well as several of his water-colours. On the top floor there is a kind of shrine to Aix's most famous visitor, Alphonse de Lamartine.

It is better to arrive at the lake at the Le Petit Port. Here, there is an aquarium that has about fifty species of freshwater fish, many of them indigenous to the lake. One of the best beaches is also situated at Le Petit Port.

An ideal way of getting to the Le Grand Port is to take the Boulevard du Lac, a beautiful spot for a stroll in the evening. On the other side of the lake is one of the area's most famous landmarks, the Abbaye de Hautecombe. This can be reached by driving round the north end of the lake, but the best way to get there is to take a boat from the Grand Port.

From the Abbaye de Hautecombe, the line of hills can be seen that dominate Aix-les-Bains and the lake from the east. Opposite is La Chambotte, and far to the right overlooking Aix is Le Mont Revard. Both can be visited fairly easily by car from the town. To get to La Chambotte take the N201 towards Annecy and at La Biolle turn left to St Germain from where there are signs to the summit. From the restaurant at La Chambotte, there is a very good view of the lake and the mountains from the Jura to the Chartreuse. To return to Aix, it is possible to retrace one's path, but it is more interesting to turn left at St Germain and continue north to the Col du Sapenay to make a circular tour. The road goes through lovely Alpine scenery, with, on the right, occasional glimpses of the agricultural region around Rumilly, known as the Albanais. After the Col du Sapenay descend by a series of hairpin bends to the marshy plain at the end of the lake, After passing through Chindrieux and Chaudieu, return on the D991 to Aix. The road goes through the village of Brison. This used to be called Brison-les-Oliviers, because it is so protected by the hills to its back that it is warm enough to grow olive trees.

The road to Mont Revard can be used as a way of getting to Chambéry from Aix-les-Bains. Continue on the D913 to La Féclaz, which has now become Chambréy's local ski resort. Shortly after, take the D912 to the right and drop down to the N6 via St Jean d'Arvey. This will go into Chambéry. However the most direct road from Aix to Chambéry is the N201 that follows the lakeside. This is quite without interest, apart from the view of the lake, but very fast. It is more interesting to leave Aix from the centre and go down the Avenue de Marlioz. This will lead on to the D991 and passes on the right the beautiful and extensive public gardens of Tresserve. On the left is the Ariana Hotel and the Marlioz Spa. This large and sumptuous complex is situated in a big park, considered very English in style by the French because of the great number of trees and flowers. The spa uses cold sulphuric spring water and is very good for respiratory ailments. It also has a fitness clinic. The Aix Racecourse and the eighteen-hole golf course are opposite the Marlioz Spa. The road to Chambéry follows the line of the foothills as it passes through Viviers-du-Lac and the flats and houses of Chambéry-le-Haut, a residential suburb, signal the outer edge of the capital of Savoie.

A Famous Savoyard from Chambéry

The Comte de Boigne

The elephant monument in Chambéry was erected in 1838 by the Grenoble sculptor Sappey to the glory of Général, the Comte de Boigne (1751 -1 830),. He had made his fortune in India and spent a great part of it on rebuilding Chambéry when he returned in 1802. The base of the monument is in the form of the cross of Savoie, and the elephants, as well as the Hindu, Persian and Mongol trophies around the column, represent de Boigne's foreign successes. De Boigne had actually been expelled from Chambéry and spent the next 35 years as a mercenary, both in the Russian and the Indian army. He returned as a hero and acted with great generosity towards the town that had earlier expelled him. He planned and organised the building of the street that now joins his monument to the castle. This rather austere street with its classical houses and porticoes, worthy of Chambéry's status as capital of La Savoie, now bears his name.

Aix les Bains and the Lac du Bourget from the summit of Mont Revard. *A

Chambéry

Chambéry was for many years a capital city and this can still be seen in the layout of the town and its buildings. While Annecy is charming and Aix has an air of luxury, Chambéry is solid and dependable. This is not to say that it lacks charm. Jean-Jacques Rousseau, one of Chambéry's most famous residents, said of the town in 1750, 'if there is anywhere in the world a town where the sweetness of life can be enjoyed with pleasant and reliable people, surely it has to be Chambéry.' This is still as true today.

Chambéry has always had an important position at the entrance to the Combe de Savoie, which was the way through the Alps on the most direct route from Paris to Italy. On the Italian side of the mountains on this route is Turin, which has always had close links with Chambéry. Many of the administrative buildings in both towns are very similar in style and design, influenced by the architecture used in the Kingdom of Piedmont.

The best point from which to start a tour of Chambéry is La Fontaine des Éléphants. This fountain is Chambéry's most photographed and well known

Brothers De Maistre

The story of these two men illustrates what internationalists the Savoyards were in the eighteenth and nineteenth centuries. Joseph, born in 1753, studied law in Turin and lived in Chambéry until 1792, becoming a Senator in 1788. Worried by the way France was developing after the Revolution, he emigrated to Switzerland and was finally made Ambassador to Russia. He spent many years in St Petersburg and wrote a number of anti-revolutionary works, one called the Letters of a Savoyard Royalist. His brother Xavier, 10 years younger, the twelfth of the fifteen de Maistre children, was also a great traveller. His earliest claim to fame was as one of the first balloonists. With a friend he flew in a hot-air balloon from the Buisson Rond Park to Challes-les-Eaux, which caused a great stir locally. After many adventures all over Europe, fighting in the Sardinian army as well as being imprisoned for duelling, he also made his way to St Petersburg. Here his brother obtained for him the position of Director of the Admiralty. He was later to become famous for his writing, his most famous novel being La Sibérienne, which was based on his knowledge of Russia.

monument, and its controversial appearance produces every sort of reaction. The people of the town call it the 'Quatre sans cul'. This refers to the fact that the four elephants appear to have no rear end!

Rather than take the Rue de Boigne direct to the castle, it is better to turn to the left along the Boulevard du Théâtre past the cinema. On the right is the entrance to the Musée Savoisien. This is housed in what was once a Franciscan friary before becoming the Archbishops's Palace. It has been meticulously restored and the buildings dating back to the thirteenth century standing round a great cloister are of interest in themselves. Inside there is an excellent permanent exhibition of life in the Bronze Age lakeside settlements that existed around Lac du Bourget. This is housed in the former refectory on the ground floor. Upstairs there is a valuable collection of medieval religious art in the form of sculptures and paintings. There is also a very good folk museum, illustrating life in Savoie through the ages, concentrating especially on the more isolated agricultural mountain communities.

After visiting the museum, the extensive pedestrian streets can be reached by going down the Rue Ducis past the Théâtre Charles Dullin. At the Place du Théâtre, turn right up the Rue de la Croix d'Or. This was the most sought after street in the eighteenth century for the aristocratic and middle-class Savoyards, who wanted a town house near the centre of power. They would call these houses 'hôtels', and many still retain the name of the original family, such as No 13, L'Hôtel des Marches et de Bellegarde. This building is a very

Les Charmettes

The house, occupied by Madame de Warens and Rousseau between 1736 and 1742, is a site not to be missed. It is 2 miles (31/4km) out of town beyond the theatre along the Rue de la République. It is now the property of the town of Chambéry. The fabric of the building was painstakingly restored in 1978, while the interior was carefully preserved, and it is now a museum dedicated to the memory of Jean-Jacques Rousseau. What is noticeable even before arriving at the house is the lack of development in the small valley that the house occupies, considering its close proximity to the centre of Chambéry. This adds to its special charm. Looking out from its upstairs windows onto the cottage garden and the beautiful countryside dominated in the distance by the Dent du Nivolet, it is easy to understand why it symbolised for Rousseau a world of happiness and innocence. The interior of the house remains as it would have been in the eighteenth century, the wallpaper in Madame de Warens' bedroom is said to be certainly from the period if not original. There is an exhibition of documents and archive material connected with Jean-Jacques Rousseau in the dining room. The small chapel or oratory, squeezed in between the two main bedrooms, is a reminder of the original reason why Madame de Warens initially took an interest in Rousseau. The house has been a place of pilgrimage since the early nineteenth century and the successive visitors' books have the names of many leading figures in the worlds of literature and politics. There is a Son et Lumière every day except Tuesday throughout July and August.

good example of an aristocratic town house of the time with its first-floor salon, its full-length windows and its balcony. Some of these houses provide an alleyway through to the cathedral behind. This used to be the chapel to the Franciscan friary, but was elevated to a status equivalent to a cathedral in 1779 and gained the name 'Métropole'. It has a particularly fine facade, which is illuminated at night. Inside there is a gilded wooden statue of Notre-Dame-du-Pilier dating from the fifteenth century, and a shrine to St François de Sales. There is also the tomb of Antoine Favre, an author, a lawyer and president of Savoie's first senate.

From the cathedral, the Métropole street goes to the main pedestrian precinct, the Place St Léger. This airy, open and lively spot is an ideal place to rest. Many of the houses have an interesting history, but none more so than No 122, the Hôtel de St Laurent. This was rented by Madame de Warens from the Comte de St Laurent, and when Jean-

Château Chambery. D

Vins de Savoie

The hillsides to the south-east of Chambéry are covered in vineyards and it is a popular excursion to follow the Route du Vin, which takes the visitor through the best wine-producing villages. The wines produced in this area have their own Appellation d'Origine Contrôlée (AOC), but in addition have the collective name of Vin de Pays d'Allobrogie. This refers to the excellent reputation that wine from this area enjoyed in Roman times, when it was made by the Allobroges, the tribe who lived in the Combe de Savoie. In 1976 the name of Allobrogie was officially granted to wines from this area. The Route du Vin hugs the base of Mont Granier as it threads its way through Aprémont, Myans and so on to St André before returning via Montmélian where there is a large cooperative.

*Above: La Fontaine des Éléphants in Chambéry. *A*

*Left: Jean-Jaques Rousseau. *A*

*The Croix de Nivolet above Châmbery. *D*

Excursions from Chambéry

The Château de Miolans is on the left of the road to Albertville and is set in a wonderful site on the hillside above the valley bottom. The castle was built on the site of an old Roman camp in the eleventh century but was constantly rebuilt and added to until the sixteenth century. Besides being a guardian of the valley, it was for many years a prison and one of its most well-known inmates was the Marquis de Sade, who was imprisoned here in 1772. The castle has a particularly gruesome oubliette, where prisoners were left and forgotten. This little room can induce a severe bout of claustrophobia. The castle is open to visitors in the summer.

Another excursion from Chambéry that is very popular with the locals is a visit to the cross, the Croix du Nivolet on the top of the Dent du Nivolet. This demands quite a walk, but is not too difficult for the able-bodied. The cross that can be seen from most directions has an interesting history. In the seventeenth century an organisation called Les Pénitents Noirs de Chambéry was formed of distinguished and influential townspeople who wanted to fight Protestantism. One of their charitable works was to give support to prisoners, especially those under sentence of death. Executions were carried out in the Jardin du Vernay and the Pénitents Noirs constructed a chapel where

Jacques Rousseau came from Annecy to join her, it was to this house that he came. But his opinion of his new home was not very good. He says in his Confessions 'the house that Madame de Warens occupied was sad and sombre and my room was the most sad and sombre in the house... it has hardly any air, no light, rats, rotten floors.' He disliked the Place St Léger so much that he claimed that it made him ill. He persuaded Madame de Warens to rent a place in the country, Les Charmettes, which is a 10-minute drive from the centre of Chambéry.

The Place St Léger crosses over the Rue de Boigne, but at this point it is best to turn left along the street towards the Château de Chambéry. Overlooking the Place du Château with its modern fountain, is a statue of the de Maistre brothers, Joseph and Xavier.

The castle behind the statue is mostly occupied by the Préfecture and only parts such as the chapel can be visited. The castle was built over a period of years in a variety of styles. The oldest sections are the Porte de la Herse (the Portcullis Gateway) and the Tour Demi Ronde (the Half-Round Tower), which date back to the twelfth century. Most of the other buildings including the Tour Trésorerie (the Treasury Tower) and the Ste Chapelle date from the fifteenth century, but many were burned in the eighteenth century and had to be rebuilt. Times for visiting the Tour Demi-Ronde and the Tour Trésorerie tend to be limited, but the Ste Chapelle is less restricted. The Turin Shroud, for so many centuries thought to be the shroud of Christ, was kept in the chapel the condemned man would spend his last night. In front of the chapel they erected a huge wooden cross. In 1860 the whole area was rearranged and this meant dispensing with the chapel and the cross. The Pénitents Noirs would only accept this if a cross was erected on the summit of the Dent du Nivolet. The first cross of iron was erected in 1861, but was destroyed by a storm in 1909. The present cross of reinforced concrete covered in metal was put up in 1910.

There are two ways of getting to the cross. The easier walk demands a longer drive taking the D912 as far as La Féclaz before turning left to the hamlet of Le Sire. After parking here, a well-marked (blue/red) path leads to the summit after about an hour's fairly gentle walk. A more difficult approach, but one involving less driving, would also mean taking the D912, but soon after passing through St Alban turning left to the village of Lorettaz. Leave the car there and follow the path marked with double red lines, pass through the hamlet of Nivolet and climb up through the trees. This path ends with a bit of a scramble and takes about 2 hours. Whichever path is taken, it is a perfect way of seeing the whole of the Pre-Alps around you, with the Lac du Bourget, Chambéry and the Isère Valley below.

from 1502 to 1578. The burn marks which disfigure the shroud were caused by a fire in 1532, which destroyed most of the chapel. It was subsequently rebuilt and the stained-glass windows date from this period

Continuing the tour of the town, there is a maze of narrow streets, such as the Rue Basse du Château opposite the castle to the left of the Rue de Boigne. These streets are now delightful pedestrian areas with interesting shops, but they act as a reminder of what medieval Chambéry must have been like before de Boigne redesigned it.

After exploring these streets, follow the extension of the Rue Juiverie that becomes the narrow Rue de Lans before reaching the Place de l'Hôtel de Ville. This is a scene of great animation on Saturday afternoons as wedding parties arrive and leave to a great blowing of car horns for the civil wedding ceremony. After passing in front of the Town Hall, make for the Rue Doppet either by way of the Place de Genève or the Rue Favre. The Rue Doppet goes towards another pedestrian area, the Boulevard du Musée. To the left is the Musée des Beaux Arts, which houses the library and some fine paintings and sculptures. The building is of great interest to the Savoyards because it was in the main hall on the ground floor that the votes were counted in 1860 when Savoie finally became part of France for good. This floor and the first floor now house the public library, which has many ancient and rare books and manuscripts as well as books for lending. It has Jean-Jacques Rousseau's testament and a thirteenth-century Bible. The

L'Abbaye de Hautecombe

In 1988 the thirty-seven Benedictine monks who lived in the Abbaye de Hautecombe took a decision that was to change the style and feel of the abbey. In 1992 they all left to continue their contemplative life in a quieter place in the Durance Valley. It has been the very popularity of the spot that has forced this decision. It is now run by members of the "Communauté du Chemin Neuf". This magnificent building nestling at the lakeside had a central place in the history of Savoie. Forty-two members of the House of Savoie are buried there, the final one being Umberto II, the last king of Italy, who was buried in March 1983. The only building that goes back to the early days of the monastery, the twelfth century, is the warehouse, the Grange Batelière. The church is well worth a visit and has a recorded commentary in English giving the background to the various wonderful statues and tombs as well as a good idea of the history of Savoy.

art gallery has one of France's richest collections of Italian paintings. There are some remarkable early medieval paintings, such as the reredos of Bartoli di Fredi taken from a church in Siena, and the famous portrait of Vecello, a masterpiece of the Italian Renaissance. There are also works by Titian, Santi di Tito, Giordano and Solimena. These are completed by a collection of objets d'art, such as ivory carvings and a very fine sixteenth-century astrolabe. The schools of painting of northern Europe are also well represented by sixteenth- and eighteenth-century works. The French school is illustrated by a collection of neo-classical works and landscapes, by artists like Watteau de Lille and Isabey.

*The old town in Chambéry. *A*

To the left of the museum is the Palais de Justice and beyond it the lovely Parc du Verney. Behind the Palais de Justice is the Lycée Vaugelas. This was one of the most prestigious educational establishments in the dukedom, named after Claude Favre de Vaugelas (1595-1650), a native of Savoie, who wrote the first real grammar of the French language. In the Place de la République between the museum and the Palais de Justice

*The Arc de Campanus at Aix les Bains. *A*

is a statue to his father, Antoine Favre, who was the President of Savoie's first Senate and a collaborator of St Francis de Sales..

There are many other places of interest in the town. They could certainly be incorporated into a walking tour, but a car might be useful since some, especially Les Charmettes, are quite a long way to walk.

Another site that merits a visit, but needs a car, is beyond the park that overlooks the town off the road to Aix-les-Bains which becomes the Boulevard de Lemenc. It got its name from the old Roman town that used to be sited on the hillside rather than in the valley like modern-day Chambéry. This went by the name of Lemincum and was centred round a Roman temple to Mercury. A lot of the Roman remains in the Musée Savoisien were excavated on this site. The church on the site of the Roman temple, St Pierre de Lémenc, can be visited by arrangement. It houses the tomb of Général de Boigne and outside against the wall is the grave of Rousseau's friend, Madame de Warens.

Returning to Chambéry, the Boulevard de Lémenc turns almost back on itself as it descends through the Parc Savoiroux. At this point, on the left, there is a statue of Jean-Jacques Rousseau. This was sculpted in 1910 by M.Valett and depicts Rousseau with walking stick in hand climbing down a rocky path. Since the road is very tricky at this point it is worth parking down near the bridge and walking up again. This will give the opportunity to have a closer look at Rousseau's statue, as well as to see the monument in the Memorial Park.

Activities in Chambéry

Every week there is a thriving market in Chambéry on Saturday mornings, and there is also a carillon concert in the castle square on Saturdays. Many sporting activities are also catered for. There is an Olympic-sized open-air swimming pool and a covered pool in the Parc de Loisirs de Buisson Rond. These are among many facilities in the old gardens of the Château de Boigne to the east of the town, just off the road to Montmélian. Also at the Château de Boigne there is a riding stables and an ice rink. Besides these permanent sporting facilities, Chambéry provides many other activities and caters for many interests. There is an Antique Dealers' Show every May, an International Folk Festival in July and the Foire de Savoie in September. There is also an annual Festival of Clowns, and every August there is a Son et Lumiére in the grounds of the Château de Boigne. It is very important to find out what is on from the excellent Tourist Information Office, because Chambéry goes out of its way to organise a great number of events throughout the year.

Instead of returning to Chambéry from Montmélian, it is a good opportunity to drive on into the Combe de Savoie to see one of the most outstanding examples of medieval fortress, the Château de Miolans. This can be reached by following the N6 in the direction of Italy, but it is more interesting to take the old road that contours round the hillside passing through the villages of Arbin, Cruet and St Pierre d'Albigny. The Château de Miolans is just beyond St Pierre d'Albigny and is set in a wonderful site on the hillside above the valley bottom.

There are two ways of getting to the cross. The easier walk demands a longer drive taking the D91 2 as far as La Féclaz before turning left to the hamlet of Le Sire. After parking here, a well-marked (blue/red) path leads to the summit after about an hour's fairly gentle walk. A more difficult approach, but one involving less driving, would also mean taking the D91 2, but soon after passing through St Alban turning left to the village of Lorettaz. Leave the car there and follow the path marked with double red lines, pass through the hamlet of Nivolet and climb up through the trees. This path ends with a bit of a scramble and takes about 2 hours. Whichever path is taken, it is a perfect way of seeing the whole of the Pre-Alps around you, with the Lac du Bourget, Chambéry and the Isère Valley below. A perfect way of rounding off a visit to the region of the Pre-Alps.

The quickest route back to Chambéry is down the D32, which meets the N6. This has always been the road to Italy crossing the Isère by the Pont Royal and following the Arc Valley to the Mont Cenis Pass towards Italy. This valley is known as the Maurienne. The easiest way to enter the Maurienne is over the Pont Royal, but there are other more interesting ways in across the mountains. One of the most well known is included as part of an excursion in Chapter 9.

Rousseau Meets Madame De Warens

Born in Geneva in 1712 of a Protestant family and effectively orphaned by the death of his mother and desertion of his father, Rousseau left the city at the age of 16 and made his way to Annecy. There, on Easter Sunday 1728, in the garden behind the Bishop's Palace, he met someone who was to change his life. There is a monument to this meeting erected at his request. The lady in question was Madame De Warens, a recent convert to the catholic faith who took Rousseau under her wing. She arranged for him to be baptised in Turin. When he returned he lived Madame De Warens on and off in Annecy, Chambéry and Les Charmettes, first as a general assistant and finally as her lover. During this time when he was creating his philosophy of the noble savage as well as studying music and botany, he continued to travel and many places in the region feature in his subsequent writings. Returing from one journey he found that he had been supplanted in the affections of Madame De Warens, which prompted him to head for Paris. Here the results of his thinking and studies bore fruit in his many works, such as the Social Contract, his Confessions and his philosophical best seller 'Julie; ou la Nouvelle Heloïse'.

*Place St Légér in Chambéry. *A*

*Le Palais de Justice in Chambéry. *A*

*Making Génépi at the Dollin Distillery. *G*

*The Dent du Chat overlooking Lac du Bourget. *A*

Places to Visit: In The Pre-Alps

Annecy and Lac d'Annecy

Excursions on Lac d'Annecy

The cruise boats set down and pick up from the Quai Napoléon III and it is possible to buy tickets either there, but information can be obtained from

Compagnie de Navigation du lac d'Annecy

2, Place aux Bois, 74000 Annecy
☎ 04 50 51 08 40
www.annecy-croisieres.com
It is possible to buy tickets from the Tourist Office, which also provides information about the town, its facilities and the villages around the lake. It is at Office de Tourisme de l'Agglomération d'Annecy, 1, rue Jean Jaurès - 74000 Annecy. ☎ +33 4 50 45 00 33
www.lac-annecy.com

Musée Régional W

MUSEE-CHÂTEAU
Place du Château, 74000 Annecy
☎ 0450338730
Open all year round. Open from 01.10 until 31.05: daily (except Tue) 10/12a.m and 2/5p.m. Open from 01.06 until 30.09: daily 10.30a.m/6p.m. Closed Easter Sun and Mon and 01.05, 01.11, 11.11, 24 and 25.12, 31.12 and 01.01.

Château de Menthon W

Château de Menthon
74290 Menthon-Saint-Bernard
☎ 0450601205
www.chateau-de-menthon.com
During May, Jun and Sept open between 14h and 18h every Fri, Sat, Sun and public holidays. During Jul and Aug open every day between 12h and 18h.

Bauges Nature Reserve

Maison du Parc, 73630 Le Châtelard
☎ 04 79 54 86 40
www.parcdesbauges.com
Open Mon to Fri 8.00–12.00 and 1.30–5.30.

Just beyond Le Châtelard is the peaceful little village of École, with the Maison Faune-Flore which is open from Jul to mid-Sept daily from 10am–7pm. From mid-Sept to Jun it is open on Sat and Sun from 1.30–7pm.

Gorges du Fier

Les Gorges du Fier, 74330 Lovagny
☎ 04 50 46 23 07
www.gorgesdufier.com
Open daily from mid-Mar to mid-Oct.

Château de Montrottier W

74330 Lovagny
☎ 04 50 46 23 02
www.chateaudemontrottier.com
In Jul and Aug open every day from 14.00 to 19.00. In Mar, Apr, May, Jun and Sept open every day except Tue from 14.00 to 18.00.

Musée de la Cloche

Fonderie Paccard, 74320 Sevrier
☎ 04 50 524 711
www.paccard.fr/musee2
Open daily in Jul and Aug. Sept–Jun, open only in the afternoon, Tue to Sun.

Aix-les-Bains

Thermes Nationaux d'Aix les Bains W

Place Maurice Mollard

73103 Aix les Bains
☎ 0 810 44 33 32
www.thermaix.com

Musée du Docteur Faure W

10 boulevard des Côtes
73100 Aix-les-Bains
☎ 04 79 61 06 57
Open daily except Tuesday from 10.00–12.00 and 1.30–6.00

Le Petit Port Aquarium W

La Maison du Lac du Bourget
Avenue du Petit-Port, 73100 Aix-les-Bains
☎ 04 79 61 08 22
www.aquarium-lacdubourget.com
Open in Jul and Aug every day from 10.00–18.00. In Feb to Mar and Oct to Nov, open every day except Tue from 14.30–17.00 and in may, Jun and Sept from 14.00–17.00.

Abbaye de Hautecombe

Abbaye d' Hautecombe
73310 Saint Pierre de Curtille.
☎ 04 79 54 58 80
www.chemin-neuf.org/hautecombe
The visit which takes about half an hour and for which there is a small charge uses headphones with a commentary in English. The Abbey is open from 10.00–11.15 and 14.00–17.00 daily except Tue.

Chambéry

Office de Tourisme

24, boulevard de la Colonne
73000 Chambéry
☎ 04 79 33 42 47
www.chambery-tourisme.com
Among many items of information, they offer an excellent map of the town with sections in English describing the various sites as well as details of Le Petit Train which leaves the Place Léger every hour from 10.00–12.00 and 14.00–19.00 from may to Sept.

Musée Savoisien W

Square de Lannoy de Bissy,
73000 Chambéry
☎ 04 79 33 44 48
The museum is open every day except Tuesday throughout the year from 10.00–12.00 and 14.00–18.00.

Les Charmettes W

890 Chemin des Charmettes
73000 CHAMBERY
☎ 04-79-33-39-44
Open every day except Tue from 1st Apr to 30th Sept from 10.00–12.00 and 14.00–18.00. From 1st Oct to 31st Mar it is open daily except Tue from 10.00–12.00 and 14.00–16.30.

Château de Chambéry

Rue Basse du Château,
73000 Chambéry
Guided tours are available in May, Jun, and Sept, daily at 10:30 and 14:30; in Jul and Aug, daily at 10:30, 14:30, 15:30, 16:30, and 17:30; in Mar, Apr, Oct, and Nov, on Sat at 14:15, and on Sun at 15:30.

Musée des Beaux-Arts de Chambéry W

place du Palais de Justice,
73000 Chambéry
☎ 04 79 33 75 03
www.chambery-tourisme.com/
Open every day except Tue and national holidays throughout the year from 10.00–12.00 and 14.00–18.00. Entrance is free on the first Sunday of each month.

Château de Miolans W

73250 St-Pierre-d'Albigny
☎ 04 79 28 57 04
The castle is open every day from May to Sept from 10.00–12.00 and 13.30–19.00, except fro Sun morning. Guided visits take place every afternoon at 13.45, 15.00, 16.15, and 17.30.

5. Lac Léman (Lake Geneva) to Mont Blanc

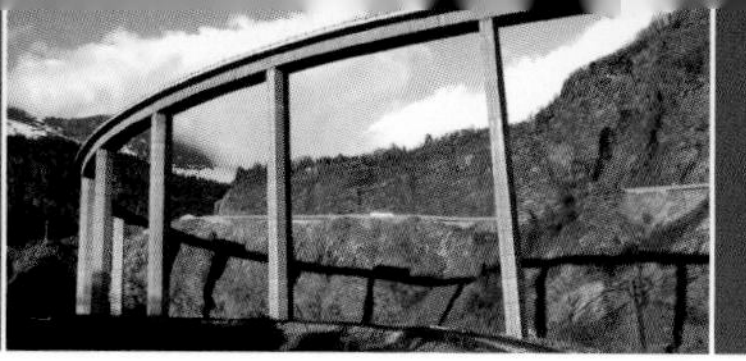

*Opposite: In Chanonix, looking down the Rue du Docteur Paccard towards the Aiguille du Midi . *B*

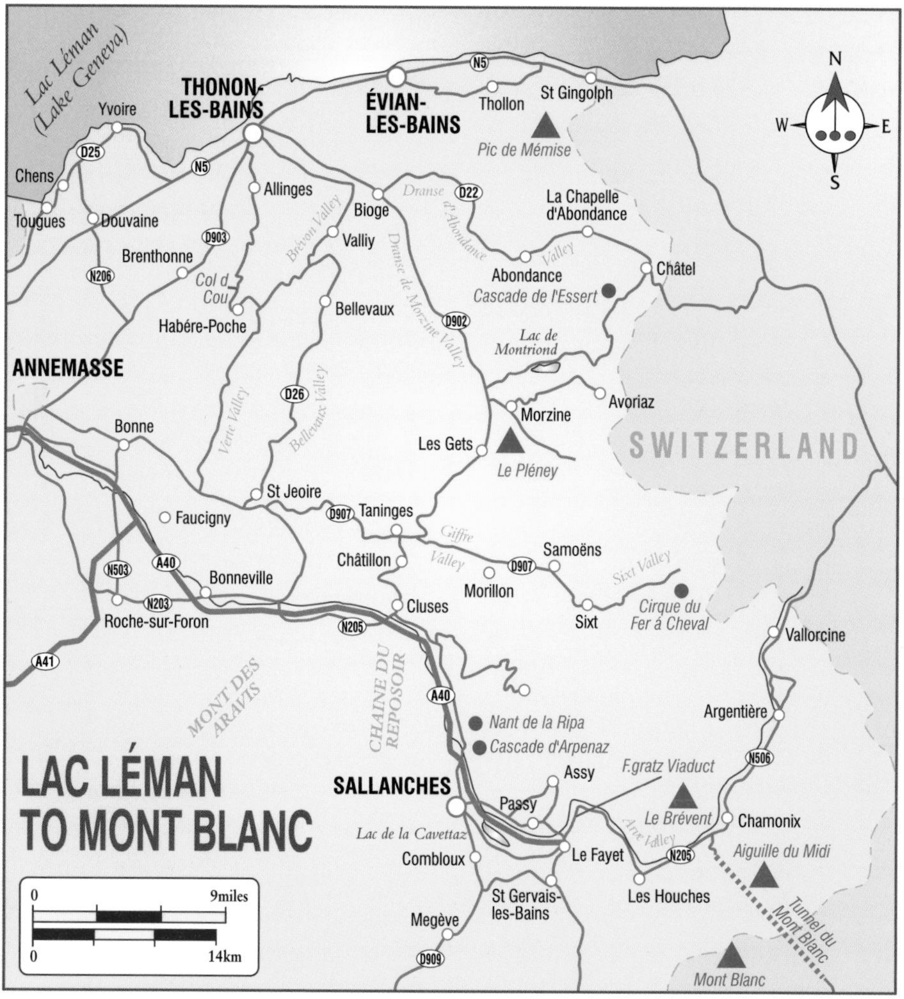
LAC LÉMAN
TO MONT BLANC
Lac Léman (Lake Geneva)
THONON-LES-BAINS
ÉVIAN-LES-BAINS
ANNEMASSE
SALLANCHES
SWITZERLAND
N
S
W
E
Yvoire
Chens
Tougues
Douvaine
Brenthonne
Allinges
Bioge
Valliy
Col de Cou
Habére-Poche
Bellevaux
Thollon
St Gingolph
Pic de Mémise
La Chapelle d'Abondance
Abondance
Châtel
Cascade de l'Essert
Lac de Montriond
Avoriaz
Morzine
Les Gets
Le Pléney
Bonne
St Jeoire
Faucigny
Taninges
Châtillon
Samoëns
Morillon
Sixt
Cirque du Fer á Cheval
Bonneville
Roche-sur-Foron
Cluses
Vallorcine
Argentière
Nant de la Ripa
Cascade d'Arpenaz
Assy
F.gratz Viaduct
Passy
Le Brévent
Chamonix
Aiguille du Midi
Lac de la Cavettaz
Combloux
Le Fayet
Les Houches
St Gervais-les-Bains
Megève
Tunnel du Mont Blanc
Mont Blanc
MONT DES ARAVIS
CHAINE DU REPOSOIR
Brévon Valley
Dranse de Morzine Valley
Dranse d'Abondance Valley
Verte Valley
Bellevaux Valley
Giffre Valley
Sixt Valley
Arve Valley
N5
D25
D903
N206
D22
D902
D26
D907
N503
A40
N203
N205
A41
N506
D909
0
9miles
0
14km

The fastest route from Lac Léman (Lake Geneva), to Mont Blanc is along the Autoroute Blanche, the quite magnificent A40. Beyond Sallanches the whole massif is laid out in all its shining splendour.

The route then proceeds towards two great feats of civil engineering, the curved Egratz Viaduct on its 197ft (60m) pillars and the 8 mile (12km) Mont Blanc Tunnel through the Alps to Italy. Many travellers have to take this high-speed route of necessity, but it is not the best way to appreciate the many attractions that this diverse area has to offer. To the north of the A40 are the regions of the Faucigny and the Chablais leading down to the French bank of Lac Léman, and the motorway passes towns of interest in the Arve Valley.

The lakeside has good beaches and towns that are beautiful to visit, besides being centres of many organised activities. The Pre-Alpine limestone mountains of the Faucigny and the Chablais are cut by attractive valleys with lovely villages, meadows and dramatic High Alpine scenery. The Arve Valley leads up, passing the town of St Gervais to the south, towards Chamonix, with its stunning views of Mont Blanc and its glaciers. Of all the regions in the Alps, this one offers the greatest variety of things to see and to do in the smallest area. It really is possible to be walking in the snow in the morning and sunbathing on the beach in the afternoon.

Lac Léman

The French section of the southern bank of Lac Léman stretches 35 miles (56km) from Hermance in the west to St Gingolph in the east. The western end is fairly flat. It forms part of the Lower Chablais plain, but the land rises towards the east, and at Meillerie before St Gingolph the mountains come right down to the water. The road at this point squeezes its way round between the lakeside and the cliffs. The lake at its widest between Évian and Lausanne is about 10 miles (16km). With a passport, it is possible to do a tour of the lake by road, a journey of 110 miles (177km). It is also possible to go round the edge of the lake by boat from Évian, which takes about 9 hours. But whichever form the tour takes, there are certain spots not to be missed, notably the little village of Yvoire, the beach at Excenevex and the spa towns of Thonon-les-Bains and Évian-les-Bains.

The Chablais has been given the name of 'Le Jardin de la Savoie', 'The Garden of Savoie', and it is particularly beautiful as it joins the lake with its chestnut trees, its flowers and its vineyards. The local wine is Crépy, and the centre of the *Appellation Contrôlée* region is the town of Douvaine on the N5 just inland at the western end of the lake. At Chens-sur-Léman there is a museum which is free to enter, the Musée du Milouti.

Driving towards Yvoire from Tougues on the D25, a left turn goes to the little village of Nernier, where there is another small museum. This houses collections of contemporary art and a permanent exhibition of the natural history of the region.

After skirting the Golfe de Coudrée, the N5 quickly reaches Thonon-les-Bains, the capital of the Chablais. The bustling centre of the town overlooks the lower port and the lake. The Place du Château refers to a castle that once

Évian Water

The road from Thonon to Évian passes through Amphion-les-Bains which is now the site of the factory that bottles Évian water. This used to be done in a building next to the station in Évian, but since the production has now reached more than 50 million bottles a month, new premises were needed. Guided visits can be made by prior arrangement at the Hall d'Information in the Rue Nationale in Évian.

stood here, but was razed to the ground in 1626. From the square the Grande Rue, a pedestrian area, passes on the left two connected churches, the Église St Hippolyte dating in its present form from 1698 and the Basilique de St François de Sales, which was built with interruptions between 1890 and 1935. The latter houses the *Way of the Cross,* one of the last paintings by the artist Maurice Denis, before he died in 1943. Opposite the two churches is the Rue de l'Hôtel de Ville, leading to the town hall, the Tourist Information Office and the Château de Sonnaz. In this ivy-covered seventeenth-century castle, there is a folk museum, which brings together many aspects of the history of the town and the region with some interesting exhibits, especially on the Stone Age lake dwellers.

The French author Henri Bordeaux, who set many of his books in the Alps, was born and brought up at No 32 Rue du Marché, which leads off to the left. Going past the Château de Sonnaz, the Place du Château is reached again with its statue of Général Dessaix, who became the leader of the Savoyard emigrés in Paris during the Revolution. From this point there are lovely views over the gardens as they drop down to the Château Mont Joux and Rives, the port of Thonon. It is a delightful walk down through the gardens, but there is a funicular for the return journey.

This road east out of Thonon towards Évian passes the park and Château de Ripaille. This castle with its four towers was made famous by its one-time resident, Amadeus VIII, the first Duke of Savoie, who was later made pope. It has a small museum in the main room, but the major feature of interest are the surrounding vineyards which produce the famous Ripaille vintage, a very light, fragrant wine with a slightly musky flavour.

Yvoire

The village of Yvoire is one of the loveliest on the lake. The present village goes back to the early Middle Ages, and the gates in the town wall have been dated at 1316. The tightly packed houses, the sloping streets leading to the fishing port and the castle are enhanced by the lack of cars. Yvoire has a reputation for the quality of its flowers and works hard to maintain its "Lauréat International du Fleurissement". The church has one of-the best examples of a traditional Savoyard *clocher à bulbe* bell-tower.

Alpine Garden

A very interesting and beautiful site in Samoëns is the Jardin Jaÿsinia, created in 1905 by Madame Cognacq, who founded the Samaritaine store in Paris, but was born in the town. Her maiden name was Jay, hence the name of the garden. It is now administered by the Natural History Museum in Paris, and is a centre for the study of Alpine plantlife. It is beautifully sited on the hillside, with a stream running through it and dammed to form little waterfalls. The entrance is off the street 50yds south of the church. The paths zig-zag through the garden, so that the visitor can see the plants laid out according to their region of origin. The higher part of the garden also provides a very good view of the town and its surrounding hills.

Évian, 'La Perle de Léman', the 'Pearl of Léman', has been a spa with an international reputation for years. The surrounding countryside, the Pays Gavot, with its soft wooded slopes, helps to give it a rather privileged ambiance. Since it is laid out along the lakeside, the visitor needs to know what he wants to do in order to know where best to park. The Centre Nautique with its swimming pool and its beach are at the entrance to the town beside the Avenue

*Balmat showing De Saussure the summit of Mont Blanc. *B*

Église St Michel in Chamonix next to the Maison de Montagne. *B

Cluses

The hills behind the convent of Le Reposoir are the Chaîne du Reposoir, a continuation of the long Aravis chain. The town of Cluses got its name because the Arve cut across this long limestone mountain chain which is a perfect example of a *cluse,* a valley cutting across a line of hills.

de Noailles. This road is named after a French poetess, Annade Noailles (1876-1933), who wrote in the Romantic style of Hugo and Lamartine and became 'the voice' of the region. although in fact she was born in Paris.

To see the centre of the town with its Town Hall, its Casino and its magnificent Palais des Festivités et des Congrès, designed and built by Novarina in 1956, it is best to park next to the Tourist Office in the Avenue du Lac. The Quai Baron de Blonay makes a lovely stroll at the waters edge, especially in the evening, and the pedestrianised Rue Nationale is an interesting walk through the centre of the town. If intending to catch a boat from Évian for one of the many excursions on the lake, it is best to drive through the town to the port at the other end beside the Jardin Anglais. Before leaving Évian, it is worth walking or driving up the hillside with its splendid hotels to get a very wide perspective of the lake and surrounding area. However the very best spot for this can be obtained by driving the 7 miles (11km) east to Évian's ski resort, Thollon, along the D24, and then taking a cable car up to the Pic de Mémise (5,500ft, 1,677m), which gives an unparalleled view of the town and most of the lake.

Meillerie, 6 miles ($9^1/_2$km) along the lakeside, is particularly pretty, squeezed in between the cliffs and the lake and surrounded by chestnut trees. Jean-Jacques Rousseau used it as a setting for various scenes in *La Nouvelle Heloïse,* and Romantic poets such as Byron and Lamartine sang its praises. Five miles (8km) beyond is St Gingolph, which is interesting, with its two communities, one French and the other Swiss, each with its own post office, Town Hall etc, and connected by a bridge over the Morge. It must be remembered that if visiting either of these towns, the only

Assy Church

The village of Assy has a quite exceptional church, the Notre-Dame-de-Toute-Grâce. This was completed in 1945 and, although designed by Novarina, is more well-known for its decoration, both inside and out. The outline with its wide roof represents the traditional mountain chalet, but the highly-coloured facade and the interior paintings are very modern. International artists such as Matisse, Bonnard, Braque and Chagall joined the many other artists to create a stunning interior. The highly-coloured mosaic facade behind the pillars was the work of the French artist Fernand Léger. In keeping with these works of art there are modern sculptures on many of the bends on the road up to the village.

way back is to retrace one's steps on the N5, unless making a round trip through Switzerland armed with a passport. Five miles (8km) inland from St Gingolph, hidden in the lee of the Dent d'Oche, is the tiny village of Novel, with its typically Alpine church that has become a sort of French Gretna Green.

Valleys of the Chablais

The main valleys of the Chablais as they stretch south from Thonon have been likened to a trident. The central prong of the trident is the Dranse de Morzine Valley, the easterly one is the Dranse d'Abondance Valley, and the westerly one is the Brévon Valley, which becomes the Bellevaux Valley.

The Dranse de Morzine Valley

The Avenue des Vallées out of Thonon leads in the direction of Morzine along the D902. The road goes alongside the rushing stream through the Gorges de la Dranse. At Bioge, the river from the Dranse d'Abondance Valley joins the Dranse from the east. The D902 continues to climb up towards one of the most exciting sights in the valley, the Gorges du Pont du Diable. The river has cut a maze of channels to a great depth through the rock. Visitors take a walkway built into the side of the towering cliff along the length of the gorge to admire its 200ft (60m) high sides and the strange shapes that the water has carved on the river bed.

After this, the road, cut into the cliffside, drops down towards the Barrage du Jolly. This is 72ft (22m) wide and because of the depth of the gorge at this point holds back over a million cubic metres of water to power the turbines at Bioge. The road continues its difficult path through the Défilé des Tines (gorge), taking a tunnel at one point through an enormous block that fell from the mountainside some centuries ago. It finally arrives in the wide St Jean d'Aulps Valley. On the left are the ruins of the Abbaye de Notre-Dame-d'Aulps, its name derived from the Latin word for Alps. The monastery was established in 1094, but was finally abandoned in 1823 and fell into its present state of disrepair,

Five miles (8km) further is the capital of the Haut Chablais, Morzine. This resort, linked to Montriond and at a higher level Les Gets and Avoriaz, is the most important tourist area in both winter and summer, but especially the latter. The cable car up to the summit of Le Pléney offers a quite superb panorama, stretching from Lac Léman to Mont Blanc. The neighbouring ski resort of Avoriaz makes a very interesting visit because of its remarkable architecture, traffic-free roads and its chapel designed by Novarina. It can be visited by taking the road to Prodain and then the cable car, or as part of a dramatic round trip taking in Super Morzine and then going round the lovely Lac de Montriond before returning to Morzine. As might be expected of such an important resort, Morzine has a very full calendar of events, from a car rally to a series of fairs and folk festivals. It has a number of tennis courts, an Olympic-sized swimming pool, a giant toboggan run and a riding centre. The Guides'

*The Mont Blanc range with the Glacier des Bossons. *B*

La Compagnie des Guides de Chamonix

In 1821 the Chamonix guides company was set up to bring together and support all the guides who were assisting the ever greater number of people who were trying to emulate Jacques Balmat's conquest of Mont Blanc in 1786. The company's role was to organise the work, look after the families and generally regularise the walking and climbing in the mountains. Article 33 of the 1872 constitution states that '.... For the ascension of Mont Blanc, a climber must have two guides and a porter. Two climbers, four guides or three guides and two porters'. This did not endear them to everyone, such as the English Alpinist Edward Whymper, who preferred to bring his own (Swiss) guides. Nowadays the guides very much put their client first and lead individuals and groups not only in the Mont Blanc Massif, but further afield, even to the Himalayas and the Andes.

Every year the Chamonix valley celebrates the history of its guides and their achievements during the Fête des Guides de Chamonix, which starts on 12th August to finish on the Feast of the Assumption (15th August). During these four days the town comes alive with events to raise money for the families and ceremonies to celebrate individual achievements, leading up to a Son et Lumiere and concerts on 15th August.

Rack and Pinion Railways

A classic excursion from Chamonix is to take the rack-and-pinion railway up to the station of Montenvers and the largest glacier in the region, La Mer de Glace. The building of this railway was an immense task, taking many years and opposed by the Mountain Guides who feared that a large part of their income would disappear. In the event, it gave them more work because they were able to guide people on a classic walk across the glacier, which they still do today.

The other rack and pinion railway, called Le Tramway de Mont Blanc starts at St Gervais. Because of the popularity of the Baths and St Gervais' reputation as a summer resort, a rack-and-pinion railway was built to give access to the town from Le Fayet at the valley bottom. This was then extended on up the mountainside to the Le Nid d'Aigle (The Eagle's Nest) at 7,826ft (2,386m) with the hope of eventually reaching the summit of Mont Blanc. It is one of the classic excursions of the region and provides a dramatic introduction to the high mountains as it rattles over the Col de Voza and finally into the great glacial amphitheatre of the Bionnassay thought by many to be the best in the Alps. Some climbers use this railway as a starting point to ascend Mont Blanc from the west via the Tête Rousse. It is possible to climb to the glacier in about half-an-hour from the station. The train journey is a long trip, it takes nearly 4 hours there and back, but is a more relaxed and natural way to get into the massif and to appreciate all its different aspects than to be whisked up by cable car. It is not necessary to go all the way to the end of the line, since even the Col de Voza at 5,420ft (1,653m) provides a good introduction to the Alpine meadows, the flowers and the surrounding mountains. The railway operates in the skiing season and in the summer from June to September.

Office in Morzine and Avoriaz also offer guided day and half-day walks to introduce visitors to the flora and fauna of the beautiful surrounding hills. They even ffer walks with donkeys.

Les Gets is worth visiting as a highly-developed summer resort and its Musée de Musiques Méchaniques (Mechanical Music Museum) is reputed to have the country's finest collection of musical boxes, pianolas and phonographs. Visits can also be made to the workshop where old instruments are restored.

The Dranse d'Abondance Valley

At Bioge there is a left turn along the D22, which arrives 17 miles (27km) later at the end of the valley at Châtel. Initially, the valley is so steep that at one point the road goes through a tunnel, and the river is used to generate electricity. After about 6 miles (9km), the valley widens, trees give way to fields that are so fertile that their abundant pasture gives its name to the valley and the villages in it. There is a breed of cattle named after the valley, the Abondance, which is a relative of the Pie-Rouge de l'Est. The cheese made from their milk looks like a Tomme from its soft crust, and Emmental from its appearance and colour.

The road continues towards La Chapelle d'Abondance in a wide-open valley covered with pastures and huge Haut Chablais farmhouses with their all-encompassing roofs and long balconies. This village, a ski resort in winter, is dominated to the north by the Cornettes de Bises.

Further on the road continues into the beautiful open Châtel Valley and an excursion worth making at this point is to the Pic de Morclan, using ski lifts. This summit gives uninterrupted views into Switzerland, especially towards the south-east in the direction of the rocky north face of the Dents du Midi.

The Brévon, Verte and Bellevaux Valleys

The remaining prong of the trident is not so clear-cut. There are a variety of ways out of Thonon to visit the lower western end of the Chablais. The most dramatic drive is to take the D26, the corniche road overlooking the Gorges de la Dranse. It skirts round Mont d'Hermone and turns up the Brévon Valley towards Vailly and Bellevaux. Just half a mile out of Vailly there is a track to the right that leads eventually to the Chapelle d'Hermone, a place of pilgrimage on 16 August every year. Shortly after this the D26 takes a left fork in the direction of Bellevaux.

The road to the right goes through the village of Lullin, with its ruined castle, and on over the Col de Terramont into the beautiful Verte Valley. At the head of the valley is the developing commune of Habire-Poche. It is a centre for traditional crafts such as wood-turning, wood sculpture and painting on wood. The Verte Valley is very open and makes good walking and picnicking country. The Tourist Office organises many accompanied walks. The village really comes into its own on its annual fête on the second Sunday in August.

The Faucigny

The village of Faucigny is to the left of the Autoroute Blanche just after its junction with the A41. Today it is a tiny hamlet remarkable only because the ruined castle there was once the home of the powerful feudal Faucigny family, that gave its name to the whole region. They owned the Giffre Valley leading up to Samoëns, but more important economically the Arve Valley leading up to Chamonix. These two valleys nowadays are called Le Faucigny, with Bonneville as its capital. Technically the region does not stretch as far west as Annemasse, but this town

The Mont Blanc Tunnel

The tunnel took 6 years to build, from 1959 to 1965, and is almost 8 miles (16$^1/_2$km) long. Its claim to fame was that it was the longest road tunnel under the Alps, but sadly it is now most well known because of the terrible event on 24th March, 1999, when 42 people lost their lives in a fire. There was strong local opposition to its being re-opened and initially only cars were allowed through. It is now open to all traffic, but under strictly controlled conditions.

The cost of carrying a kilo of merchandise through the Alps by road has been costed at nearly four times as expensive as by rail and at present a number of "tunnels de base" (at almost sea level) are being built or planned. A rail tunnel, 35 miles (54 kms) long is being planned to take traffic from Lyon to Turin. When it is completed in 2018, it might reduce the non-stop procession of lorries through the Mont Blanc tunnel.

is certainly a good starting point to explore the region's two valleys.

The Sixt and the Giffre Valleys

The Sixt Valley is named after the village of Sixt at its head. It would be worth the 30mile (48km) journey up the valley just to see this village and the dramatic scenery behind it, the famous Cirque du Fer à Cheval — the Horseshoe Amphitheatre. However it is one of the prettiest and most impressive valleys in Haute Savoie with many points of interest throughout its length. Leaving Annemasse by the Rue de Faucigny the D907 goes towards Bonne, alongside the River Menoge. On the left is the impressive hillside of Les Voirons. After opening out, the valley becomes tighter at St Jeoire which was the birthplace of the French engineer, Germain Sommeiller, who was responsible for the Mont Cenis Railway Tunnel among other projects. His statue stands in the main square.

Beyond St Jeoire in the direction of Sixt the D907 passes high above the meeting of the Risse and the Giffre that comes down the main valley. The confluence is used as a power source by the extensive electro-chemical factory in the valley. At this point look south right into the other valley of the Faucigny, the Arve Valley. After passing Mieussy, with wonderful views of Mont Blanc, the road drops down into a gorge, the Étroit-Denté, which acts as an entrance to the open central section of the valley between Taninges and Samoëns. Taninges is an important crossroads, as the Route des Alpes crosses the D907. It has a well preserved section of older houses, a hump-backed bridge and a lovely market place. By taking the road south to Châtillon and turning left along the D4, it is possible to continue along the southern side of the Giffre to the picturesque summer resort of Morillon. This village has many organised activities, a fair on the

Peloton de Gendarmerie de Haute Montagne (PGHM)

The clatter of an over head helicopter can often be heard in the Chamonix valley. This will be the PGHM either responding to a call or carrying out training.

There are four PGHM groups in France, four in the Alps and one in the Pyrenees. The members of the groups are officially policeman, either Gendarmes or from the CRS, normally used for crowd control. The groups were formed in 1958 to carry out the duties imposed on the local prefect by La Loi Montagne. Prior to this rescues were carried out by anyone available and this lack of structure had lead directly to the deaths of two young climbers in the Mont Blanc Massif. La Loi Montagne was a direct result of the strength of public reaction to the disorganised approach to safety in the mountains. Helicopters began to be used in 1967 and a special air section has been based at Chamonix since 2004.

The PGHM has responsibility not only for assisting and rescuing but also for completing the legal dossier which is needed in the case of a fatal accident.

It takes seven years to train to be a member of the PGHM and apart from other skills each member must acquire the expertise of a qualified mountain guide and a national ski instructor. In spite of these skills, 46 Gendarmes have died since 1958 while carrying out their work.

first Sunday in August, a cross-country cycling rally at the end of August and many courses, such as tennis coaching. For other activities it is linked with the region's main town of Samoëns, 3 miles (5km) away.

Samoëns is a good centre for exploring the surrounding region, but with its history as a stonemasons' centre and its first prize for floral decoration, the town

*The Egratz viaduct taking the motorway towards Chamonix and the Tunnel du Mont Blanc. *A*

*Mont Blanc seen from the village of Combloux. *B*

Cable Cars in the Chamonix Valley

It is easy to gain access to the highest mountains around Chamonix by using any one of the four main cables cars. The highest (for many years the highest in the world but now over taken by the Mérida Cable Car in Venezuela) is the Aiguille du Midi. Using this it is possible to gain a height of 3842 metres. Opposite the Aiguille du Midi is the Brévent, rising to 2525 metres. This has the best possible views of Mont Blanc and its neighbouring 'Aiguilles' (needles). Further up the valley on the same side is La Flegère and facing this across the valley is the Grands Montets, which reaches 3300 metres. An additional cable car, not visible from the valley, is the smaller cable car which crosses the massif to the Pointe Helbronner on the Italian side. This quite extraordinary and absolutely unique crossing (only available in the summer) takes 30 minutes to cover the 5 kms with frequent stops to take photographs.

All the cable car companies, as well as the two rack and pinion railways, have joined together to form the Compagnie du Mont Blanc, which offers a Multipass Mont Blanc. This can be quite a saving on paying for each ride individually over a number of days.

is of interest in itself. As a holiday centre, it has a great range of activities, many centred on the Lac aux Dames Leisure Centre with its swimming pool, beach and toboggan run. It also has a riding centre and tennis courts. The picturesque centre of the town is renowned for its 50ft high lime tree, reputed to be over 500 years old. The church, which has a twelfth-century clock tower is a monument to the skill of the local stonemasons, with its sculptures and its portico resting on carved lions. There is an impressive awning over the doorway covered in little copper tiles. The fountain beside it with its four masks and ornamental ironwork is dated 1763, and on the old presbytery building there is a complex sundial showing the times in different countries. The Stonemasons' Association still exists in the town and guided visits can be made to the exhibition hall.

From Samoëns the road continues past the Aiguille du Criou and on up to Sixt, a good centre for exploring this part of the Haut Faucigny, but at this point it is difficult not to be drawn into Cirque du Fer à Cheval. The road ends beneath the towering cliffs of the Tenneverge which rises 6,560ft (2000m) above the valley at this point. The whole area is now a Nature Reserve and classified as a Grand Site de France. At the end of the road there is a café and ample parking space. To experience the grandeur of the site and the sounds of the many mountain streams and waterfalls, take the path away from the café towards the Fond de la Combe. It is not necessary to walk the full distance to the source of the Giffre, which takes about an hour, in order to escape the cars and people.

The Conquest of Mont Blanc

The most photographed monument in Chamonix is Salmson's statue of the guide Jacques Balmat pointing out the summit of Mont Blanc to Horace de Saussure. In 1764 the latter had offered a prize for anyone who could show that there was a safe way to reach the summit. Nothing happened for over 25 years until Jacques Balmat, a hunter and crystal gatherer, was caught at high altitude and had to bivouac in a crevasse. On returning he went for medical advice to Doctor Paccard, who announced him fit and by so doing realised that contrary to general opinion it was possible to spend a night at high altitude. Together they decided to attempt the climb. On 7th August 1786, they slipped out of the town at 4.00pm and by 9.00pm they were at 2300 metres. They slept until 4.15am, when they began again and climbed all day. At 5.30pm people in Chamonix could see them below the summit, which they reached at 6.23pm on the 8th August 1786. They spent another night on the mountain on the way down and both suffered from temporary snow blindness, but they had shown that the summit could be reached safely. Among those who were led up the following year was Horace de Saussure, the scientist from Geneva, who had set the whole process in train nearly 30 years earlier.

The Arve Valley

An exploration of this valley could start at Annemasse although it is beyond the Faucigny, but being in Annemasse would give the opportunity of first going south on the N206 and taking a cable car from Veyrier up to the very northernmost point of Mont Saléve. This point, Les Treize Arbres, a corruption of Trois Arbres, named after three isolated trees that stood there, gives a clear view of Geneva, the whole of the Chablais, the Faucigny and the Mont Blanc massif, a good introduction before going into the mountains.

From Annemasse, the road and the motorway follow the river. Five miles (8km) beyond Bonneville, the capital of Faucigny, is reached. It has an attractive square, surrounded by arcades, and down by the river, the Quai de l'Arve is lined with plane trees. As in many Savoyard towns there is a monument to the fallen of the Franco-Prussian war as well as World War I, but the most striking monument is the 70ft (21 m) high column, surmounted by a statue of King Charles-Felix.

Continuing towards Cluses, a right turn can be taken into the Foron Valley. This would lead to the village of Le Reposoir, a Carthusian monastery that was abandoned, turned into an hotel and later in 1932 taken over by a very strict order of Carmelite nuns. This impressive building on an interesting site can be visited but only by prior appointment.

Cluses is dominated by the Pointe de Chevran, which rises above the gorge cut by the Arve to the east of the town. It is famous as a centre for clock-making and the manufacture of screws or any metal objects made by precision turning. The French for this is *décolletage,* a word that has other connotations in the English language! This sort of manufacture has traditionally been carried out in small workshops, many of which can be seen in the surrounding villages, notably Scionzier, but it is increasingly being carried out in larger factories. The clock-making industry in Cluses was given great encouragement in 1848 by the setting up of a Royal School — L'École Royale de l'Horlogerie. The builing was bought by the town of Cluses in 1992 and is now a museum. The National School made the monumental electric clock on the Town Hall in 1901.

Cluses is well-known today as the motorway exit and starting point for reaching the resort of Flaine 12 miles (19km) away in the mountains to the east, at the foot of the Désert de Plate. Just after the *cluse* is at its tightest with the motorway, the road, the railway and the river squeezed side by side, there is a left turn at Balme, the D6, that leads up towards the resorts of Les Carroz and Flaine. It is not an easy road and there is no other way out of the valley, but both resorts are well geared up to receive visitors who want an active stay. There are tennis clubs, swimming pools, an eighteen-hole golf course and a permanent programme of activities. Flaine offers two sorts of pass that give access to all these activities. The more expensive, the *Pass Vitalit,* includes horse-riding and golf tuition. Because Flaine is a cul-de-sac and the mountains beyond are a nature reserve, it is possible on organised walks to come across

Grande Traversée des Alpes

This is an association which acts as a network of support, bringing together public bodies and tourist offices to co-ordinate the creation, upkeep and management of long distance routes and trails across the Alps. Some of these such as the Via Alpina and Les Chemins du Soleil touch on the region, but one which goes right through it is 'La Route des Grandes Alpes'.

Since the beginning of the 20th century, there has been a lot of pressure to create a direct route for motorised traffic from the Mediterranean to Lac Léman. This would mean crossing some very inhospitable land and high mountain passes. A route which could be covered by open-topped coaches was opened in 1930, but it was by no means direct. It took the opening of the Col de l'Izoard in 1934, the Col de l'Iseran in 1937 and the Cormet de Roselend in 1970 to create a route that could be said to be direct.

In 2004 the definitive route was formally agreed and 'La Route des Grandes Alpes' was opened to great acclaim. It can be done in 2 days by car but this seems to be against the spirit of the enterprise because the purpose of the route is to enable people to appreciate the history and culture of the different regions it crosses. The number of cyclists using overnight stops recommended by the association has increased by 30% and motorcyclists by 42% since the formal opening of the route.

badgers, marmots and even chamois. There is a little museum of clock-making, Le Musée de l'Horlogerie, at Les Carroz.

If not going to Flaine, the road from Cluses to Sallanches continues next to the motorway. The village of Magland is known for its smoked sausages. At Oëx take a detour to the left to get a close view of two waterfalls. The first, the Nant de la Ripa, comes down a staircase of twenty-six individual steps, while the second, the Cascade d'Arpenaz, falls 750ft (228m) in a straight line, often being blown away as a sort of heavy mist.

At Sallanches there is one of the best views of the Mont Blanc massif in its entirety, rising 13,120ft (4,000m) above the town to the summit of Mont Blanc itself. This view is enhanced by seeing it in the evening as the rays of the setting sun give the snow a delicious pink tinge. Because of its privileged site and easy access, Sallanches has become very popular as a centre from which to explore the area.

The town of Sallanches was destroyed by fire in 1840 and rebuilt along nineteenth-century Savoyard lines, imposing blocks and straight streets, many lined with trees. The centre of the town is the huge Place Charles-Albert, with a fountain and a statue of *Peace* surrounded by lions, celebrating the centenary of the Revolution.

To the south of Sallanches on the hillside are the lovely villages of Cordon and Combloux. They are worth an evening detour taking the D113 for their exceptional views, which give them the name of Le Balcon du Mont Blanc. On 15 August, lovers of history will find Cordon very interesting. Among other celebrations, there is a parade in authentic dress of the Napoleonic era as well as some military manoeuvres of the period.

The Lower Arve Valley to Chamonix

The Egratz Viaduct shows the way into the Gorges de Servoz and on up the Arve Valley, but it is well worth holding back. To the south of the entrance to the valley is St Gervais and to the north the Plateau d'Assy. In order to appreciate the magnificence and grandeur of Mont Blanc, there are many points from which to view it, and everyone forms different opinions of the best. A visit to St Gervais and then Assy before entering the valley will create a broader perspective of the massif than going direct to Chamonix.

St Gervais can be reached from Sallanches by going along the valley bottom and turning right at Le Fayet, where the park of the Établissement Thermal is on the right. A more interesting approach would be to continue through Combloux and at the roundabout near Megève turn left down through the woods to St Gervais. The town is entered over the Pont du Diable (the Devil's Bridge), and the quality and style of the hotels at the lower end of the main street give an indication of its popularity as a spa and health centre during the *Belle Époque.* It is worth parking in the square by the church and Town Hall. Behind the Tourist Office there is a long walk down the hillside to the L'Établissement Thermal, in its lovely park, set round the River Bon Nant and the Crépin and Bains waterfalls.

Facing St Gervais across the Arve Valley is the Plateau d'Assy. This is also a health resort. In the days when consumption was so prevalent, the pure air and warmth on this south-facing, protected plateau were considered to be very effective in helping to cure it.

It is possible to stay on the northern side of the valley and drive through the village of Servoz. In its initial stages, this route gives a very good view of the Egratz Viaduct on the opposite side of the valley. The difficulty of introducing the railway into the valley can be seen by the dramatic bridges that take it over the road on its journey through the gorge. Just after the second railway bridge, the valley widens and a bulky sloping concrete aqueduct takes a stream over the newly constructed road. There is a right turn here to the village of Les Houches, an increasingly popular resort in both winter and summer, with a full programme of organised activities. Facing Les Houches on the northern side of the Arve is the animal park on the Balcon de Merlet. It is in a wonderful position and it harbours animals as diverse as chamois and llama. From the Parc de Merlet it is possible to see the way that Mont Blanc is climbed from the east. There are many mountain huts used by climbers on their ascent, but the most well-known is Les Grands Mulets that is clad with metal. This can sometimes be seen glinting in the sunlight above the junction of the two glaciers that seem to tumble into the valley. Half-way up to the park on the right, there is a pathway to the huge high statue of Christ the King that can be seen from the valley. This was erected in 1834, and on the chapel wall there is the bust of Pope Pius Xl, a very keen mountaineer. A short drive above Les Houches, on the south side, there are two cable cars, one to Prairion and the other to Bellevue, which provide stunning views of the Upper Arve Valley,

From Les Houches, the road goes directly along the valley bottom to Chamonix, passing the reservoir that feeds a power station at Passy. A mile beyond this, the road to the Mont Blanc Tunnel goes off to the right. To the right of the road is the spectacular end of the Glacier des Bossons. The great blocks, the *séracs,* that break away from the end of glaciers can be quite clearly seen.

On a clear day, the mountains on both sides of the valley leading up to Chamonix, especially the long line to the south, are quite overwhelming. The road into Chamonix goes under the cables of the Aiguille du Midi cable car and swings round left until it reaches the Place du Mont Blanc. There is usually ample parking here. If not, a left turn goes to the station to the right of which there are more spaces. Opposite the station is what was once the little English church surrounded by a cemetery with the remains of British climbers who died on the mountain. For historians of mountaineering there is another cemetery the other side of the railway line beyond the Montenvers rack-and-pinion railway station. The headstones there read like a roll call of famous European mountaineers. The most famous English name is that of Edward Whymper, the conqueror of the Matterhorn. The most well-known French climber buried there is Lionel Terray, an inspirational mountaineer and writer, who climbed everywhere in the world and recorded it in a wonderful book, entitled in English "The Conquistadors of the Useless".

The centre of Chamonix, Avenue Michel Croz, has now been made into a pedestrian area and is named after a nineteenth-century mountain guide. The road from the main station towards this precinct passes on the left the wooden building of the French Alpine Club. Above the door it has the legend in French, 'Where there's a will there's a way'. In the old Chamonix-Palace is the Musée Alpin, which has many old prints of the valley such as one showing de Saussure's climbing of Mont Blanc as well as many items showing the development of mountaineering.

Walking through the precinct, notice the statue of Dr Paccard (the first man to climb Mont Blanc in 1786) in front of the Salle Michel Croz. The Arve has been covered over at this point, but can be seen emerging in front of the statue. Carry on past the statue towards the Town Hall, beyond which is the church. To the right is the Maison de la Montagne. This is the base for the mountain guides in Chamonix. In front of the building is a statue of Jacques Balmat, Dr Paccard's guide. There is an excellent Information Office to the left of the church. There is a very good sports centre and swimming pool, just north of the Place du Mont Blanc.

From Chamonix there are many ways of getting into the mountains, the most traditional being to take the rack and pinion railway from the main station in Chamonix. From the upper station, there is an excellent view across the glacier to the towering pinnacle of the Dru. Looking up the glacier, the first pyramid-shaped mountain is the Grands Charmoz and far away at the top of the valley the near vertical north face of the Grandes Jorasses can be seen. When the railway was built, it ran alongside the glacier, but the glacier is shrinking. It has been precisely calculated that the glacier has retreated 2 and a half miles (4kms) in one hundred years. Now it is necessary to take a cable car to get down to the glacier from the station. A cave is carved out into ice, it has to be re-shaped every year so that visitors can experience the strange sensation of walking inside the glacier. In the cave there are all sorts of objects carved out of ice.

The best way to view the Mont Blanc massif is to go by cable car to the summit of Le Brévent. The cable car station is up an extremely steep little road behind the church, the Route des Moussoux. It is possible to go half-way up in the cable car, by stopping at Plan Praz. It gives a very good view of the Aiguilles, the Needles, the jagged range of mountains opposite. The name Plan Praz means flat meadows, and although that is a bit of an exaggeration, it is possible to walk along very well-marked paths. The view from the summit of Le Brévent, at 8,282ft (2,525m), is much wider and embraces the whole of the massif, the Arve Valley and all the limestone peaks looking into the Faucigny and Chablais to the north.

Looking south from Le Brévent, there is the block of the Aiguilles facing, with the Mer de Glace 'pouring' out of its valley to the left and the large Glacier des Bossons to the right of it. The road leading up to the tunnel is very obvious just below and to the left of this glacier. To the right of the Glacier des Bossons is the smaller Glacier de Taconna. The actual summit of Mont Blanc is sometimes difficult to distinguish, because from this angle it is not as pointed nor as dramatic as many of the slightly lower peaks that surround it. It is the highest point of the block of mountains behind and to the right of the Aiguilles.

Every Aiguille (needle shaped summit) opposite has a name but the most famous of them all is the Aiguille du Midi at 12,600ft (3,842m). This peak has the distinction of having its cable car, transporting people from the valley bottom to its summit 9,184ft(2,800m). The Aiguille du Midi cable car allows access to the very highest mountains. The station is situated to the left of the road from St Gervais with a very good parking area. Because of the change in height, take warm clothes, and sunglasses are especially important to protect the eyes from the light reflected from the snow.

The cable car from the Plan de l'Aiguille, the mid-station, to the summit takes about 5 minutes. This is one of the longest sections of cable without supporting pylons anywhere in the world, being over 2 miles ($3^1/_4$km) in length. The Aiguille du Midi has two summits, one made even higher by the telecommunications tower on top. The cable car arrives at the slightly lower one, the Piton Nord. There is an exit point for skiers and climbers, as well as an observation platform. To get the very best view, having come this far, it is worth crossing the bridge and taking the lift up to the summit of the Piton Central. This gives the most complete view of the Alps, and on a clear day it is possible to see far into Italy with the Monte Rosa to the south and the Matterhorn to the east.

Other Excursions

The Aiguille du Midi, the Brévent and Montenvers are the three classic excursions from the town, but the Arve Valley does not end at Chamonix. The train and the road continue on up the valley and eventually reach Switzerland. Five miles (8km) beyond Chamonix is the little village of Argentière. The road goes to the left here and climbs to skirt round the mountain ahead with the lovely name of Les Posettes. The road leaves the Arve Valley at this point, since the source of the Arve is near the Col de Balme, the Swiss/French border, high above the villages of Montroc and Le Tour. Argentière is a very good centre for exploring the highest points of the valley. The Glacier d'Argentière and the Glacier du Tour approach the village from the south. The Glacier d'Argentière can best be seen by taking the new Grands Montets cable car. The Glacier du Tour can be seen from the village Le Tour, where it is also possible to get a cable car to Charamillon, or further on to the Col de Balme. This gives the opportunity for easy high-altitude walking.

From Argentière, the road to Switzerland goes over the Col des Montets after passing through Trélechamp. The view of the Glacier d'Argentière with the Aiguille Verte and the top of the Aiguille du Dru behind it is very striking from here. At the Col there is the Aiguilles Rouges Nature Reserve, a natural history museum, and marked nature trails. Further on at Le Buet, a road to the left goes to the lovely Cascade de Bérard, and beyond an hour's walk up to the Chalet de Pierre à Bérard.

Since passing the Col des Montets, the road has been coming down the La Vallée d'Eau Noire (Black Water Valley). It was once called the Le Val aux Ours (Valley of the Bears), and this gave the name Vallorcine to the last village in France before crossing into Switzerland at Le Châtelard.

W = Perfect for Wet days

Lac Léman to Mont Blanc

Lac Léman

Yvoire

Le Labyrinthe - Jardin des Cinq Sens à Yvoire
Rue du Lac
74140 Yvoire
☎ 04 50 72 88 80
www.jardin5sens.net

The garden is open to visitors every day from May to Sept 10.00–19.00. In Apr it is open 11.00–18.00 and in Oct 13.00–17.00.

Musée Milouti

Granges de Servette
74140 Chens-sur-Leman
☎ 04 50 94 12 92

This small museum, housed in farm buildings in the middle of the fields, is open every afternoon in Jul and Aug.

Thonon

Le musée du Chablais *W*

Château de Sonnaz
74200 Thonon-les-Bains
☎ 04 50 71 56 34

This museum in its spectacular house with wonderful views of the lake is open every day in Jul and Aug 10.30–12.30 and 15.00–19.00. In other months it is open from Wed to Sun from 14.30–18.00.

Château de Ripaille

Avenue de Ripaille
74200 Thonon-les-Bains
☎ 04 50 26 64 44
www.ripaille.fr

There are guided visits to this castle, set amongst its vineyards. In Jul and Aug they are at 11.00, 14.30, 15.15, 16.00 and 16.45. In other months they are in the afternoon. It is closed in Dec and Jan.

Évian

Cruises on the Lake

Association "Mémoire du Léman"
Kiosque Place du port de commerce
74500 Evian les Bains
☎ 04 50 70 26 38
www.barquelasavoie.com

This is the address to hire a beautiful traditional lateen sailing boat "La Savoie", which has been restored and is run by volunteers, but tickets are available to individuals.

Office du Tourisme

Place d'Allinges
74501 Évian les Bains
☎ 04 50 75 04 26
www.eviantourism.com

This is the starting point for many excursions and walks around the town. There is so much organized that it is an essential visit to get the most from the town and the surrounding area.

Cont'd overleaf

Cont'd from previos page

W = Perfect for Wet days

Places to Visit: Lac Léman to

Évian Water W

The bottling plant is just outside Évian at Amphion and visitors are welcome but they must check in at:
Le Hall d'Information
19, rue Nationale
The visits are free but a small charge is made for the bus journey.

Les Jardins de l'eau de Pré Curieux

Chemin des marronniers
74500 Évian les Bains
☎ 04 50 75 61 63
www.precurieux.com
This water garden and small museum can be reached by solar powered boat from the centre of Évian. Tickets can be bought at a kiosk opposite the Casino. There are three boats a day every day in Jul and Aug at 10.00, 13.45, and 15.30. In May, Jun and Sept they operate from Wed to Sun.

Valleys of the Chablais

Gorges du Pont du Diable W

Le Jotty
74200 La Vernaz
☎ 04 50 72 10 39
These caves are open from May to Sept 9.00–18.00. The guided visit lasts about an hour.

Musée de la Musique Mécanique W

74260 Les Gets
☎ 04 50 79 85 75
www.lemuseedesgets.free.fr
The museum hosts a festival from 14th–18th Jul. The Museum is open every day from 14.30–19.30. Annual closure is Nov to 20th Dec.

L'écomusée de Samoëns W

Le Clos Parchet
☎ 04 50 34 46 69
www.le-clos-parchet.com
This typical Savoyard farmhouse hosts a good little museum of local life. It is open in July and August on Tue, Thur and Fri from 14.30–16.30. In other months it is open on Thur from 14.30–16.30.

Ancienne Chartreuse du Reposoir

Fréchet
74950 Le Reposoir
☎ 04 50 98 18 01
The church of this Carmelite Convent can be visited on Sat and Sun 8.30–12.00 and 14.30–18.30. Guided visits to the cloisters take place at 15.15 on Sat and Sun.

L'École Royale de l'Horlogerie W

Musée de l'Horlogerie et du Décolletage
Espace Carpano et Pons
100, place du 11 novembre
74300 Cluses

☎ 04 50 89 13 02
Open in Jul and Aug from Mon to Sat 10.00–12.00 and 13.30–18.00. From Sept to Jun open 13.30–18.00

Lower Arve Valley to Chamonix

Railway from Chamonix to Montenvers
Aiguille du Midi cable car
Tramway from St Gervais to Le Nid d'Aigle

These three ways of gaining access to the high mountains around Chamonix have, since 2000, been run by:

La Compagnie du Mont Blanc

35 place de la Mer de Glace
74400 Chamonix
☎ 04 50 53 22 75
www.compagniedumontblanc.fr
Times can vary and are sometimes affected by the weather but up to date details are always available from the office or the company's website which has pages in English.

Le Musée Alpin *W*

89, avenue Michel Croz
74400 Chamonix
☎ 04 50 53 25 93
This museum occupies a building that was one of Chamonix's grandest hotels and it houses every kind of document and artefact concerned with the conquest of mountain peaks. It is open every afternoon 14.00–19.00

Compagnie des Guides de Chamonix

Maison de la Montagne
190, place de l'Église
74400 Chamonix
☎ 04 50 53 00 88
www.cieguides-chamonix.com
They have information about every kind of activity from walking in the mountains above Chamonix to accompanying climbers on the hardest routes. Good English leaflets and website.

6. La Savoie

*Below: The road to Arêches in Beaufort. *A*

The region that forms a crescent round the Mont Blanc massif is so full of interest and provides so many facilities for every kind of activity that any town could act as a base from which to go out and explore. The town perhaps best situated as a starting point to see the whole area is the 1992 Winter Olympic town of Albertville. The opening and closing ceremonies took place in the futuristic-looking Ice Stadium, specially built for the occasion on the edge of town, with the mountain La Belle Étoile as a backdrop. This town stands at the junction of two important rivers, the Arly and the Isère, and is a bustling commercial and industrial centre in the valley of the Isère.

From Albertville the eyes are drawn upwards to the little village on the southerly slope overlooking the town. This is Conflans, named after its position on the confluence of the two rivers. It is a truly medieval town, a collection of houses huddled closely round the church with its traditional onion-shaped dome, at one time a very important religious centre. Cars should be left in the visitors' car park below the town. The road into Conflans goes through the very deep Porte de Savoie which gives a good indication of the protection afforded by town gates in the Middle Ages. Passing a fountain, enter the narrow main street, with the houses pressing in on both sides. Towards the main square, there are more shops with attractive shop signs outside. Past the church that towers above the houses on the left, is the square with its fountain, lime trees and window boxes bulging with flowers. The town opens out a little here, and on the right beyond the square is a large building, the red-brick Maison Rouge, dating back to 1390. This one-time convent now houses a very good little museum, with permanent exhibitions of Savoyard furniture, and a history of skiing. One exhibit, unearthed locally by a priest and local historian, L'Abbé Hudry, is a set of Roman scales. These highlight the importance of Conflans as a border town, since they would have been used for weighing goods for tax and toll purposes.

Returning to Albertville, the road crosses into the town over the Pont des Adoubes. This is named after a tool used in leather-working that indicates a staple industry of the town at one time. There is another reminder of the history of the town in the name of the street alongside the river, the Quai des Allobroges, so named after the tribe that occupied this region at the time of the Romans' arrival.

The Aravis Region and the Arly Valley

To the north, there is a series of small hillsides dotted with hamlets and cultivated strips. Beyond these, the mountains rise to over 9,840ft (3,000m). The largest, shaped like a slightly flattened pyramid, has the delightful name of La Belle Étoile. The mountains to the west overlooking the Combe de Savoie are the southern edge of the region of the Bauges. Between these mountains and La Belle Étoile, there is a pass, the Col de Tamié, the only way north out of the valley of the Isère at this point. There are a number of roads out of Albertville in the direction of the Col de Tamié, but the most direct goes through the village of Mercury. This cannot be missed because the village church has a quite extraordinary statue on the top of the church tower and forty-four gilded statues as well as the largest bell in the valley.

Climbing the hillside above Mercury with a great gilded statue on its church the view behind begins to transform as it gets wider. Mont Blanc comes into view beyond the mountains to the east, Le Grand Arc on the other side of the valley, with the river Isère, the motorway and the railway running along the valley bottom. By the lower pass, the Collet de Tamié hidden in the trees to the left, there is one of the many military forts in the area, built to protect the valley. Instead of going straight on to the main pass, the Col de Tamié, there is a little road to the right that passes a small hamlet and climbs across sloping meadows up the side of La Belle Étoile. Down below to the left, on the other side of the valley, the buildings of L'Abbaye de Tamié can be seen. Just beyond the meadows it is possible to park in the trees and the more adventurous can climb La Belle Étoile from here. So much height has been gained by road that it is not very arduous, and many locals do it as an afternoon outing. The path is very clearly marked, but, although quite within the capacity of any able-bodied walker, it must be treated with some seriousness, particularly in the upper sections. Returning to the road, a right turn goes towards the Col de Tamié, where the meadows, especially in springtime when they are knee-deep in flowers, are delightful.

After leaving the abbey, the Faverges road north drops slowly but steadily alongside the stream, the Bard de Tamié, which will eventually end up in the Lac d'Annecy. The valley opens out at Seythenex. This village boasts a 98ft (30m) waterfall and a cave. Drop down

La Savoie becomes part of La France

Although Savoy became part of France in 1860, many would still say that they are Savoyard first and French second. In fact, although the men of Savoy (Yes, only the men) voted by more than 99% to join France rather than remain part of the Kingdom of Piedmont and Sardinia, some still have not apparently come to terms with being French and "Savoie Libre" can be seen scrawled on road signs and bridges. Despite this massive majority, there was one stipulation – that the name should live on, as it does in the names of the French Departments. Napoléon III celebrated the event with a formal visit to the region and the famous Fête du Lac held in Annecy every August commemorates this visit. A more sombre memorial is to be found on the many war memorials, where it is not the fallen of the two World wars, but the fallen of the France's disastrous war with Prussia in 1870 who are remembered. These are particularly poignant because just a decade earlier the men of Savoy would not have been involved.

*Cable Cars at La Plagne. *A*

through pleasant agricultural countryside to Faverges, a small town, on the Annecy-Ugine road. Cross the town and take the Dl2 north in the direction ofViuz, where there is a very old church with some Roman remains and an archaeological museum. This road goes in the direction ofThônes.

Although the road continues up towards the Col de la Croix-Fry, it is better to return and make for Thônes. This little town is very well sited to act as a base for exploring the lovely region between Lac d'Annecy and the Aravis mountains. There is a little museum in the town, devoted to the history of the region and its traditions and Les Amis du Val de Thônes usually have an exhibition of country life in their base by the church. There are also folk festivals, a Foire d'Artisanat, a craft fair, over the weekend nearest to the 15th August and a Foire St Maurice, a celebration to mark the descent of the sheep from the mountains. Many towns hold these *fêtes de descente des alpages* around the end of September. Thônes, like many towns in this region, claims to be the capital of Le Reblochon, the local cheese and there are many places to find out about this famous cheese, such as the Cheese Cooperative, SICA des Alpages, just outside the town on the Annecy road. The church has a particularly fine traditional onion-shaped dome. A plaque on the front of the church commemorates the dead from a bombing raid on 3 and 4 August 1944. This is linked to the position of the town and the surrounding area as a centre of Resistance during the war.

Two miles ($3^1/_4$km) along the D909 in the direction of Annecy there is a further and more dramatic reminder of this period, the Cimetière des Héros des Glières. This is the burial ground of 105 Resistance fighters who died trying to keep open the Plateau des Glières on the hills above for parachute drops. The small museum near the cemetery shows what conditions were like and explains how 465 Resistance fighters fought off the Vichy forces and only succumbed to the onslaught of a small army of 12,000 German soldiers after nearly two months. The memorial with the names of the dead bears the message *Vivre libre ou mourir*, 'Live in

L'Abbaye de Tamié

On the road from Albertville to Faverges, a left turn leads up to the L'Abbaye de Tamié. Before the Abbey just after the car park, there is an excellent visitors' centre which describes the life of the monastery. The Cistercian monks are renowned for their cheese, the Tomme de Tamié, as well as for their life of prayer. Visitors are very welcome in the church. High Mass on a Sunday morning is an unforgettable experience for its simplicity, its wonderful singing, and its atmosphere of calm and peace.

freedom or die' and at the other end of the cemetery there is a simple granite stone with a bronze sword set in the Cross of Lorraine.

Back through Thônes, the D909 north-east goes to St Jean-de Sixt. Before turning right to La Clusaz, a detour left along the D4 will lead to the resort of Le Grand Bornand, which has very varied and full programmes of summer-time activity.

Back in St Jean-de-Sixt, take the D909 right to La Clusaz, the capital of the region. Although Clusaz is most well known as a ski resort, it has maintained its old charm as a true Savoyard mountain town. It caters for every kind of outdoor activity in the summer and has recently become a centre for cross-country cycling (VTT) and many events throughout the summer celebrate its agricultural past.

Behind the town is the line of Aravis mountains, that are crossed at the Col des Aravis, 5 miles (8km) away. This road is not kept clear throughout the year.

Megève

In winter, this charming little town has maintained the atmosphere of an original ski resort with sleigh rides and *après ski* entertainments in an authentic setting. The centre is barred to traffic. Megève which has the highest number of top quality hotels after Aix and Evian has a feeling of elegance. Perhaps this is why many internationally famous film stars and singers have their winter chalets here. Throughout the year and especially in the summer, there are organised activities, exhibitions and fairs. There are also many sporting events and facilities, centred on the excellent sports centre, the Palais des Sports, which is open to the public.

To visit the town, park in front of the Palais des Sports and cross the main road into the town centre. The town has an interesting history. It got its original charter in 1282, and in the centre it still has the feel of a small medieval town with its church, its *donjon* and its narrow streets. These can be explored on foot or in one of the pony traps which stand in the main square. The road west of the centre leads to a little garden with a delightfully graceful statue. The town has two museums, the Musée de Megève and the Musée du Haut Val d'Arly. The former concentrates on life in the town at the end of the nineteenth century, while the latter gives an insight into Savoyard art and traditions.

It can be closed by snow up to April, but when it is open, it provides one of the most picturesque drives in the Alps, with dramatic views of Mont Blanc.

The descent down the Arondine Valley is steep and windy and needs some care. After La Giettaz, there is a waterfall on the left, the Cascade du Dard, that can be spectacular after rainy weather. Seven miles (11km) later the road reaches Flumet, a true Alpine crossroads with roads in all four directions. Because of its position, a castle was built here in the twelfth century, but the only fortification now remaining is the church bell-tower. The most striking feature is the River Arly that has cut a deep gorge at this point. A mile south of Flumet is the delightful Alpine village of Notre-Dame-de-Bellecombe. To get there, cross the bridge over the Arly, the Pont de l'Abime, from which the river can be seen many feet below. Look back to see the line of houses built on a ledge with a sheer 150ft drop into the river.

Before returning towards Albertville, down the Arly Valley, a 6-mile ($9^1/_2$km) detour in the opposite direction along the N212 goes along a wide-open green valley through the village of Praz to Megève, the doyenne of French Alpine resorts.

The N212 goes back through Praz, named after the surrounding meadows *(prés)*, and through Flumet, before dropping steeply down into the Gorges de l'Arly. The river, renowned for its trout fishing, at this point is many feet below the road, which is set into the cliffside in a dramatic setting. At a hairpin bend 2 miles (3¼km) later by the Pont de Flon, there is a small right turn to the village of Héry. This is the corniche road on the upper slope of the gorge. Instead of descending on the main road down the gorge, this road can be taken not only to visit the isolated and peaceful village of Héry in its picturesque setting with views into and across the gorge, but also for its descent into Ugine, the town at the other end of the gorge. Just before dropping down into Ugine on this route, there is on the left the tower of the castle that protected the valley at this point. Ugine is dominated nowadays by the steelworks. The N212 follows the River Arly back to Albertville.

Le Beaufortain

To enter Le Beaufortain, cross the Pont des Adoubes in the direction of Conflans, but be ready to turn left immediately after the bridge and climb out of the Combe de Savoie. The D925 climbs steeply, before levelling out by the village of Venthon. After this, the road enters a very steep gorge, the real entry into the valley. This is the site of the first and oldest of all the hydro-electric schemes in the area. It was first started in 1888 using the power of the River Doron. Because this fluctuated so much, the owner thought of bringing water from the Lac de la Girotte, over 20 miles (32km) away. Against some local opposition and after 11 years' negotiation and work, he succeeded in getting water from the lake. The pipes can still be seen coming down the hillside feeding the power station in the valley bottom.

After crossing the River Doron by the Pont de Roengers, there is a left turn to the village of Queige. The hillsides around Queige, helped by its south-facing prospect, account for 36 per cent of all the cultivated land in Le Beaufortain.

The road in the valley makes its way to Beaufort crossing and recrossing the Doron. Beyond the final gorge, there is a garage to the right, and standing in a small meadow opposite is a perfect example of a Savoyard farmhouse with living area, barn and grain store all under one roof, with cut logs piled outside acting as extra insulation against the elements. The N525 passes Villard-sur-Doron on the south-facing slope. A mile later, a left turn goes off in the direction of Hauteluce and the Col des Saisies.

The entry into Beaufort is not particularly pretty with garages and works strung out along the road, but the very centre has a lot of charm. It is best to park in the large car park to the right on the other side of the River Doron. Opposite the car park is one of the most important attractions in the town, the Beaufort Cheese Co-operative. Although some cheese is still made in small *fruitières* on the high-altitude meadows, most is now made in Beaufort. Visitors are very welcome to the factory to see the processes that go to make this *Prince des Gruyères*. What they will not see is the cattle being milked. This goes on in the farms, but in summer it is sometimes still possible to see them being milked in the open air in mobile milking parlours. These can

*The church spire at Thônes. *A*

be seen in operation in the surrounding hills, but especially above Arêches. The milking, which can take four hours in the morning and three in the afternoon, is done by highly specialized teams which stay up in the mountains with the cattle from May until they come down in September.

There are three bridges over the Doron. The original packhorse bridge can be seen on the left of the modern one. Across the bridge, the buildings are packed so close together that their eaves almost touch in places. Most churches in Savoie are worth visiting to see the expertise in wood-carving that went into making the pulpit and the reredos. However, the pulpit in the church at Beaufort is acknowledged to be the finest in the region, with its ornate canopy and many sculpted figures made in 1722 by Jacques Cléran. The four figures around the pulpit are the four church fathers, St Ambrose, St Gregory, St Augustine and St Jerome.

Looking at Beaufort nestling peacefully in its valley, it is difficult to believe that 5 miles (8km) behind it and 3,936ft (1,200m) above, is the largest high-altitude reservoir in France, the Lac de Roselend. This was created by the building of the Roselend Dam between 1955 and 1960. It is reached by driving through a gorge, the Défilé d'Entreroches, and up the D217 by a series of hairpin bends. The original village of Roselend was drowned by the waters of the reservoir, but a left turn at the top of the climb goes past a copy of the village chapel to a cafe and some

Traditional Tarine Dress

Throughout the area folk festivals are held in the summer, when the beautiful Tarentaise costumes are much in evidence. These are occasions to see ladies wearing the traditional costume and the head-dress known as La Frontière Tarentaise or La Pointe Tarine, a black closefitting cap with three points, one over each temple and a central one over the forehead. It is embroidered and laced with gold, and can take up to an hour to fit correctly.

buildings. The road then continues on up to a pass, the Cormet de Roselend, before it drops down dramatically into the Tarentaise Valley. But to stay in Le Beaufortain, it is best to turn back and follow the road round the lake to the dam. There are a number of points at which to see the dam from close quarters.

After driving along the dam, the road goes to the Col des Prés, below which is an interesting botanical walk, and then back into Le Beaufortain. About a mile before Arêches in the valley bottom, a take the turn to the village of Boudin. This village is a conservation site because of the magnificent farmhouses, built in traditional style, that seem to rise up the hillside along the line of the stream. The village and its little chapel are worth a detour on foot to get the

Left: Megéve town centre. *A

Below: Barrage de Tignes. *D

Parc National de la Vanoise

Since Roman times the ibex (le bouquetin) had been hunted but not only for its meat. Its horns, which can grow up to a metre in length, were thought to have aphrodisiac qualities and deep in its heart it has a cross shaped cartilage which was thought to have magical properties and was sought after as a talisman. By the 19th century it was all but extinct because of over hunting. The Gran Paradise national park was established in 1922 on the Italian side of the Alps with the express purpose of saving them. This was seen to be so successful that the French created the Parc National de la Vanoise in 1963. Since then the number of ibex has increased until there are now about 1200. There seems to be some kind of self regulation because it has stayed at this number for some years. This self regulation is the subject of a number of in depth studies.

The national park is a major centre for conservation with great emphasis on environmental protection, but was also set up to welcome and inform the public. It is organised into two zones. The peripheral zone covers 28 villages, including most of the well known ski resorts such as Tignes and Val d'Isère. The central zone is highly protected with very strict regulations. Bordering this zone are 5 nature reserves.

Apart from ibex, there are chamois, marmots and over one hundred types of bird, including Golden Eagles as well as a huge variety of wild flowers.

The only way to explore the central zone is on foot, starting at entry points such as pva. Two long distance paths, the GR5 and GR55 cross the park. Camping is strictly forbidden, but there are over 40 mountain huts for overnight stays. The central zone covers 528 square kms (203 square miles), it has many peaks over 3000 metres (9850 feet) high and 500 kms (300 miles) of footpaths.

feel of a real mountain community as it would have existed before the days of modern communication.

Arêches, a base for the 1924 Winter Olympics, is still a skiing centre and in summer a walking centre with many walks into the mountains to the south, notably via St Guérin to the Cormet d'Arêches or Le Planey to the Col de la Bathie. These routes provide fairly easy access to mountains such as Le Grand Mont at 8,813ft (2,687m) that dominate the valley. Until 1950, Arêches had an anthracite mine producing up to 600 tons a month, but any suggestion of such activity is completely gone and it has now become above all a holiday village. The road back to Beaufort drops down by a series of bends giving a good view of the town.

Excursions from Beaufort

The best view of the Hauteluce Valley is to be seen from the road that goes up to the Col des Saisies. At the first bend in this road, there is a much photographed view of the village with its very elegant onion-shaped church tower, and the valley rising to the Col du Joly with the Mont Blanc massif as a backcloth. It is possible to drive all the way up to the Col du Joly, where there is a welcoming café and some of the best views of the Mont Blanc massif. The Col du Joly is on the famous Tour du Mont Blanc and walkers participating in this 10 day walk round the periphery of the Massif usually stop at the café which also acts as a mountain hut.

The Col des Saisies (named after all the contraband goods seized by the frontier guards) has developed very quickly as a ski resort, and this has changed its character and its appearance. It is an international centre for cross-country skiing and a very good place to take up or to practise this increasingly popular sport. It has some of the best-prepared and most attractive runs in the Alps for this kind of skiing. Its attraction as a downhill resort has been increased by the sons of the ski shop owner, Franck and John Piccard, reaching Olympic standard and winning medals. In the summer it is a very good base for walks or picnics, either on the hill to the north, the Chard du Beurre, or on the more easily approached Signal de Bisanne with its restaurant, which gives one of the finest views of the Alps because of its central position.

Before leaving the Col des Saisies, notice in the car park the memorial to the RAF who parachuted in weapons and munitions to the Resistance forces in a huge daytime airlift in June 1944. This was highlighted in the autobiography of the most famous writer in the area, Roger Frison-Roche. Soon after the car park there is a picturesque road to the left through the village of Crest-Voland and down into the Gorges d'Arly by the Pont de Flon. A most impressive drive down the gorge, through tunnels and over bridges between steep cliffs on either side, leads down to Ugine and back to Albertville.

La Tarentaise

The River Isère from its source down to Albertville cuts its way through the mountains in a zig-zag pattern. The region through which it flows is called the Tarentaise after the Latin name of its main town *Darentasia,* now Moûtiers. The name Tarine is used for all things connected with the region. Stocky Tarine cattle are now reared throughout the Alps and have a very good grass to milk conversion rate. The traditional ladies' head-dress of the region is the Pointe Tarine.

Turning right at Albertville out of the Combe de Savoie or looking into the Tarentaise from Conflans, it is evident that it is the start of a different world. The valley is deeper and the mountains are higher as the wide Combe de Savoie is left behind. The region falls into three quite distinct areas. La Basse Tarentaise, the Lower Tarentaise stretching from Albertville to Moûtiers, La Tarentaise Centrale, Central Tarentaise from Moûtiers to Bourg-St Maurice and La Haute Tarentaise, the High Tarentaise

Roger Frison-Roche (1906 – 1999)

Well known for his writing, his travelling and his exploration, Frison-Roche was first and foremost a man of the mountains, specifically the French Alps. His parents had left their little village above the town of Beaufort to find work in Paris, but such was his love of the mountains that he returned as a child to spend summers with his grandparents and extended family. In his autobiography (Le Versant du Soleil) he describes the working life of an alpine farm in the early 20th century. On leaving school he went to Chamonix where he worked for the Tourist Office and perfected his climbing and skiing, for which he won many prizes. His climbing ability and achievements were so outstanding that he became the first 'étranger' (person not born in Chamonix) to be invited to become a guide. He took up journalism and in this capacity gave the first radio report from the summit of Mont Blanc in 1932. His journalism took him to Algeria, where he wrote his first book 'Premier de Cordée' (first on the rope) which was filmed in 1943. He was captured by the Germans while covering the Allied advance in Africa in 1942, but escaped while being transferred back to France and joined the Resistance in the Beaufort area. After the war he settled in Chamonix and undertook many expeditions to the Sahara, to Lapland and to the Canadian north, all of which resulted in well received books. When the bicentenary of the conquest of Mont Blanc was celebrated in Chamonix in 1986 Frison-Roche was the official commentator. He died in Chamonix in December 1999 at the age of 94.

*Courcheval Chalet. *D*

from Bourg-St Maurice into the mountains past Val d'Isère. Although the lower end used to be famous among tourists for the spas at La Léchère and Salins-les-Bains, it is now more notorious for its rather dirty factories and its power stations.

The section from Moûtiers to Bourg-St Maurice is primarily agricultural, but a far richer harvest is gained from the hundreds of thousands of skiers who visit the resorts of La Plagne, Peisey-Nancroix, and Les Arcs throughout the year. Above Bourg-St Maurice are the mountains of the Tarentaise with the ski resorts at Val d'Isère and Tignes, near where there is also a high-altitude dam. To the south of the Tarentaise is France's first National Park, the Parc National de la Vanoise. There are many points of entry, but the best is in the little village of Pralognan, almost in the centre of

Famous Regional Cheeses from La Savoie

Although Savoie is the home of the celebrated Beaufort cheese, the region is more generally associated with the Tomme De Savoie cheese. Unlike Beaufort which is a full milk cheese, Tomme De Savoie uses skimmed cows milk and can have a fat content as low as 20%. The word 'Tomme' means a disc of cheese in the local dialect and for this reason is often followed by the name of the place where it is made, e.g. Tomme de Tamié. There is a local cheese called 'Tome', but this is the trade name acquired by the cheese makers of the Bauges region.

After the cream is skimmed off, it is pressed to extract the whey and then left to mature for several months. During this time it acquires its thick brown rind which gives it a distinct appearance. The taste is nutty, slightly salty and more mild than its rough exterior would suggest. The rind is not usually eaten. Slimmers might appreciated the 20% cheese, but to obtain the authentic flavour of a Tomme de Savoie, it really needs to have about 40% fat content.

The other very well known and highly regarded regional cheese is Reblochon. This cheese, which is made from unpasteurised milk and often cannot be exported for this reason, is made in the area between Annecy and La Clusaz. Its name is said to come from the farmers' ruse to keep their rents low. They had to pay rent according to the milk yield, so they would only half milk the cows and when this lower production was marked up they would "reblocher", i.e. remilk getting a milk rich in fat. It takes five litres of whole milk to produce one cheese which will weigh about 500 grammes. There are two types, Reblochon Fermier which has a green tag and Reblochon Fruitier which has a red tag, the former from farms in the Thônes valley and the latter from cooperatives.

the park. This is reached from Moûtiers by the D915 that wends its way up the valley of another river with the name of Doron. Above this road to the south is France's most well-known and celebrated skiing area, the Trois Vallées. The 'Three Valleys' come down to the Doron Valley and at the head of the valleys are such famous names as Val-Thorens, Méribel and Courchevel.

Throughout many months of the year, the Tarentaise is a cul-de-sac, but in the summer various high-altitude passes are open. The Petit St Bernard Pass above Bourg-St Maurice leads into Italy and the Col de l'Iseran, one of the highest passes in Europe, above Val d'Isère, takes the road out of the Isère Valley and into the valley of the River Arc to the south. This valley, La Maurienne, can also be reached by taking the Col de la Madeleine from Notre Dame-de-Briançon. If intending to take these routes, it is essential to look out for roadside signs advising on whether the passes are open.

Lower Tarentaise

Five miles (8km) into the valley a profusion of high-tension wires can be seen on the left of the road. These wires plus a long concrete channel carrying water out of the hillside are the only evidence of the power station of La Bâthie, that gets its water from Lac de Roselend high in the Beaufortain. There are administrative buildings and offices, but nothing can be seen of the generating plant from outside, since it is all hidden deep in the mountain.

After La Bâthie the traveller in a hurry will take the newly constructed expressway contouring along the mountainside with wonderful views across the valley. The old N90 goes through the most industrial part of the valley. At Notre-Dame-de-Briançon, there is a right turn onto the D94 out of the Tarentaise towards the Col de la Madeleine. This was for many years the highest road in the Alps frequently used by the Tour de France and villages such as Celliers clinging to the mountainside are fascinating.

Although it has never been discovered for certain exactly which road Hannibal took to cross the Alps, the National Electricity Company (EDF) have assumed that he took the Tarentaise route and have named the dam between Aigueblanche and Moûtiers after Hannibal's steps Les 'Echelles d'Annibal'. The waters of the dam are used nearly 10 miles (16km) away. A tunnel takes them to the power station at Aiguebelle in the Maurienne Valley, another example of the imaginative way the difference in height of two neighbouring valleys is used to advantage.

The most striking thing for a traveller arriving in Moûtiers is the size of the road network bypassing the town. If travelling on a Saturday in winter, the reason is clear. This is traditionally the change-over day for most flats and hotels, and skiers from the Trois Vallées, as well as Les Arcs, La Plagne and Val d'Isère arrive and leave on this day. Since all these resorts can accommodate well over 100,000 visitors and most travel by road through Moûtiers, the casual visitor should avoid this day if possible. It was Moûtiers' position as crossroads and staging post that made it the capital of the area in the days when it was still called *Darentasia*. A monastery was established here in the fifth century. The abbot was elevated to the position of archbishop by Charlemagne in return for ruling the town and the valley. The monks continued as feudal overlords of the Tarentaise throughout the Middle Ages and provided at least one Pope, Innocent V, an illustration of the position of the Church in medieval power politics. The Cathédrale St Pierre remains as a monument of these days, with its bishop's seat, its statues and its thirteenth-century Madonna, all sculpted from wood.

Central Tarentaise

The N90 out of Moûtiers used to be squeezed between the mountain and the river. It was so crowded and dangerous that it lived up to the name of 'Couloir de la Peur' (Corridor of Fear). This old road is no longer much used since a modern expressway has been cut through the mountain, one of the obvious benefits of the 1992 Winter Olympics. Gradually the valley opens after the village of Centron, named after the early inhabitants of the Tarentaise, the Centrons.

The main village in Central Tarentaise between Moûtiers and Bourg-St Maurice is Aime. Aime's most important building is the lovely Romanesque Basilique St Martin next to the main road. The basilica dates back to the eleventh century, but was built on the site of a Roman temple. Inside the church are many stones dating back to this era. The expertise of the builders of the time can be seen by visiting the crypt, which supports the main structure. There is a museum in the town, Musée St Sigismond, housed in an old chapel displaying Roman and Dark Age artefacts, found in the vicinity. Sadly, the name has nothing to do with love – it is a corruption of the Latin word for axis!

Aime is the starting point for the road to La Plagne, the well known all-year-round ski resort, where the 1992 Winter Olympics bob sleigh competitions took place The extremely expensive bob sleigh run can be seen in the village. One of the highest sections of the ski resort, 'Aime 2000' - called Aime Deux Milles - is named after the village. Although the road (the D220) has many hairpin bends it is not difficult and is worth taking. The whole of the Tarentaise opens out and some cable cars above the resort go up to over 9,840ft (3,000m). Skiing is possible all the year round, but it is not necessary to ski to take the cable cars and they provide an unforgettable view of the Alps in every direction. To the north is the Beaufortain and Mont Blanc, to the south the Vanoise and the resorts of Méribel and Courchevel can be seen in the valleys 12 miles (19km) away.

Six miles (9kms) beyond Aime, the N90 passes a right turn to the resort Peisey-Nancroix and reaches Bourg-St Maurice. This town, known as *Bergintrum* in Roman times, was an important crossroads and staging post, as well as agricultural centre for the Tarentaise. It is reputed for its fruit trees, mainly apples, its honey and its Tarine cattle. Bourg-St Maurice, or Le Bourg as the local Savoyards call it, is as well-known nowadays as the railway terminus, used by holiday-makers and skiers visiting the many resorts in the Tarentaise, such as Val d'Isère and les Arcs.

*A goat on the roof! *D*

As with many resorts, Les Arcs began as a single skiing area, served by a road and a *télécabine* from the valley, but has developed at a great pace. It now comprises three separate skiing villages, Arc 1600, Arc 1800 and Arc 2000, stretching up the mountainside to the summit of the Aiguille Rouge at 10,580ft (3,226m). The development of the resort was assisted by the creation of a revolutionary teaching technique, the Ski Évolutif, where the skier progressed from very short manageable skis to longer skis as he or she became more proficient. Although this has lost some credence now, it put Les Arcs on the map. Les Arcs is now concentrating on a programme of summer activities, which perhaps makes it the best adventure centre in the region, It has golf tuition on a very good eighteen-hole course, it specialises in tennis tuition, and it has an established reputation for its music and dance. However it offers many more active sports such as cross-country cycling, high-altitude walking and climbing, white water canoeing and grass skiing. In fact Bourg-St Maurice is an international centre for canoe and kayak championships in late July. Arcs Aventures, run by the Mountain Guides Office, offers 'passes' for different sports.

*Walking in the Vanoise. *D*

*Beaufort–a true Alpine town. *A*

*A Tarine cow about to enter a mobile milking parlour. *A*

The accessibility of the resort, its wonderful situation facing the Mont Blanc massif and the very well-developed programme of activities make it a very good centre for an activity holiday.

High Tarentaise

From Bourg-St Maurice, the Tarentaise continues south on the D902 towards the source of the River Isère. But before taking this route, it is worth following the main N90 north as it climbs out of the valley and heads over the mountains towards Italy, via the Col du Petit St Bernard. After the village of Séez, the N90 forks left and rises fairly gently in a series of bends. There are very impressive views down on to the Isère Valley with the village of Ste Foy in the bottom, dominated by the imposing Mont Pourri to the south. The snowy peaks of the Vanoise can be seen in the background. The road goes up through the fast developing resort of La Rosière, which now has a full programme of summer activities. The road then enters a rather desolate region for 5 miles (8km), before it reaches a large rectangular building, the 'Hospice'. This fell into disrepair but is being renovated. The most striking monumentis the Colonne de Joux, a monolith on which there was at one time a statue of Jupiter, but mow a statue of St Bernard. To the right is an Alpine garden, the Chanousia, created by the rector of the Hospice between 1859 and 1909, Canon Chanoux, who was also responsible for the statue of St Bernard, on the Colonne de Joux.

Down in the Isère Valley, the road along the High Tarentaise towards Val d'Isère and the Col de l'Iseran, becomes the D902. In the village of Séez, a right turn leads to the road to Les Arcs and the dam and power station of Malgovert. This is linked now to a higher dam at Tignes, 18 miles (29km) up the valley. The D902 goes alongside the River Isère for 5 miles (8km) and climbs up towards the village of Ste Foy. This is an important village in the High Tarentaise, and traditional Savoyard costume is still worn here by ladies on many occasions.

It is well worthwhile turning and taking the road that goes along the top of the dam towards the village of Tignes 3 miles (5km) up into the mountains.The modern architecture of the buildings seems at a variance with the surrounding mountains, particularly the superb Grande Motte in the background. It is extremely well-equipped as a centre, especially for summer skiing with huge cable cars going right up to 11,316ft (3,450m), and it provides for many other activities such as sailing on the lake. Although the cable cars provide the visitor with a quick access to the Parc National de la Vanoise from the east, serious walkers find Tignes a good setting-oft point by following the GR55 up to the Col de la Laisse and into one of the park's central areas, the Vallée de la Laisse to the south of the Grande Motte.

The only way back down from Tignes is by the same road, crossing once again over the dam. A right turn leads towards Val d'Isère. The road passes through a series of tunnels and galleries, providing protection against stone falls and avalanches. Just after the last of these, the extended resort of Val d'Isère is reached. Although very attractive in winter, when everything is covered in a deep layer of snow, it has to be said that all the work on the mountainsides to protect the resort from avalanches has not left it looking very attractive in the summer. Val d'Isère provides easy access to the surrounding mountains. The Rocher de Bellevarde 9,269ft (2,826m) is now reached by the famous 'Funival', an express train that rises up a tunnel cut into the mountain. The Tête du Solaise at 8,367ft (2,551 m) is further south and can be reached by cable car. The latter, with its café on the summit and its wonderful views of the High Tarentaise and the Lac du Chevril, provides the better views despite its lower altitude. There is also the road leading up to the Col de l'Iseran, but because of its altitude it is only open for about 3 months of the year. Even though this 10-mile road goes up through rather inhospitable-looking country, it is worth taking for the view from the Belvédère de la Tarentaise, back down the Isère Valley and the Chapel of Notre-Dame-de-l'Iseran at the col. This road, constructed in 1936, is particularly useful in the summer for crossing from the Tarentaise to the Maurienne Valley to the south and forms an important link in La Route des Grandes Alpes.

The Mountains of La Vanoise

To the south of Moûtiers, there are many roads leading into the mountains. They usually follow the line of a stream as it flows down to join the Isère. Since the original Savoyard word for stream was *doron,* each name begins with this. The main road towards the Parc National de la Vanoise, the D915, follows the Doron de Bozel, but just after crossing the Isère bridge out of Moûtiers, there is a road to the right, the D915A, that goes up alongside the Doron de Belleville. This leads up the first of the three valleys, with its resort of Les Menuires and Val Thorens. It is a 25-mile (40km) cul-de-sac, but unlike some other valleys, which have become over-developed as skiing areas, it has some delightfully authentic Savoyard villages, such as St Jean-de-Belleville and St Martin-de-Belleville, near which there is a pretty Romanesque chapel at Notre-Dame-de-la-Vie, dating back seven centuries.

To approach the National Park, follow the D915 to Pralognan, which lies at the very edge of the park, surrounded on all sides by high mountains. There are pretty shaded picnic sites in the woods beside the road to the village. Pralognan is an excellent base from which to explore the park, in fact its main interest lies in the many entrances into the high mountain areas that it affords. For those interested in walking in the park and getting to know it well, a specialist *TopoGuide* to the paths (such as the GR55) or guide books with itineraries can be bought in the village or neighbouring towns. They are well illustrated and even without a good knowledge of French the reader can get a great deal of information of a more specialist nature on where to go and what to see.

Beyond the village, a road goes east to the little hamlet of Fontanette. There is ample parking here beside the café at the foot of the valley that comes down from the centre of the Vanoise massif. This valley was formed by the Glacier

*Horse-drawn taxis waiting in Megéve. *A*

de la Grande Casse, which has now drawn back up the mountainside. There is a well signposted pathway to the Col de la Vanoise, the old mule track across the mountains. It is quite a steep 3-hour walk to reach the Col and the Félix Faure hut beyond. This is the classic entrance into the Vanoise, undertaken in 1897 by the then President who left his name to the original hut. A modern hut, which is more like a high altitude café has been built nearby. The Col de la Vanoise is the watershed between the Tarentaise to the north and the Maurienne to the south. It provides excellent views of the surrounding glaciers and summits, such as the Grande Casse to the north-east, at 12,634ft (3,852m) the highest peak in the Vanoise.

*A statue in Megéve. *A*

Places to Visit: La Savoie

Albertville

Albertville Olympic Centre W

Maison des Jeux Olympiques
11, rue Pargoud, 73200 Albertville
☎ 04 79 37 75 71
This museum, which also houses temporary exhibitions, is not on the Olympic site but in the town centre. It is open from 9.30–12.30 and 14.00–18.00 except Sun and national holidays. During Jul and Aug open daily from 9.30–19.00, but from 14.00–19.00 on Sun and national holidays.

Musée d'Art et d'Histoire W

Maison Rouge
Grande Place, 73200 Conflans
From 16 Jan to 31 May and from 1 Oct to 30 Dec, open from 14.00–18.00. From 1 Jun to 30th Sept open from 10.00–19.00.

The Aravis Region and the Arly Valley

L'Abbaye de Tamié W

Col de Tamié, 73200
☎ 04 79 31 15 50
www.tamie-abbaye.com
The visitors' centre at the start of the drive up to the Abbey is open every day from 10.00–12.00 and 14.30–18.00

Grotte et Cascade de Seythenex

Seythenex
www.cascade.fr/fr/grotte
The site is open everyday from mid-May to mid-Sept. In May, Jun and Sept it is open from 10.00 to 17.30 and in Jul and Aug from 9.30 to 18.00.

Musée Archéologique de Viuz W

Route de Viuz
Faverges
☎ 04 50 324 599
Open throughout Jul and Aug fomr Mon to Fri 14.30–18.30 and on Sat and Sun 16.30 – 18.30.

Les Amis du Val de Thônes W

1 rue Blanche
74230 Thônes
This Association hosts very interesting exhibitions on aspects of life in the Thônes Valley every year at its centre by the church. The centre is open throughout Jul and Aug from Tue to Sat 10.00–12.00 and 16.00–18.30 and at the same times on Sat only in Sept.

Coopérative du Reblochon de Thônes

Route d'Annecy
74230 Thônes
☎ 04 50 02 05 60
This cheese making cooperative welcomes visitors from 9.30 on weekdays.

Cimetière des Héros des Glières

The monument on the Plateau des Glières and the cemetery can be visited but the museum is at present undergoing reconstruction.

Cont'd overleaf

Cont'd from previous page

W = Perfect for Wet days

Places to Visit: La Savoie

La Clusaz

Office de Tourisme

161, place de l'Église
74220 La Clusaz
☎ 04 50 32 65 00
The Tourist Office is very good on guided walks and cross-country cycling (VTT) routes.

Musée de Megève

66 rue Comte de Capré
74120 Megève
☎ 04 50 21 27 28
This museum with exhibitions about nature in the mountains is only open on Sat from 14.00–18.00.

Musée Rural du Haut Val d'Arly

88, ruelle du Vieux Marché
74120 Megève
☎ 0450 587 524
This museum, set in reconstructed 19th Century farm building, is open every day except Sun from 14.30–18.30.

Le Beaufortain

Beaufort Cheese Co-operative **W**

73270 Beaufort sur Doron
☎ 04 79 38 33 62
www.fromage-beaufort.com
There is a permanent exhibition above the shop and it is possible to visit the "caves". It is open 8.00–12.15 and 14.00–18.30 every day from May to Sept. From Oct to Apr it is open 8.00–12.00 and 14.00–18.00. In Jul and Aug there is a beautiful film "Au Pays du Beaufort" for which there is a small charge.

Col du Joly

Restaurant d'altitude Chez Gaston

Col du Joly
73620 Hauteluce,
☎ 04 79 38 80 66
During the drive or walk up to the Col du Joly from Hauteluce it may not be apparent but there is a welcome café/restaurant at the top.

Col des Saisies

Office de Tourisme

316, avenue des Jeux Olympiques
73620 LES SAISIES
☎ 04 79 38 90 30
www.lessaisies.com
The Tourist Office is very helpful in ensuring that visitors get the most from this beautiful region on the very edge of the high Alps.

La Tarentaise

There are a number of places where information may be gained about the National Park. One, easily approached by car, is:

Parc National de la Vanoise

105 Place de la Gare
73700 Bourg St Maurice
☎ 04 79 07 04 92

Information is also available at most of the ski resorts and where a number of walks commence.

Parc national de la Vanoise

73710 Pralognan-la-Vanoise
☎ 04 79 08 76 17
www.vanoise.com

Moûtiers

Musée des Arts et des Traditions Populaires W

This is housed in the Bishop's Palace and is open every day except Sun and national holidays from 9.00–12.00 and from 14.00–18.00.

La Léchère

Société des Eaux Thermales de La Léchère W

"Village 92"
73260 La Léchère
☎ 04 79 22 60 30
www.la-lechere.com
The resort's Wellbeing Centre is open from Mon to Sat from 14.00–20.00 between Jan and Oct. It particularly caters for occasional visitors, who can pay per session.

Musée archéologique et minéralogique Pierre Borrione

venue de Tarentaise
73210 AIME EN TARENTAISE
☎ 04 79 55 67 00
www.aimesavoie.com
Visits, which are free, can be made between 15.00 and 18.00 on Sat and Sun throughout the year.

Bourg-St Maurice

Musée du Costume de Bourg-Saint-Maurice W

Place de l'Église
Hauteville-Gondon,
Bourg-Saint-Maurice
☎ 04 79 07 09 01
☎ 04 79 07 27 29
Open from 14.00–18.00 daily except Tue throughout the summer months.

Jardin alpin de la Chanousia Col du Petit Saint Bernard

This garden, at an altitude of 2188 metres, is only open in the summer from Jul to Sept. It can be visited daily from 9.00–19.00. There is a small charge.

Tignes

Golf du Lac de Tignes

Val Claret
73320 ignes
☎ 04 79 06 60 00
www.tignesreservation.net
This 18 hole golf course is the highest in Europe at 2100 metres.

Val d'Isère

Club 4X4 des Aigles

73150 Val d'Isère
☎ 04 79 06 02 06
www.4x4valdisere.com
The course for 4X4 vehicles is in Bellevarde. To get there it is necessary to follow the "Chemin des Coves", which is not metalled and crosses a number of streams.

A great variety of other activities are offered at Val d'Isère and the Tourist Office has information about activities in the summer and winter

Tourist Office

BP 228
73 155 Val d'Isère
☎ 04 79 06 06 60
www.valdisere.com

7. Grenoble & the Grésivaudan

*Below: Cable Cars crossing the Isére on their way to the Bastille. *A*

Grenoble

Grenoble is an exciting city, it is animated, lively and full of interest. It has always been the capital of the Dauphiné, but in recent years it has acquired a reputation as the capital of the Alps. There are many reasons for its pre-eminence, economic, political and educational, but the underlying reason is its situation. Lying as it does on the confluence of the Isère and the Drac, it has had room to expand up the flat alluvial valley bottom in three directions. The fertile valley of the Grésivaudan stretching north-east towards Chambéry, the onetime bread bowl of the Alps, is on the doorstep. It is close to natural resources. Hydro-electric power from the surrounding mountains helped the growth of many industries, and in recent years its attractive position so close to the skiing resorts and the Hautes Alpes has made it easy to recruit highly qualified personnel for the increasing number of high-tech businesses that have sprung up. The economic dynamism of the city has been assisted by the university and the colleges, which have put Grenoble in the forefront of scientific research and cater for 35,000 students.

Grenoble is now very large, and stretching along the valleys in three directions, it has engulfed many outlying communes. This is one reason for the success of the city, since these communes joined with Grenoble in a voluntary association for joint town planning and joint services, under a scheme devised by a one-time mayor, Hubert Dubedout. As a result of this expansion, a car is needed to see the whole of the city. However it is best to explore the centre on foot.

There are a number of car parks in the centre of Grenoble, but the best is the car park under the new Musée de Grenoble, which is in the centre of the city and is well sign-posted.

Before beginning to explore Grenoble, the best way to get a full view

The Founder of Modern Grenoble

Hubert Dubedout can be said to personify the progress of Grenoble. He was a scientist at the newly-founded Nuclear Centre, not in any way interested in politics, but fed up that the water supply to his flat kept failing. He successfully led a campaign to force the mayor to do something. To do this, he set up a non-party political group, whose only brief was to improve local services and local planning. As the head of this group he contested local elections and was to be elected as mayor for nearly 20 years. In a way he was very fortunate, since the outgoing mayor, a fiery dynamic character by the name of Albert Michallon, had almost single-handedly secured the Winter Olympic Games of 1968 for Grenoble. This meant a complex programme of construction and co-ordinating for the new mayor, but at least three-quarters of it was to be funded by central government. Many buildings, particularly three apartment blocks near the new museum, and roads date from this period. Besides the obvious structures, such as the ice rink and the Olympic Village, the station, the post office and many of the inner and outer ring roads were built for the Olympics. This gave Grenoble a sense of modernisation that spread to other areas of the city.

of the city is to take the Téléphérique de la Bastille, a cable car that rises in a few minutes from the water's edge to the top of the Fort de la Bastille on the opposite bank. The cable car station can be reached in a few minutes from the Musée de Grenoble by going down to the River Isère and turning left. A return ticket can be bought, but a single is to be recommended for anyone fit enough to walk back down the hill on the opposite side of the river. Not only is it a pleasant stroll, but it also provides an opportunity to visit sites of interest on the right bank. There is a viewing terrace at the level of the cable car station on the Fort, but it is better to climb the few steps on to the top of what is now the restaurant. This large flat area gives views in every direction. For the more adventurous the Bastille has its own Via Ferrata, named "La Prise de la Bastille", the Storming of the Bastille.

Down below the various stages of the development of the city can be made out by the colour of the roofs, the shape and size of the buildings and the layout of the streets and roads. The very oldest settlement was on the

Museums in Grenoble

Grenoble boasts 11 museums and all are of interest, but two stand out as quite exceptional. They are the Musée de Grenoble and the Musée Dauphinois.

The present Musée de Grenoble, Grenoble's Art Gallery, was opened in 1994 to house the various collections which the city had acquired going back to 1796. This magnificent building has a collection of art, thought to be the best held in any provincial Art Gallery in the world, which stretches in an unbroken line from the 12th Century. It features works by Canaletto, Matisse and Picasso. There are 1500 works of art in 65 rooms and outside in the 2 hectare grounds are numerous sculptures and pieces of modern art. To round off a visit, it has a very good café/restaurant!

The Musée Dauphinois was set up in 1906 in the convent chapel, but later took over the whole convent of Ste Marie d'en Haut across the river from the Musée de Grenoble. The main purpose of the museum is to illustrate the different lifestyles that have developed in the mountains of the Dauphiné. The gloves and glove-making machinery, the porcelain and earthenware, the fine furniture, all made in the region with some interesting pieces from the Queyras, are always exhibited in some form. Of all the folk museums in the Alps, it is one of the best-equipped and most imaginatively presented. The museum also houses an Alpine Library and has become a regional centre of information for researchers into the history of the Alps, with rare manuscripts, documents and books.

Corner of Place St André, showing statue of Bayard. *A

right bank some way above the river. The medieval town is centred round the Church of St André, which can be clearly seen from the Fort, not far from the river and cable car station. It has a spire rising from a tower, adorned at each corner with smaller spires.

The Right Bank

At the upper Téléphérique station, after taking in the wonderful view which encompasses the whole of Grenoble, the Belledonne massif beyond and even on occasions Mont Blanc itself, there is a lovely walk down through the Parc Guy-Pape, leading into the Jardin des Dauphins that ends up opposite the Place de la Bastille/Place Hubert Dubedout. The walk ends by the Porte de la France, the gateway that protected the town from the west, when it was entirely walled. Nearby there is a statue of the mounted Philis de la Charce, a regional heroine, a sort of local but later Joan of Arc, who helped in 1692 to save the Dauphiné region during one of the many attacks by the Savoyards. But this descent leads away from the two other sites of great interest on the right bank, the Musée Dauphinois and the Church of St Laurent. It is very difficult to reach any of these right bank sites by car and

Horse riding in the hills outside Grenoble. *C

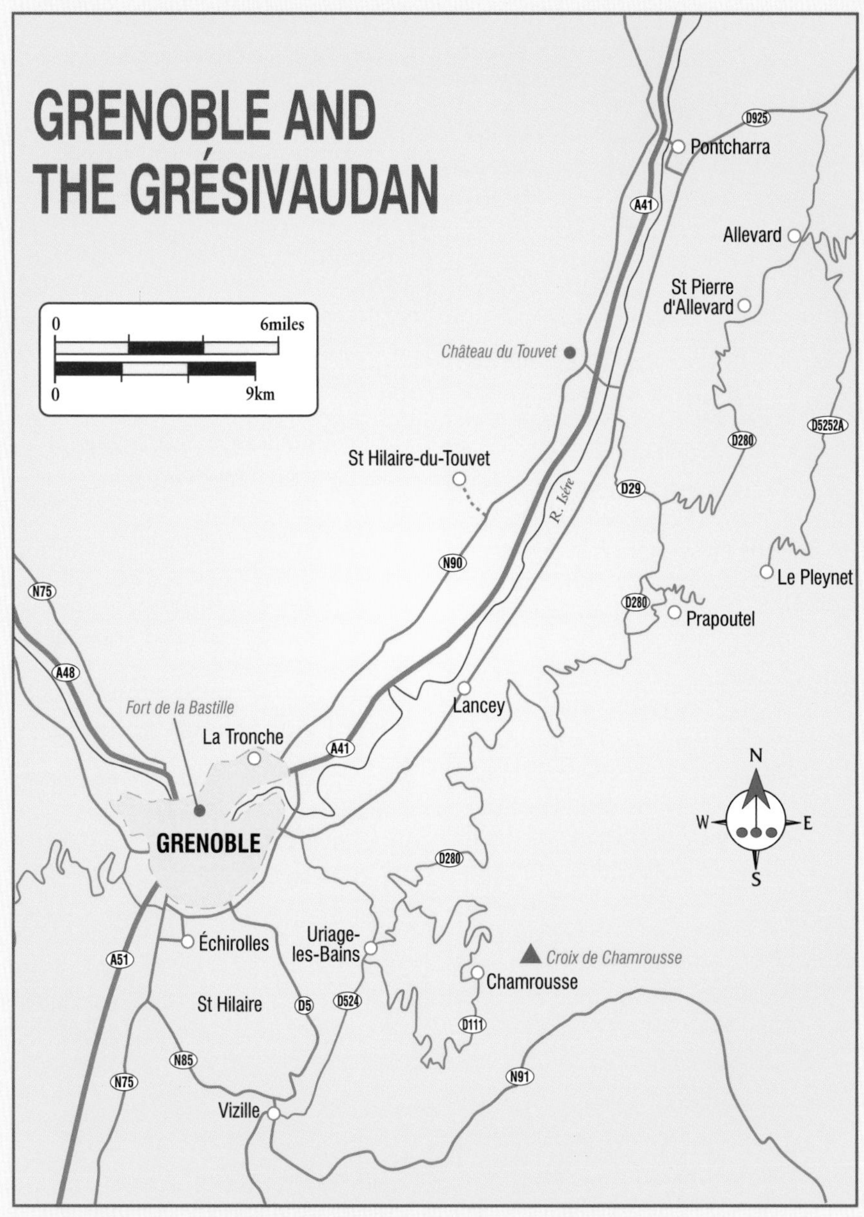

if not visiting by walking down from the Bastille it would be better to leave the car parked on the left bank and walk across one of the bridges. Below the pedestrian way and steps up to the Musée Dauphinois, in the Place de la Cymaise, there is a statue of a lion and a snake, the famous Fontaine du Lion, the lion symbolizing the River Drac which had flooded Grenoble on many

Grenoble's most famous author

Stendhal was the nom-de-plume of Marie-Henri Beyle, born in 1783 in Grenoble at No 14 Rue Jean-Jacques Rousseau. He is most well-known as the author of Le Rouge et Le Noir (Scarlet and Black). The events mirror the fate of a young man guillotined in the Place Grenette on 23 February 1828, an event that Stendhal probably saw, and used as the inspiration for his novel. Stendhal wrote other novels, but is especially known for his travel writing. He very early got the 'travel bug', and he especially loved Italy, where he situated his final novel, the Chartreuse de Parme. His books, such as Les Promenades dans Rome and Les Mémoires d'un Touriste, bring his travels in the early nineteenth century vividly to life. A visit to the museum, once Grenoble's Town Hall, shows that he is still popular 150 years after his death. It also takes the visitor back to that era, not only with its exhibits, but also with its beautiful parquet floor and panelling.

occasions and the Isère symbolized by the snake.

While on the right bank, it is worth visiting the Church of St Laurent, a 5-minute walk above the river. This is of particular interest for historians, because the floor of the Romanesque twelfth-century church has been taken up to reveal a chapel underneath, dating back to the fifth century, which makes it one of the oldest churches in France. The architecture and in particular the marble columns and the capitals at the top, carved with leaf patterns and birds, show the sophisticated state of decoration at that time. It is worth noting that there are organised walks around Grenoble, many with English-speaking guides, and most start from the Church of St Laurent.

From the church, the city centre is reached by taking the first bridge over the Isère, the Pont de la Citadelle, or continuing a little and taking the footbridge, Le Pont St Laurent. Just before the Pont de la Citadelle, a square tower can be seen on the opposite side of the river, the Tour de l'Isle. It used to be part of the town's defences and originally served as the Town Hall.

The Left Bank

After crossing the river, a right turn along the Quai Stéphane Jay, followed by an immediate left turn, comes into the wide-open Place St André, surrounded by the oldest buildings in the city. This is the heart of the medieval city and gives a clue to the development of the city during the Middle Ages. On the break up of Charlemagne's empire, there was in every town great tension between the bishops and the nobility. In many cases the bishops won, but decidedly not in Grenoble. This is seen by the relative position today of the centre of the town grouped as it is round the Place St André with the cathedral some way off to the east. The Church of St André was the chapel of the Albon family, who ruled the region, almost independent of their supposed sovereign, the Holy Roman Emperor. Guiges IV, Lord of Albon, was given the name of Dauphin in 1133 and his lands became the Dauphiné. When one of his successors sold the region to the King of France, Philippe VI, in 1349, he made it a condition that the eldest son of the King of France should always be named the "Dauphin". Back in the days of the Albon rule, the Dauphin had a Council, which sat in a building on the site of the Palais de Justice opposite the church. The Dauphins' palace has also been replaced, but there is still a relic, the Tour du Trésor, that forms part of the Palais de Lesdiguières behind the Church of St André.

The Church of St André was built in 1228, entirely of brick. The stone facade and the bas-relief over the door were added last century, as were the stained-glass windows. After entering the north door and walking towards the main altar, there is a plaque on the wall that tells how the Duc de Lesdiguières foreswore his Protestantism in 1622 thanks to the persuasive power of St François de Sales. It highlights how the duke, a follower of Henry IV, helped to put an end to the Wars of Religion by allowing both Catholics and Protestants to practise their faith in peace, after he had invaded and defeated the city in 1590. He was helped in this by Henry V's Edict of Nantes in 1596, giving freedom of faith to Protestants.

To the left of the main altar is the dark and rather gloomy mausoleum of the Chevalier Bayard, whose interesting life story will be seen when discovering his birthplace at Pontcharra at the other end of the Grésivaudan Valley. It is worth saying that the church is very dark and fairly gloomy, and there are printed invitations to turn the lights on.

In the centre of the Place St André, there is a full-sized statue of Bayard with some welcome cafés behind, of which the Table Ronde claims to be the oldest in Grenoble. This is quite likely, because the presence of the Palais de Justice would have made this square the busiest and most important in town.

The Palais de Justice has a very interesting facade. Originally built in 1453, it was considerably enlarged in 1539. The oriel window in the centre is the chapel, to the left of which is the older Gothic building. To the right of the chapel is the pure Renaissance extension, built on the orders of François I, who is better known for the beautiful Château de Chambord on the Loire. The bas-reliefs make interesting viewing. The snails are said to symbolise the slow pace at which government and the law operate!

The Rue Berlioz goes out of the Place St André back towards the cable car station, passing in front of the Municipal Theatre. The Rue Berlioz is named after the musician who was born in Côte St André, 30 miles (48km) west of Grenoble just beyond the increasingly well used Grenoble Airport. On the left is one of the remaining vestiges of the old town wall. By passing the Palais de Lesdiguières, the fourteenth-century Tour du Trésor incorporated into it can be seen. This palace was the town residence of Lesdiguières, his country residence was the imposing Château de Vizille, which is described in Chapter 9. He was responsible for rebuilding the city, encircling it with

Le Petit train de Grenoble. *A

new and longer walls, and creating an atmosphere of peace and religious tolerance within it. His palace was bought in 1719 as a Town Hall, then became the préfecture, and now houses the Musée Stendhal.

The park in front of the Palais de Lesdiguières with its statue of Hercules in the centre is very formal, but the trees provide a welcome shade on a hot day. An alleyway at the far side of the park leads towards the present-day centre of the town, the Place Grenette, the middle of a large network of pedestrian streets. The cafés stretch out invitingly into the Place, and a variety of international chain stores and fast food restaurants can be found in the streets beyond. The Place Grenette was just outside the walls of the old town in the time

of the first Dauphins. It was a market place, mainly for the sale of grain, hence its name. It was also, as Stendhal saw, the place of execution - the site of the town guillotine. Nowadays it is the bustling commercial hub of Grenoble, a pedestrianised square, where strolling players often perform and people are able to relax. The only vehicle allowed to cross the square is the petit train de Grenoble, the little train that threads its way through the town on a 35-minute run. The departure point is in the Place Grenette just opposite the cafés. Trams also cross the far corner of the Place, as they make their way up and down the Rue Félix Poulat.

Before continuing a tour of the old town, it is worth a 3-minute walk from the Place Grenette along the Rue de

France's most famous Knight

Bayard was born in Pontcharra in 1476, and after serving as a page in the court of the Duc de Savoie, he crossed over to France to become the most famous knight of his time. He was to lead many of the French king's invasions into Italy, and after gaining a reputation for valour and integrity - a sort of medieval Lancelot - he was killed on the field of battle in 1524. The Bayard museum gives an idea of Bayard's life with an audio-visual exhibition, as well as concentrating on the wider aspects of the idea of the Chivalry of his period.

la République to the excellent Tourist Information Centre in its complex of modern buildings, which include the Post Office.

Back towards the Place Grenette, a right turn goes towards the Grande Rue, past the lovely nineteenth-century fountain, the work of the sculptor Sappey. This street, the main road in medieval times, used to be called the Rue du Puits, since there was a well in the little Place Claveyson at the other end of the street. The first building on the left, behind the fountain, is the house of Stendhal's grandfather described in his biography La Vie de Henry Brélard as the surgeon M. Gagnon. Almost opposite this house is the Rue Jean-Jacques Rousseau. This also has connections with Stendhal, since he was born in 1783 at No 14. He was not to live here for long, because his mother died when he was young, and he spent a large part of his boyhood with his grandfather. Both are undergoing an extended renovation and might not be open for some time.

Further down the Rue Jean-Jacques Rousseau, on the left-hand side, No 4 is a typical eighteenth-century town house. It belonged to the Barnave family. There is a street named after Antoine Barnave, who became a lawyer and was one of the architects of the French Revolution. As will be seen when visiting the Château de Vizille (see Chapter 9), the Revolution was initiated by the middle and upper classes, many of whom like Barnave were to end under the guillotine when they lost control of the Revolution that

The birth of Hydroelectric Power

In the village of Lancey, just outside Grenoble, the French engineer Aristide Bergés used the river, which rushes down from the Belledonne Mountains, in 1869 to generate electricity. He was the first man in the world to do this and named his invention 'houille blanche' - white coal, a name still used today in French to describe hydro-electric power. Aristide Bergés used electricity to power a paper mill in the valley, and now there is a museum on the original site given over to the generation of electricity in the Alps and the local paper-making industry. Its opening hours tend to be flexible, so it is worth checking in Grenoble or at a local tourist office.

they had set in motion.

A left turn at the end of the Rue Jean-Jacques Rousseau goes towards the Cathédrale Notre-Dame, passing a beautiful fountain by the Place Notre-Dame. This fountain is called La Fontaine des Trois Ordres, the 'three social orders' that make up the nation. The cathedral beyond on the right-hand side is an amalgam of different churches. The Église St Hugues, the chapel on the left inside the cathedral, was the original thirteenth-century church with the other parts added later. The most famous item is a stone ciborium, or resting place for the consecrated communion hosts, to the right of the High Altar. This tall construction, in flamboyant Gothic style dates from about 1500. It was carved of local stone, and standing 46ft (14m) high, is a fine example of the delicacy and artistry that stonemasons could achieve at this time.

The Rue Brocherie, the main street in Roman times, leads to the little Place aux Herbes, the one-time commercial centre supplied by boats that would tie up at what is now the Place de Bérulle.

Some historians say that the French Revolution began not at the Bastille in Paris, but in the Place de Bérulle in Grenoble. In 1788, the King suspended the Grenoble Parliament, and troops were sent in to disperse the members. The reaction of the townspeople was to pull slates from the roofs and hurl them at the soldiers, who retreated in disarray. This was the famous Journée des Tuiles, 7 June 1788. Because many more troops arrived and threatened the town, the parliament met instead a month later at the Château de Vizille, and a train of events began that led to the downfall of the monarchy.

Via Ferrata

Via Ferrata, literally "Iron Ways", were first used by the Italian military in the Dolomites on the border with Austria, but have recently been introduced into the French Alps with more added every year. One of the easiest to reach is the Via Ferrata on the Bastille in Grenoble. This starts in the park below the Bastille by the Porte de France and is in two sections, the second being the more demanding. There is another at Crolles with a variety of routes of differing standard. Although the metal ropes and walkways provide protection, it is strongly recommended that Via Ferrata are not used by the inexperienced without a guide.

Other Things to Do and See in Grenoble

The Place de Verdun with the Préfecture (1866) facing it from the south used to have in the centre a statue of Napoleon seated on his favourite horse. This fine statue has been removed to the field above the Lac de Laffrey at the exact spot 12 miles (19km) south of Grenoble where Napoleon was met by the Royalist troops as described in Chapter 9.

The Rue Haxo to the left of the Préfecture goes past the Jardin des Plantes towards the Boulevard Jean Pain and the Parc Paul Mistral on the other side. In the Jardin des Plantes is the Musée d'Histoire Naturelle. On the ground

*Musée de Grenoble. *A*

*Jardin de Ville, in front of the Stendhal Museum. *A*

Coupe Icare

Paragliding is practised throughout the Alps and many centres cater for beginners, who can fly tandem with an instructor for an unforgettable view of the mountains. One school of paragliding is at St Hilaire du Touvet, north of Grenoble, overlooking the Grésivaudan near the top of the St Hilaire Funicular railway, but this village is known throughout the world of paragliding for its annual Coupe Icare (Icarus Cup). This is an international paragliding festival, held every September with competitions, films and events attracting people from all over the world. The highlight of the Coupe Icare has become the Concours de Déguisements (A Fancy Dress Competition) when the "sails" come in all shapes, sizes and colours.

floor there is an exhibition of animal life in the mountains and rivers, and on the first floor there is a wonderful collection of minerals and fossils. The Orangerie is used for temporary exhibits.

The Parc Paul Mistral, named after a former mayor who organized an international fair on hydro-electric power in 1925, is a lovely park surrounded by many buildings of interest. It is possible to park just off the Place Paul Mistral at the corner of the park, where there are monuments to the Déportés and the Diables Bleus, the 'Blue Devils', a nickname for the Resistance fighters of the Vercors. In the park there is an odd-looking, high tower, the Tour Perret, a relic of an international exhibition held in the park in 1927, but the present-day attraction of the park is the new Town Hall. Organised visits to the Town Hall are possible, but anyone can go into the main vestibule and admire the sculptures and tapestries.

*The Belledonne Mountain range, overlooking the Graisivaudan Valley. *C*

Around the other side of the park are some of the main buildings associated with the Winter Olympic Games. There is a skating rink and an open-air speed-skating arena, but the eye is drawn to the Palais des Sports, which can seat 12,000 spectators. Its imaginative design was copied for the Palais de Congrès in Paris.

The Grésivaudan

This valley, sometimes written as the Graisivaudan in English, stretches 25 miles (40km) north-east of Grenoble. It is the southern part of the Alpine Furrow, the 'Sillon Alpin', a continuation of the Combe de Savoie. Although its present shape owes a lot to glacial erosion, and many of the foothills are in fact lateral moraines, its initial formation was the result of a lifting and a cracking of the earth's crust, leaving the huge cliffs of limestone, such as the Dent de Crolles, pointing skywards. This long chain of limestone cliffs separates the Grésivaudan from the Chartreuse, with only two roads managing to penetrate its length. On the opposite side of the valley is the equally impenetrable Chaine de Belledonne, with many peaks nearly 9,840ft (3,000m) high. The interest in the Grésivaudan lies on the foothills on both sides of the valley. Before the taming of the River Isère, the roads up and down the valley passed through a succession of delightful villages which have now been effectively bypassed by the motorway and main road in the valley bottom.

If exploring the Grésivaudan from Grenoble, leave the city by taking the Avenue Maréchal Randon via the Place Dr Giraud to avoid missing a beautiful museum in the suburb of La Tronche. This is the Musée Hébert in the house where the painter Ernest Hébert lived for most of his life (1817-1908). The house is a fine example of a typical nineteenth-century Dauphinois country house set in a lovely park. Besides paintings and drawings by the artist, the museum also has furniture and household objects of the period.

After visiting the museum, a right turn down the Chemin de la Carronerie leads along to the N90 and into the valley. To reach the first major point of interest, the Funiculaire des Petites Roches up to St Hilaire du Touvet, continue on the N90, although it is quicker to use the motorway and leave it at Le Rafour. The lower station is in the village of Montfortjust beyond Crolles. The railway was built for a very practical reason, to get people and provisions to the many health hydros on the plateau of Les Petites Roches, 2,624ft (800m) above the valley. It is now mainly for tourists, but it is an unforgettable experience. As the train is hauled up a slope with an average rise of 65 per cent which reaches a record-breaking 83 per cent at one point, the view over the valley and the Alps beyond gets wider and more spectacular the higher it goes.

The Grésivaudan is dotted with small castles and stately homes. Many are still in private hands and cannot be visited, or only by prior arrangement, such as the château at Crolles. Five miles (8km) beyond the funicular railway, the château at Le Touvet is open at weekends. With its lake and formal gardens it is a good example of these small castles which often date back to the thirteenth and fourteenth centuries. In the Château du Touvet there is a fine collection of furniture and manuscripts, with a lot of emphasis on the days of the monarchy.

It is worth crossing to the other side of the valley at Le Touvet and going along the D523 to Pontcharra. This rather industrialised little town was at one time an important border point between the Dauphiné and Savoie. Just to the south of the town is the Château Bayard, now a museum to the memory of this knight, whose statue stands in the Place St André in Grenoble. The signposts in the town are to the 'Musée Bayard'. The views all around the château, but especially back down the Grésivaudan, are superb.

The road through the Gorges de Bréda is one of the ways to visit the town of Allevard, hidden in its valley behind the hill with the odd name of Brame Farine. This lovely town on the River Bréda was once very well-known as a spa. Nowadays the villages around and above it are established small ski resorts, but this has not yet spoilt the peaceful country atmosphere of this little valley. The closest resort is the Collet d'Allevard, and a drive up the winding road gives a very good outlook over Allevard, as well as a view up the Bréda Valley in the direction of the major skiing area, the Sept Laux. This lovely green valley with its typical villages and hamlets is worth exploring, and from Le Pleynet, the resort at the end, a ski-lift open on Mondays, Tuesdays and Thursdays allows access into the mountains.

Le Pleynet is one of the many resorts that make up the Sept Laux complex, the others are all on the Grésivaudan side of the mountains. They can be reached by turning left at St Pierre d'Allevard in the direction of Theys. Although not always an easy road, this is a delightful drive along the old road from Savoie to Grenoble. The main resort on this slope is Prapoutel, which is to the left 2 miles (31/4km) beyond Theys at the Col des Ayes. In the summer, there are many organised activities at Prapoutel, such as tennis and mountain bike riding, as well as horse riding.

The road from Allevard, the D280, continues to contour round the hillside. Although there are many roads down to the valley bottom, it is worth continuing until a mile after the village of St Mury Monteymond. Just as the road rounds the hill, there is a cross about 50yd off the road to the right. This cross, the Croix de Revollat, gives a superb view of the Grésivaudan and the Chartreuse on the other side with the Dent de Crolles looking very impressive towering above the valley. The road continues to skirt round the foothills of the Belledonne, passing the village of Lancey, where hydro-electricity was invented by Aristide Bergès in 1869.

Chamrousse

The Croix de Chamrousse is the final summit before the Belledonne range peters out and drops into the Drac Valley. It could be seen from the Fort de la Bastille behind the rounded foothills that surround Grenoble to the south-east. Chamrousse has become Grenoble's local ski resort, and because it is so close and so easy to reach, it tends to become very crowded in winter. However in spring and summer it is an essential excursion from Grenoble, not only to visit the summit with its wonderful views, but also to see the lovely villages in the foothills.

The route direct from Grenoble to Chamrousse is the D524. This is reached by taking the N87 that begins behind the Parc Paul Mistral. As the road passes under the motorway, it becomes the D524 that follows the line of the River Sonnant as it flows down from St Martin between the foothills. In Uriage-les-Bains, a left turn to St Martin and a right turn in the village goes up to Chamrousse, 10 miles (16km) beyond. The road goes through the Forêt de St Martin and provides superb views of Grenoble in the valley through the trees.

Chamrousse is composed of two villages, Le Recoin and Roche Béranger. It is claimed that downhill skiing was introduced to France in 1881 by Henri Duhamel in Chamrousse. The activities in the resort are now spread between the two villages. Roche Béranger is the larger of the two and has a large campsite. It is particularly well-known as a rally point for caravans because of its position and its relatively easy access.

Since Chamrousse is only 15 miles (24km) from Grenoble and offers a variety of activities as well as courses in tennis and horse riding, it is becoming known as a very good base in the summer for exploring the region and participating in outdoor sports. As with most summer resorts, it is possible to buy a carte station to gain access to these activities. In the resort it is possible to hire mountain bikes or all-terrain motorbikes, as well as participate in

Another View of the Belledonne range. *C

guided walks in the mountains. Hang-gliding is also taught, and there are special lessons for beginners.

It is possible to get high into the mountains by taking the cable car from Le Recoin to the summit, the Croix de Chamrousse. This gives unparalleled views of Grenoble and the valleys that lead towards the city. The pyramid-shaped Taillefer is on the other side of the deep Romanche Valley to the south-east. The Drac Valley comes in from the south, the cluse of the Isère lies ahead, and the Sillon Alpin of the Grésivaudan with the Chartreuse behind it goes off to the north. The hills of Central France can be seen behind the Chartreuse and the Vercors.

Le Touvet - the garden of the Château du Touvet. *C

The resort is particularly worth visiting around 14 August, when there are inter-village games, a lumberjack competition and firework shows.

To return to Grenoble, follow the road which loops round through the trees before coming back to Uriage-les-Bains. After dropping down the first series of hairpin bends, at the Col Luitel, there is a road to the left that ends up in the Romanche Valley. It is worth following this road until the cross, from where there is an impressive view of the valley below. The road down into the Romanche Valley is not easy, so it is best to return to the D111 and descend to Uriage, passing an old monastery building in a clearing on the left half-way down. Those towing caravans should use this road for going up to and returning from Chamrousse.

*The Dent de Crolles, overlooking the valley of the Graisivaudan. *A*

It is wider and has easier gradients than the other road. In addition the old buildings provide a good resting place half way up. From Uriage it is easy to return to Grenoble or turn left to Vizille, the gateway to the Romanche Valley, described in Chapter 9

*Place Grenette, Grenoble. *A*

Grenoble & the Grésivaudan

Grenoble & surrounding area

Musée de Grenoble W

5 place de Lavalette, 38000 Grenoble
www.museedegrenoble.fr
This museum, the most prestigious in provincial France, is open every day except Tue from 10.00–18.30.

Musée Stendhal

Ancien Hôtel de Ville de Grenoble
1, rue Hector Berlioz
38000 Grenoble
☎ 04 76 54 44 14
This museum, in association with Stendhal's birthplace and his grandfather's house, is closed for renovation and will be reopened after an assessment of the best way to present the life and achievement of Grenoble's most famous son has taken place.

Téléphérique

Téléphérique Grenoble-Bastille
Quai Stéphane Jay, 38000 Grenoble
☎ 04 76 44 33 65
www.bastille-grenoble.com
The cable car is open all day every day with minor restrictions, e.g. a later starting time on Mondays (11.00 rather than the normal 9.15).

Musée Dauphinois W

30 rue Maurice Gignoux
38031 Grenoble
☎ 04 76 85 19 01
www.musee-dauphinois.fr
This museum is open every day except Tuesday from 10.00 – 19.00 from 1 Jun to 30 Sept and from 10.00–18.00 from 1 Oct to 31 May.

Église St Laurent W

Place Saint Laurent
38000 Grenoble
☎ 04 76 44 78 68
www.musee-archeologique-grenoble.com
This museum is open every day except Tue, the 1 Jan, the 1 May and 25 Dec from 9.00–12.00 and from 14.00–18.00.

Via Ferrata de la Bastille

Bureau des Guides
Maison de la Montagne de Grenoble
3, rue Raoul Blanchard
38000 Grenoble
☎ 04 38 37 01 71
www.guide-grenoble.com
It is possible to do the via ferrata without a guide but most unadvisable!

Musée Hector-Berlioz W

69 rue de la République,
38 261 La Côte-Saint-André
☎ 04.74.20.24.88
www.musee-hector-berlioz.fr
The museum is free of charge and open every day except Tue 10.00–19.00 from 1 Jun to 30 Sept and 10.00 – 18.00 from 1 Oct to 31 May. It is closed on 1 Jan, 1 May and 25 Dec.

Jardin des Plantes and the Musée d'Histoire Naturelle

Musée d'Histoire Naturelle de Grenoble
1 rue Dolomieu, 38816 Grenoble
☎ 04 76 44 05 35
www.museum-grenoble.fr
Open every day except Tue, Sun and National Holidays from 9.30–12.00 and 13.30–17.30. On Sat and Sun it is open from 14.00–18.00.

Caves de la Chartreuse **W**

10 Bd Edgar-Kofler, 38500 Voiron
☎ 04.76.05.81.77
www.chartreuse.fr
Open from 1 Apr to 1 Nov, including Sat, Sun and Holidays, 9.00–11.30 and 14.00–18.30. Entrance is free of charge.

Musée du lac de Paladru

Maison de Pays, 38850 Charavines
☎ 04 76 55 77 47
http://museelacdepaladru.com
Open every day in Jul and Aug from 10.00–12.00 and 14.00–1900.
In Jun and Sept open from 10.00–12.00 and 14.00–18.00.
In May, Oct and Nov open from 14.00–18.00 only on weekends.

The Grésivaudan

Musée Hébert **W**

Chemin Hébert
38700 la Tronche
☎ 04 76 42 46 12
Open every day except Tue from 10.00–18.00 from 1 Oct to 31 May and from 1 Jun to 30 Sept10.00–19.00. Entrance is free of charge.

Funiculaire des Petites Roches

Le Funiculaire
Gare de Montfort, chemin Polonais
38660 Lumbin
☎ 04 76 08 00 02
www.funiculaire.fr
Simultaneous departure from upper and lower stations on the hour from 10.00 until 18.00 with additional trains at 13.30 and 19.00 on Sun and holidays.

Musée Bayard **W**

Château Bayard
38530 Pontcharra
☎ 04 76 97 68 08
www.wheelabrator.com/bayard
Open from the beginning of May until the end of Sept. In May, Jun and Sept open at weekends from 14.00–18.00. During Jul and Aug open every day except Tue from 14.00–18.00.

Musée Jadis Allevard

Parc des Forges
38 580 Allevard
☎ 04 76 45 16 40
The museum is open in May, Jun and Sept from 15.00–18.00 and during Jul and Aug every day from 10.0 –12.00 and 15.00–18.00.

Lancy

Musée De La Houille Blanche **W**

Maison Bergès,
Lancey
Grenoble
☎ 04 76 45 66 81
This museum is open from Tue to Sat throughout the year.

Chamrousse

Office de Tourisme

42, place de Belledonne
38410 Chamrousse
☎ 04 76 89 92 65
www.chamrousse.com
☎ (0)4 76 89 92 65
The Tourist office has a lot of information about walks in the Belldonne massif and other activities in this high altitude resort, only a few minutes drive from Grenoble.

8. The Chartreuse & the Vercors

*Opposite: Hang-gliding in the Chartreuse. *C*

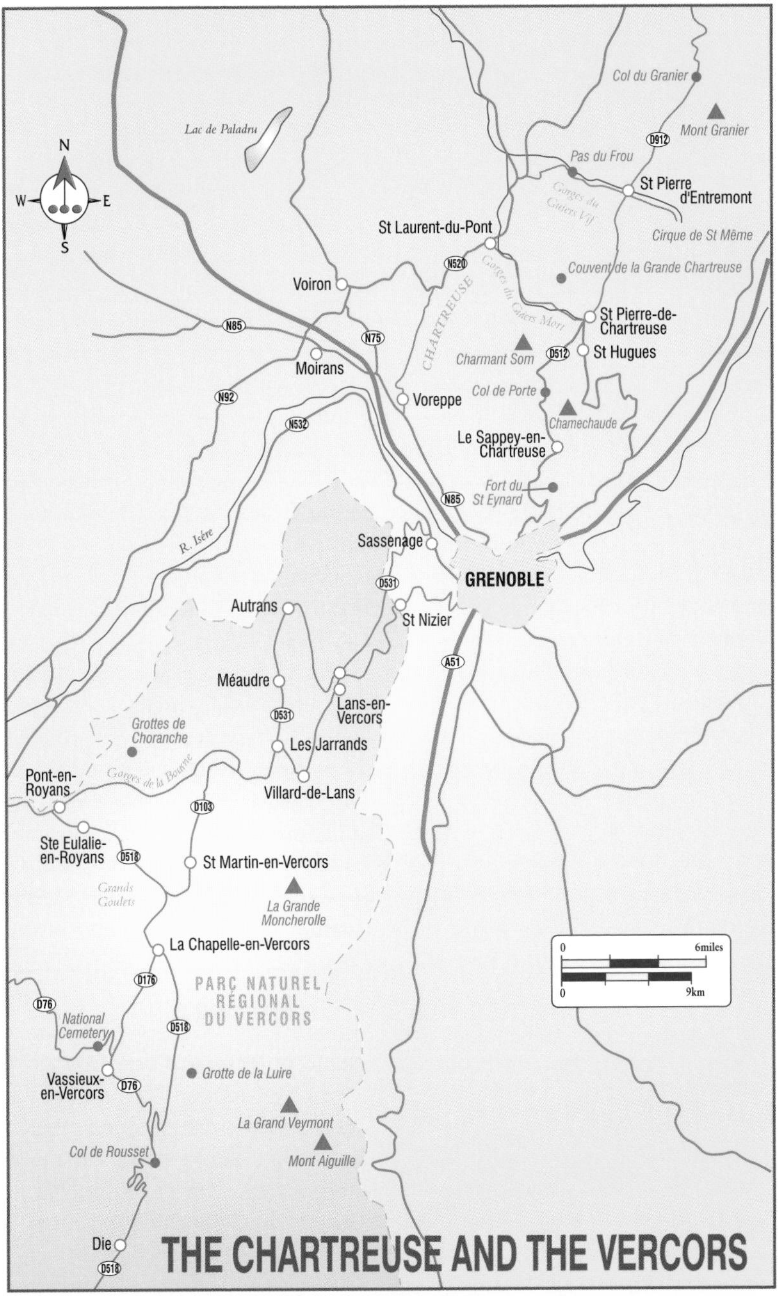

THE CHARTREUSE AND THE VERCORS

N
W
E
S

Lac de Paladru
Col du Granier
Mont Granier
D912
Pas du Frou
St Pierre d'Entremont
Gorges du Guiers Vif
St Laurent-du-Pont
Cirque de St Même
N520
Couvent de la Grande Chartreuse
Voiron
Gorges du Guiers Mort
CHARTREUSE
St Pierre-de-Chartreuse
N85
N75
Charmant Som
D512
St Hugues
Moirans
Col de Porte
Voreppe
N92
Chamechaude
N532
Le Sappey-en-Chartreuse
Fort du St Eynard
N85
R. Isère
Sassenage
GRENOBLE
D531
Autrans
St Nizier
A51
Méaudre
Lans-en-Vercors
D531
Grottes de Choranche
Les Jarrands
Pont-en-Royans
Gorges de la Bourne
Villard-de-Lans
D103
Ste Eulalie-en-Royans
D518
St Martin-en-Vercors
Grands Goulets
La Grande Moncherolle
La Chapelle-en-Vercors
0
6miles
0
9km
D176
PARC NATUREL RÉGIONAL DU VERCORS
D76
National Cemetery
D518
Vassieux-en-Vercors
D76
Grotte de la Luire
La Grand Veymont
Col de Rousset
Mont Aiguille
Die
D518

These two limestone massifs are separated by the valley of the River Isère as it flows north-west out of Grenoble.

The city is a good starting point from which to visit either of these mountain regions. Using Grenoble as a base would mean an excursion of about 50 miles (80km) to see the Chartreuse to the north and about 80 miles (130km) to see the Vercors to the south. This means that a visit to either region could be a day's excursion. But these would be the minimum distances needed to visit most of the sites of immediate interest in the two regions. They would need to be extended to reach many of the less well-known parts. Alternatively, each region has small towns in the centre with developing tourist facilities that might act as a more satisfactory starting point to get to know it well.

Both the Chartreuse and the Vercors are centres for outdoor activities, involving a great variety of sports from caving to hang-gliding. They are especially popular with walkers. Most of the hills and high points are accessible to reasonably fit walkers, even the magnificent Chamechaude in the Chartreuse and the Grand Veymont in the Vercors. Nowadays mountain-biking is becoming increasingly popular as a way of getting deep into the hills and exploring them. This sport lends itself particularly well to the Vercors, where the first World Championships were held in 1987. Both regions have a very wide variety of wildlife, the Vercors was made a Parc Naturel Régional in 1970, while the Chartreuse, also created a Parc Naturel Régional in 1995, is particularly well-known for the richness and variety of its flora at every level. It is a mixture of herbs found in the region that form the basis of the famous drink of the same name, La Chartreuse Verte.

The Chartreuse and the Vercors were both equally impenetrable until comparatively recently because of the steepness of their outward-facing cliffs. Even by today's standards some of the roads in and out are wonderful feats of engineering. Both massifs have an average height of about 3,280ft (1,000m), although the peaks in the

Cement from the Chartreuse

The Chartreuse has a perfect combination of limestone and clay for making Portland cement and it is claimed that modern cement was invented here by Louis Vicat in 1812. The mountains are honeycombed with mines which still extract 720 tons of rock a day to be turned into cement, but there is not much evidence of this. One of the outlets, which can be seen squeezed into the Gorges du Guiers Mort in a most unexpected site, has been providing cement, used specifically for the facades of buildings, for many years.

Vercors are higher. This means that the air is very clear, and with a low population and an almost complete lack of industry its purity is very noticeable to the visitor. It is this factor combined with the relative isolation that gives both areas their charm.

The Chartreuse

The Chartreuse massif does not cover a very large area, it is only 25 miles (40km) long and 10 miles (16km) wide. It is cut off by surrounding valleys in such a way that it has a sense of isolation from the surrounding mountains. Within the massif there is a long valley that stretches down the middle, La Grande Vallée de Chartreuse, but this is split up into many smaller areas, called *bassins,* by ridges that cut across the valley. This has meant in the past that the different communes remained very isolated, relying on farming, forestry and in some areas cement manufacture.

The isolated nature of the massif was the main attraction for St Bruno, who in 1084 after studying in Reims and Paris chose the contemplative life and settled with six companions to form a monastery deep in the mountains. The presence of the monastery, La Couvent de la Grande Chartreuse, has had a permanent influence on the massif, and the word Chartreuse signifies the religious establishment as much as the region. Around the monastery there is a *Zone de Silence,* and this could almost be a description of the massif. A very short way from Grenoble and the valley of the River Isère, or Chambéry and the great trunk roads to Italy, the massif is a quiet retreat, where it is easy for the visitor to return to nature. Even in the height of the summer when the villages tend to become more crowded, it is possible to get off the beaten track very quickly.

Green Chartreuse

The word 'Chartreuse' to many people means the green or yellow liqueur which has been made by the monks since the early seventeenth century. Since 1935 this has not been done at the monastery, but in the town of Voiron on the edge of the region. It is worth making a detour via Voiron to see the "caves" where the liqueur is made and stored. It is the largest liqueur cave in the world, and as well as the original liqueur the monks also make a digéstif, the Elixir Végétal, and recipes for all these are closely guarded secrets, but they are based on local herbs and young pine buds. The liqueurs mature in oak casks that line the 492ft- (150m-) long caves. There is an interesting audiovisual show giving the history of the order and how the liqueur has been made over the years. There is also a free tasting, and the caves are open every weekday throughout the year and at weekends as well in the summer.

There are roads into the Chartreuse from every direction, although some, such as the one from the Grésivaudan over the Col du Coq are quite difficult. One way is from Chambéry, passing below the huge cliff face of Mont Granier and going south over the Col du Granier along the D912. However Grenoble is the most popular starting point.

From Grenoble to the Couvent de la Chartreuse

Voiron, the modern day home of Green Chartreuse, is 15 miles (24km) north-west of Grenoble on the N75, which runs parallel to the motorway, the railway and the river along the valley bottom with the high mountains of the Vercors to the left. The town is industrial and it is at a crossroads. It tends to be dominated by traffic in a one-way system round the centre which has been pedestrianised. The Gothic-style church in the middle, built in 1873, with its elegant high twin spires and the Town Hall with its art gallery merit a visit. Visitors are also welcome at the Rossignol ski factory on the edge of the town, as well as at the distillery.

As the road out ofVoiron towards the Chartreuse, the D520, climbs the hill-side, there is a good view back over the town with the distillery in the middle. The road threads its way through the Gorges de Croissey before reaching St Laurent-du-Pont, 10 miles (16km) from Voiron. This used to be called St Laurent-du-Désert,'St Laurent-in-the-Wilderness'. This wilderness was the area surrounding the monastery and is entered via the Gorges du Guiers Mort. About a mile into this deep gorge there are some ruined buildings and a forge by the river. The buildings formed the original Chartreuse distillery until they

*Chartreuse - cross country sking. *C*

were destroyed by a landslide in 1935. This spot is called the Fourvoirie, a corruption of the Latin words *Forata Via,* meaning the excavated road. It was constructed by the monks in the sixteenth century to enable them to trade with the outside world. Just beyond the buildings is the Entrée du Désert. This was originally a gate beyond which women were not allowed! The road climbs higher up the side of the gorge through a series of tunnels until it crosses to the other side over the Pont

St Bruno, a bridge of a single arch above the river. Beyond this the road passes at one point between the cliff and an isolated 393ft- (120m-) high limestone block, the Pic de l'Oeillette. This was once the site of another gate guarding the route to the monastery or "couvent" as it is called in French.

The present monastery, built in 1688, is just over a mile (2km) by foot further up the valley, and although it is not possible to visit it, a short walk into the hills behind is worthwhile to appreciate fully its isolated but beautiful position. The best view of the monastery is gained by walking past it and on up to the Chapel of Notre-Dame-de-Casalibus, or the Chapelle de St Bruno. From La Correrie to the two chapels is a round trip of 5 miles (8km), but it gives a chance to experience the calm and quiet of the valley on even the busiest day.

From La Correrie the one-way system guides the visitor towards St Pierre-de-Chartreuse, the tourist centre of the region.

La grande Vallée de la Chartreuse

From St Pierre-de-Chartreuse it is 15 miles (24km) back to Grenoble past the Chamechaude mountain that looks its most dramatic from this angle. However the village's central position gives a good opportunity of exploring the region to the north. St Pierre is becoming well equipped as a resort as well as being a touring centre. It has two swimming pools, tennis courts and a pony-trekking centre. It is sometimes possible to take the cable cars up to get into the hills above, and in summer mountain-biking and hang-gliding are practised from the top. The tourist office will give details of nature rambles that can be taken in the company of a forestry commission officer. It has two good camp and caravan sites and every kind of accommodation from hotels to *gîtes d'étape* and mountain huts.

Past the cable car to the Scia and over the Col du Cucheron with superb views of the Charmant Som and the Chamechaude to the rear, the D512 drops down into St Pierre d'Entremont 12 miles (19km) to the north. This village is on the Guiers Vif, which is the border between the Savoie and Isère departments and was until 1860 a national frontier between France and Savoie. The village is still split with two *mairies* - Town Halls. On the approach to the village from the Col du Cucheron valleys can be clearly seen running off the Bassin de St Pierre to the east, north and west. All of them are worth exploring.

The valley to the north is a continuation of La Grande Vallée to the Col du Granier. The road passes through the Gorges d'Entremont and on through the village of Entremont-le-Vieux. All the time the huge wall of Mont Granier becomes more and more impressive as it towers over the valley. There is an hotel and cafés at the Col and a short walk beyond them gives the most comprehensive view of the mountains back down the full length of the Grande Vallée - in the middle the Grand Som and the Chamechaude, and to the east the Dent de Crolles. There are also excellent views into the Combe de Savoie with the Bauges behind it and on a clear day Mont Blanc in the distance. The Col du Granier is an exceptional site not to be missed.

Lac du Paladru

From Voiron, before going towards the Chartreuse, it is a short 6-mile (10km) detour to the Lac de Paladru to the north. This lake, set in soft rolling hills is very well-organised for water sports and bathing. It has seven beaches, four of which are near the village of Charavines. Besides these facilities, it has become well-known for archaeological reasons. When a new port was being built in 1971, the well-preserved remains of a medieval village were discovered in the mud. All the finds have now been transferred to a museum in the village of Charavines, the Maison de Pays. This also shows remains of earlier habitation back to the Neolithic era, as well as an audio-visual presentation of how underwater digs are carried out.

Another excursion from St Pierre d'Entremont is the valley to the east going into the Cirque de St Même. This 5-mile round trip takes the visitor to the impressive 1,640ft- (500m-) high amphitheatre. Halfway up the cliff-face the Guiers Vif emerges from a cave and descends to the valley bottom in magnificent waterfalls.

The road east of St Pierre d'Entremont follows the Guiers Vif into the gorge that it has cut in the limestone. Until 1867 there was a sort of roadway alongside the river at the bottom of the gorge, but this was finally washed away and a new road was cut into the side of the cliff. It is the most impressive route in the Chartreuse and calls for strong nerves in places as it juts out from the side of the cliff over the gorge 500ft (152m) below. Extreme care needs to be taken as the Pas du Frou is approached. There is a lovely statue of Notre-Dame-du-Frou at the side, as well as a memorial to a cave diver who lost his life exploring the subterranean streams in the rock below. The road continues on down to St Christophe-sur-Guiers. From here it is possible to visit the Grottes des Échelles described in Chapter 3.

The most direct route to Grenoble goes back through St Pierre-de-Chartreuse along the D512. Two miles (3kms) south of St Pierre there is a turning to the hamlet of St Hugues. This has become internationally famous and has received over two million visitors in twenty years because of the interior decoration of its church. From the village of St Hugues it is possible to drive along a difficult road over the Col du Coq past the towering Dent de Crolles and into the Grésivaudan. At the col will be seen the rather sad spectacle of a defunct ski resort, a victim of global warming! The GR9 footpath crosses the road just after the Col du Coq and serious walkers use this as a starting point for walking to the top of the Dent de Crolles after first crossing the Col des Ayes to the north. The paths they take can be seen from the road, etched into the grassy slopes.

An easier way to gain height if intending to climb one of the Chartreuse's main peaks is to return to the D512 and just before the Col de Porte turn right in the direction of the Charmant Som. Although the road is very steep in places, it gains so much height that from the end of the road it is only a 40-minute walk to the top of the mountain. The road ends in the meadows above the tree-line so that the walk is clear to see in every direction, but most interesting is the view of the monastery deep in its valley to the north.

From the Col de Porte the road goes towards Grenoble through the village of Sappey, a growing tourist centre. Beyond the village a left turn along the D57A goes up through the trees to the Fort du St Eynard, which is over a hundred years.

The Vercors

The Vercors is now a Parc Naturel Régional measuring 40 miles (64km) from north to south and 25 miles (40km) from east to west. It is split almost half and half between the departments of the Isère and the Drôme. More than half of the region is covered by forests of pine, larch and beech trees, but there are many large clearings in the woods as well as wide-open spaces in some of the upland valleys. The Vercors is composed of two quite distinct areas. The valleys in the north around Villard-de-Lans and Méaudre are soft and accessible, but further south the countryside is altogether more wild.

The long valley down the centre of the southern Vercors, the valley of the River Vernaison, marks a dividing line between the 'lower plateau' to the west and the 'upper plateau to the east. The upper plateau rises up above the treeline to the summits of La Grande Moucherolle and Le Grand Veymont, and since any water quickly sinks through the limestone, this part of the Vercors can be rather arid and devoid of much lush vegetation, although it is good walking country, but remember to carry enough to drink!

The limestone rock of the Vercors is honeycombed with subterranean passages, caves and potholes. For many years the world record for underground exploration was held by the Caving Club of the Seine, who reached a depth of 3,936ft (1,200m) in the Vercors entering the system through the Gouffre Berger, an enormous natural pothole in the north of the region. This is not a

*Cross-country cycling in the Vercors. *C*

visit for the amateur and in fact was off-limits to everyone for a time, and now visits have to be booked in advance.

Sadly, for many Frenchmen the name Vercors has become synonymous with the Resistance's battle with the Germans in July 1944. The Vercors, because of its natural defences and geographical position, was isolated from the main theatres of war, and the Resistance movement used this isolation in order to build up the area as a base from which to operate but were eventually defeated.

Le Couvent de la Grande Chartreuse

It is not possible to drive right up to the monastery itself. The road stops at the car parks that serve La Correrie. This is the building that used to be occupied by Le Père Procureur, the business manager of the monastery. It was also used as a hospital for the monks in case of illness. Nowadays it has been converted into a museum showing the life of the monks. There is a reconstruction of a monk's cell and a very good impression is conveyed of the rigorous life of a contemplative monk. The average number of visitors a year is over 100,000 and for this reason it is best to avoid periods which will obviously be busy. In this way it will be possible to get the real flavour of the 'Zone de Silence', which surrounds the monastery.

*The 'Pas de Frou' in the Chartreuse. *A*

The Northern Vercors

A tour of the northern part of the Vercors starting and finishing in Grenoble is about 80 miles (130km). An extension of this taking in the central valley and the lower plateau would add about 50 miles (80km), but it might be very demanding to do this all in one day because of the difficulty of some roads and the nature of the terrain.

The N532 out of Grenoble passes through the town of Sassenage, famous for its *cuves* and its stately home, the Château de Bérenger. The *cuves* are the pools in the caves. Both can be visited,

The tragedy of Mont Granier

On 24th November, 1248, after days of torrential rain huge blocks of limestone came away from the mountain. As they fell, they broke the surface of the softer marl below and triggered an enormous tsunami of mud, earth and stone which gathered speed and carried everything before it. As the huge wave crashed down it wiped out all the villages below and killed over 5000 people, leaving a lake of mud in the valley 7 kilometres wide and up to 40 metres deep in places. Seen at close quarters from the Col du Granier, the enormity of the catastrophe can really be appreciated.

although the château is only open in the afternoon and the *cuves* cannot be visited by children under six, even accompanied by their parents. The caves, one above the other connected by a waterfall were reputed to be the home of the fairy Mélusine, a mermaid. According to the legend she was murdered by her husband when he discovered that she was a mermaid, and the legend says that the *cuves* were her tears - in fact, more prosaically, they are a resurgence of the waters from the Gouffre Berger 6 miles ($9^1/_2$km) away to the north-east. Another legend is that she was bathing in the *cuves* when spotted by her future husband. It is this legend that has been taken up by the basrelief over the front door of the château. Before leaving Sassenage, it is worth buying some Fromage de Sassenage, which has a good reputation and is not unlike Roquefort in appearance, but softer and milder.

The N531 climbs up the hillside behind Sassenage, giving extensive views over Grenoble and the Chartreuse. After passing the col near a telephone antenna, the road goes alongside the River Furon through a series of pleasant and not very steep gorges. Later, between the road and the river there are some perfect picnic spots in the meadow. The first village is Jaume on the edge of Lans-en-Vercors, where on the left can be seen La Magie des Automates, a museum of automated dolls.

Rather than continue the 5 miles (8km) down the wide valley of the Bourne towards Villard-de-Lans, it is worth turning right, skirting round the Forêt de Guiney and crossing over into the Méaudret Valley. There are two villages in the valley, Autrans and Méaudre. Both are excellent places to use as a base for a holiday, since every sort of activity is organised, from caving to archery. It is possible to get a season ticket giving access to all these activities. As with many holiday villages, the Syndicat d'Initiative will send precise details of all the activities and who is organising them. One of the reasons for the organisation of all these activities in the summer is that in winter both villages are popular cross-country ski resorts and they have good facilities for visitors.

The road south of Méaudre meets the

D531 again at Les Jarrands and a right turn leads towards Pont-en-Royans. This is one of the great routes out of the Vercors, the Gorges de la Bourne. It was completed in 1872. The cliffs rise up above the road and almost block out the sunlight. In the old days the mule drivers would struggle down this gorge, often crossing and recrossing the river on cable bridges to get goods into and out of the Vercors. One of the main items would have been charcoal, which was one of the staple industries of the upper regions of the Vercors. Three miles (5km) later the D531 forks right towards La Balme after first crossing the Pont de Goule Noire. After this village the road is cut into the cliff side and gradually descends with the River Bourne at times 330ft (100m) below on the left with the massive cliffs rising up on the other side of the gorge.

As the gorge opens out, there is a large sign indicating the 'Grottes de Choranche' to the right. A good but initially very steep road rising even higher leads up towards the caves. There is an outer cave open to all, the Grotte de Gournier, and a deeper cave, which is visited with a guide. The significant feature of the Grottes de Choranche is the formation of needle-like stalactites, hanging in their thousands from the roof and reflected in the water. Some of them are 10ft (3m) long and very thin, but hollow. The special lighting shows them to very good effect and makes them almost appear transparent. They are thought to be unique in Europe. At the entrance there is a little museum showing how the caves have been used by different civilisations since Stone Age man first came to the area about 70,000 years ago. From the car park can be seen the Falaise de Presles (cliffs), a favourite haunt of rock-climbers, with the Cascade de Gournier cascading down in wet weather.

As the D531 continues towards Pont-en-Royans, it passes through the village of Choranche with its lovely shaded market place. Although the cliffs are still as impressively high, the gorge has opened out completely and there is a feeling of space until Pont-en-Royans is reached. This town is sited on a very narrow gorge spanned by a single bridge. The most remarkable feature of the town is its houses perched on the rock and in places built into it as they overlook the river. These are best observed by not crossing the river but by continuing parallel to it along the Avenue Thiers. This is also the route to be followed for going back into the Vercors after perhaps visiting the centre of the town on the other side of the river. The Bourne has been dammed just below the town and it looks very quiet and peaceful to the left of the road after its tumultuous descent from the Vercors. From the point where the road moves away from the river there is a very good view back into the gorges that go deep into the Vercors. The Gorges de la Boume are behind the town to the left, the Petits Goulets gorge is just to the right of it, and some way to the right is the wide gorge known as the Combe Laval. On a clear day and with good eyes a thin line can be seen crossing the far cliff of the Combe Laval about 4 miles (6km) away. This is the most famous road in the Vercors, La Route de Combe Laval, which traverses the sheer 2,460ft

Fort du St Eynard

This fort was one of a series built as a direct result of France's defeat by Prussia in 1870. For many years it was derelict and dangerous to enter, but is now being repaired and has an attractive café as well as small museum depicting the days when it was occupied as a small garrison. The view from the fort is absolutely stunning, with Grenoble laid out below and the Oisans and Obiou massifs beyond. Immediately south can be seen the whole eastern edge of the Vercors.

(750m) cliff-face before contouring round and dropping into the valley at St Jean-en-Royans.

Continuing past the Pont-en-Royans bridge without crossing over into the town, the D518 goes to Ste Eulalie-en-Royans, where a left turn takes it back into the Vercors through a very impressive series of gorges. These gorges were formed by the River Vernaison, the chief river of the southern Vercors as it found its way down from the mountain before meeting the Bourne and flowing into the Isère. The road through the gorge was completed in 1851 after more than 10 years of planning and construction. It was the only means of linking the villages on the

Houses in Pont en Royans above the River Bourne. *C

St Hugues de Charteuse

This church has become internationally famous because of the wonderful interior decoration. From the outside the church has no distinguishing feature, in fact it is the Chamechaude rising up behind it that catches the eye, but inside, the pictures, tapestries, stained-glass windows and statues add up to create an indelible impression. They are all the work of one man. In 1953 Jean-Marie Pirot, a young art teacher from the École des Beaux Arts in Grenoble was asked to decorate the church. This simple request turned into a life's work. The artist, now using the pseudonym Arcabas, has constantly added to the work until now the walls are covered and there is a glow of orange and gold as the visitor enters the church. Brochures and audio-descriptions are available in the church porch to help in understanding the artist's intentions. Although the paintings might not be to everyone's taste, the overall effect especially when the sun lights up the interior is very powerful.

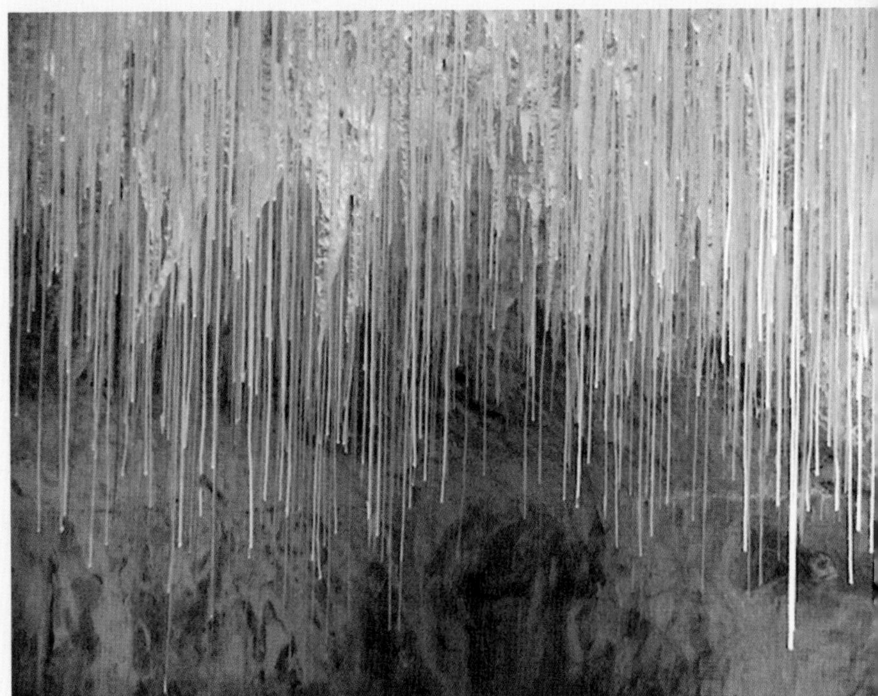

*Stalactites in the Grotte de Choranche. *C*

Vercors plateau to the western plain, and because this route was so well used, other roads such as the Gorges de la Bourne and the Combe Laval road were undertaken later in the century.

The word *goulet* has links with the English word 'gully' and the depth of the gorge at various points creates the image of a deep gully. After leaving Ste Eulalie, the road goes straight into a gorge, the Petits Goulets, and by a series of tunnels and embankments rises up into a slightly more open valley. Soon the little village of Echevis can be seen below grouped around its church. The road then rises with a series of hairpin bends as the valley becomes tighter. The river is some 984ft (300m) below at this point and the walls of the gorge ahead seem to close up. This is the Grands Goulets, and the road goes through several tunnels and galleries as it threads its way through the gorge, which is so tight that light hardly enters it even on the brightest day. As the road emerges from the final dark tunnel, it comes into the bright light of the upper valley and a feeling of freedom and space. Just by the exit from the Grands Goulets is the village of Barraques-en-Vercors, so named because it was the workers' barracks during the long years needed to construct the road. A new tunnel of 1700 metres is being constructed to bypass this difficult route.

Returning towards Grenoble, leave the D518 at Les Barraques-en-Vercors and take the D103. It goes through St Martin-en-Vercors. The old dairy in this village has been transformed into a Caving Centre, which highlights the importance of the region for cavers. In the centre of the village in front of the church is a lime tree planted in 1597 on the orders of Sully, Henry V's chief minister. This is evidence that the village and indeed the area were given financial help to grow and develop during this period. Beyond St Julien, the road passes over the Col de l'Écharasson before joining the upper part of the Gorges de la Bourne and following the River Bourne to Villard-de-Lans. This town, set in a wide open valley is the tourist capital of the Vercors and has every facility with particular emphasis on health and outdoor activities. It has a series of ski-lifts and cable cars that take the visitor high into the mountains on the eastern edge of the Vercors around the summit of La Grande Moucherolle. These operate summer and winter from Le Balcon de Villard, also known as La Côte 2000, just above the town. There is every type of accommodation in the town and surrounding area, but particular attention is paid to children. There are many hostels that cater for them in groups, but perhaps more important for the visitor seeking outdoor exercise, there are many nurseries and 'Garderies d'Enfants' that look after children up to 10 years old during the day. Addresses for these as well as a Tourist Guide that has some pages in English are available from the Tourist Office.

The town is surrounded by wide thoroughfares designed to keep passing traffic away from the small narrow pedestrianised streets in the centre. Arriving from the Gorges de la Bourne, turn left at the roundabout and then right at the second junction. This will bring the visitor to the main car park in front of the Tourist Office. From here it is best to walk to see the centre

Resistance in the Vercors

Although evidence of the resistance can be seen throughout the Vercors, particularly in the south, Vassieux-en-Vercors has the most poignant reminders of the heroism and the tragedy with its Musée de la Résistance, its memorial and its Cimetière National a mile to the north. The museum is the work of a Resistance fighter, J. La Piscirella, who assembled every sort of object, photograph or weapon that would serve as a reminder of that tragic time. It is now laid out in two rooms, one devoted to the events in the Vercors and the other to the war in general. Nearby there is a modern memorial with panes of glass instead of tombstones, which might not be to everyone's taste, but the church with its striking triptych by Camelo Zagan is worth seeing.

Above the National Cemetery, at the Col de la Chau there is a most impressive National Memorial Museum, set in the contour of the hill overlooking Vassieux. It was opened in 1994 by the Prime Minister. The Car Park is on the left at the Col, but those who might not be able to walk the long, winding path down to the Museum and back can park in front of the Museum by turning left before the Col.

La Grotte de la Luire, south of La Chapelle-en-Vercors, was used as a hospital by the Resistance during the war and on 27 July the wounded and the medical staff were taken completely by surprise by the SS. Fourteen wounded were immediately shot and there is a monument to them nearby, eleven others were taken to the village of Rousset and executed there. The doctors were executed in Grenoble and the nurses were sent to a concentration camp in Germany. It is necessary to know facts such as these to understand why the whole region continues to be a place of pilgrimage for so many French people.

of the town, which is not very extensive, composed mainly of two streets leading off a delightful main square. It is noticeable that the gable ends of some of the houses, even the most modern, are stepped in the traditional Vercors manner. This tradition can be seen on buildings in the northern Vercors, but are rare further south.

To visit the cable car, drive back out of town by the same road and skirt round passing the turn towards Pont-en-Royans. The next turn to the right leads to the ruins of the village of Valchevrière, purposely never restored after the war. The road to it has now become a pilgrimage, an outdoor version of the 14 Stations of the Cross, leading to the final cross, the Croix de Valchevrière. It is a return journey of 10 miles (16km) to the ruins of the village.

If not taking the Valchevrière road, there is a fork a mile-and-a-half later and the left-hand road goes up to the cable car. The right-hand road leads to Corrençon-en-Vercors, a good starting

*The Monastery of the Great Chartreuse. *C*

*A colourful dragonfly - an entry in the Coupe Icare. *D*

*The road down from the Col du Rousset towards Die. *A*

point for walks, but more popular as a ski resort in winter. The cable car does not go to the summit of the ridge, it needs at least an hour's walk to get from the cable car station to the eastern edge. However it is quite easy walking and very open, the Tourist Office will help with detailed maps. It is worth the walk for the view from the ridge looking down the Drac Valley and across to the

*Mont Aiguille, first climed in 1492! *C*

Taillefer ahead and the Obiou to the south-east, as well as the line of hills leading to the isolated block of Mont Aiguille to the south.

Besides being a great walking country, the whole of the mountainside above Villard has become a centre for mountain bikes. These are carried up to altitude and retrieved at the end of the day so that the whole time can be spent at height. Many organisations that specialise in this are based at Villard-de-Lans and an annual race the Transvercors VTT is run here every September.

From Villard-de-Lans, there is a different and attractive road back to Grenoble, the D531. This goes past Lans-en-Vercors, it then climbs the wooded hills with superb views over the Furon Valley, the main route into the Vercors. Three miles (5km) beyond Lans-en-Vercors, there is a good view right down the very deep Gorges du Bruyant to the left. It is worth stopping in St Nizier to visit the viewpoint and orientation map, showing the mountains from the Chartreuse right round to the Massif des Écrins, with Mont Blanc in the background. St Nizier is developing as a ski resort because of its proximity to Grenoble. It was very badly damaged in July 1944 and the cemetery commemorating the fallen during this sad episode is just below the village. The road drops steeply through a series of hairpin bends and 4miles ($6^1/_2$km) later to the left is the Tour sans Vénin after the village of Pariset. This gets its strange name of the 'Tower without Poison' from the story of the owner returning from the Crusades with a sack of soil. He scattered this sacred earth around his castle and since then no poisonous snake has ever been spotted there. From this point the mountains to the south, the Dévoluy massif, can be seen effectively blocking off the Drac Valley and acting as a frontier post between the Northern Alps and the Southern, leading to the Maritime Alps.

The road then descends through an area of woods and rocks, called the Désert de Jean-Jacques, where Rousseau used to wander and collect plants. The road then continues on to Seyssinet and returns to Grenoble over the Pont-du-Drac.

The Southern Vercors

La Chapelle-en-Vercors is the chief village in the southern part of the Vercors. It is a very well-equipped tourist centre with several hotels, a good municipal camp site, sports facilities and a riding school. The entire village has been rebuilt since the events of July 1944 and on 25 July every year there is a ceremony in the Cours des Fusillés in memory of those who died. The only building left standing was the church with its typical square stone clock tower with small pointed steeple. It has been very well restored. La Chapelle is a centre for cavers who have a hostel there, and it is possible to join organised caving visits, many of which are organised for beginners. Often cave visits start by dropping down one of the many natural wells or *scialets* that can be found in the surrounding countryside. There is a festival of caving films, called "spéléovision" in the village every year at the end of August.

Leaving La Chapelle-en-Vercors, the D518 continues south along the valley of the River Vernaison. Five miles (8km) along the valley there is a well-signposted turn to the left leading to the Grotte de la Luire. This is of great interest, not only for its curious geology, but also because of its historical associations. After parking, there is a short walk through trees to 'La Grotte'. The pathway leads up towards the cave entrance under its huge canopy. At the back of this opening is the entrance to the cave and its subterranean passages. At the back of the interior cave is a pothole that cavers have explored and found to go down a depth of at least 724ft (250m). In times of flooding it can be very dangerous. It is a kind of release valve for the extended network of underground rivers that drain the hills to the east. In very wet conditions, water has been known to rise quickly up the pothole and the cave itself has been filled. These occasions are fairly exceptional and ordinary visitors to the cave would not be in any danger.

After passing through Rousset, the road climbs the hillside, and although the road to Vassieux-en-Vercors leads off to the right, it is worth going on to the Col de Rousset, with the small ski resort of Beurre above, and passing through the tunnel. It is possible to park at the southern end of the tunnel, from where the view south is breath-taking as the road theads its way down into the Drôme Valley with the town of Die, famous for its bubbly wine, Clairette de Die, at the foot of the mountain. It might be possible to see flying high above the mountainside one of the vultures which have been brought back to the village of Chamaloc.

Returning through the tunnel, the road bears left and after passing over the Col de St Alexis drops down to the rather bare plateau of Vassieux-en-Vercors. This village has also been totally rebuilt since the war,

South of Vassieux along the D615 is a quite different site of historical interest. A few years ago a prehistoric 'workshop' was discovered with flint tools in different stages of production. This has now been set out as a museum with a projection room, a viewing room and information panels. It makes a fascinating visit since it brings to life the way that the early inhabitants of the Vercors would have lived 5-6,000 years ago.

Passing the turning to Font d'Urle, a developing little ski resort in a dominating position over the Drôme Valley, the road enters the Forêt de Lente. This huge wooded area is renowned for its wildlife. Three miles (5km) after entering the Forêt de Lente, there is a very pleasant 500yd walk through trees to the left of the road to the Grotte du Brudour. The huge cavern with its monumental entrance acts as a resurgence for the water that has fallen on the higher cliffs to the south. The D76 continues after passing the village of Lente in the middle of its open clearing to Col de la Machine, beyond which is the impressive Combe Laval.

Until 1897, wood and charcoal had to be hauled up over the Montagne de l'Écharasson to the west of the Col de la Machine, but in that year the dramatic road alongside the Combe Laval was completed. For nearly 3 miles (5km) it is cut into the cliff-face, with a sheer drop of 2,132ft (650m) in places to the River Cholet below and some people might find driving along it quite unnerving. After the Col de Gaudissart at the end of this exposed part and a short drive through trees, there is a very sharp left-hand bend, with an impressive viewpoint. This gives a clear and impressive view of the district of Royans below with Ste Eulalie and Pont-en-Royans further north at the mouth of the entrances to the Petits Goulets and the Gorges de la Bourne. Two miles ($3^1/4$km) later, the road reaches St Jean-en-Royans. The newly opened Musée de l'Eau is certainly worth a visit before returning to Grenoble along the Isère Valley or through the Gorges de la Bourne.

*St Pierre de Chartreuse. *A*

*Mont Granier. *A*

*Boating on Lac Paladru. *C*

Places to Visit: The Chartreuse

The Chartreuse

Parc Naturel Régional

Maison du Parc
38380 St-Pierre-de-Chartreuse
☎ 04 76 88 75 20
www.chartreuse-tourisme.com
The English language website is under construction but this site can be used to download documents about the Park and its activities in English.

La Couvent de la Grande Chartreuse **W**

Musée de la Grande Chartreuse
La Correrie
38380 St Pierre de Chartreuse
☎ 04 76 88 60 45
www.musee-grande-chartreuse.fr
This excellent introduction to life in the monastery is open every day from May until Oct. From Jun until Sept it is open from 9.30–18.30 and the other months from 10.00–12.00 and 14.00–18.00.

St Hugues

Musée Départemental d'Art Sacré Contemporain **W**

Eglise St Hugues
38380 St Pierre de Chartreuse
☎ 04 76 88 65 01
www.arcabas.com
The website which is in English gives the background to the artist's thinking. The church is open every day except Tue from 10.00– 8.00. It is closed on 1 Jan and 1 May.

Fort du St Eynard

38700 Le Sappey en Chartreuse
☎ 04 76 85 25 24
www.fortsteynard.com
The café and the museum are open from 1 May to 1 Nov. This is a site not to be missed!

The Vercors

Parc Naturel Régional

Maison du Parc
255, chemin des fusillés
38250 Lans en Vercors
☎ 04 76 94 38 26
www.parc-du-vercors.fr
A lot of good information in English about the park of particular interest to naturalists and bird watchers.

Cuves de Sassenage

The caves, called "Cuves de Sassenage" are open every day 10.00–18.00 from May to Oct. The gardens of the nearby Chateau de Bérenger can also be visited at the same time.

La Magie des Automates **W**

Musée des Automates
38250 Lans en Vercors
☎ 04 76 95 40 14
www.magiedesautomates.com
Open throughout the year 14.00–18.00 Mon to Sat and on Sun and National Holidays from 10.00–18.00.

Grottes de Choranche W

38680 Pont en Royans
☎ 04 76 36 09 88
www.grottes-de-choranche.com
All visits to the caves are guided. In Jul and Aug the guided tours take place every 30 minutes between 10.00 and 18.30. In Apr, May and Sept they are from 10.00–12.00 and 13.30–18.00.

Villard-de-Lans

Office du Tourisme

101 Place Mure-Ravaud,
38250 VILLARD-DE-LANS
☎ 08 11 46 00 15
www.villarddelans.com
The Tourist Office has a lot of good information in English about walks and other activities. The website is also in English.

Grotte de la Luire

Saint Agnan en Vercors
☎ 04 75 48 25 83
www.grottedelaluire.free.fr
Open every day from Apr to Oct.

Clairette de Die

Cave de Die Jaillance W

Avenue de la Clairette
26150 Die
www.jaillance.com
The wine distributors also host temporary exhibitions related to their wine and local life.

Vassieux-en-Vercors

Musée de la Résistance W

26420 Vassieux-en-Vercors
☎ 04 75 48 28 46
This small museum, set beside the church and the memorial garden, is open from mid-Jul to mid-Aug from 10.00–19.00. In Mar, May, Jun, Sept and Oct it is open 10.00–12.00 and 14.00–18.00.

Mémorial de la Résistance W

Col de La Chau
26420 Vassieux-en-Vercors
☎ 04 75 48 26 00
www.memorial-vercors.fr
Open from May to Sept 10.00–18.00 and from Oct to Apr 10.00–17.00.

Le Musée de la Préhistoire W

26420 Vassieux-en-Vercors
www.prehistoire-vercors.fr
This prehistoric 'workshop' is open every day in Jul and Aug 10.00–18.00. In Apr, May Jun and Sept 10.00–12.30 and 14.00–17.00.

Musée de l'Eau W

38680 Pont en Royans
☎ 04 76 36 15 53
www.musee-eau.com
This new and imaginatively constructed museum is open all year. In Jul and Aug it is open from 10.00–18.00. In other months it is open from 10.00–12.00 and 14.00–17.30.

9. Hautes Alpes

*Below: Meltwaters from the Glacier Blanc near Pré Madame Carle. *A*

East of Grenoble the mountains of the department of the Isère merge into the northern section of the suitably named department of Hautes Alpes before meeting the Italian border.

The mountain ranges at this point are the dividing line between the main French Alps to the north and the Southern Alps which become lower as they stretch down towards the Mediterranean. Because many summits are lower, the average height of the region is not as great as in the Mont Blanc massif or the Vanoise, but the mountains here live up to their name of 'Hautes Alpes', since they are generally more impenetrable. The valleys in this region cut deep, which often makes for difficult driving, whether threading one's way along the valley bottom or climbing up the side to reach the more open mountain sides above. Typical of this is the Oisans region, which is centred on the middle section of the Romanche and is the most popular tourist area. The region of Hautes Alpes boasts some of the highest passes in Europe as well as the highest village and the highest town in Europe and a large section is in one of the biggest National parks, Le Parc National Des Écrins.

The two main valleys running west to east, the Maurienne and the Romanche, both lead towards quite accessible passes into Italy. From the Maurienne into Italy there is now a road tunnel as well as a railway tunnel, and the Col de Montgenèvre at the head of the Romanche Valley is, at 6,068ft (1,850m), the lowest pass from France into Italy. This has meant that throughout history the valley bottoms have been active and busy, forming major lines of communication. This, combined with the proximity of hydro-electric power, has encouraged the growth of heavy industry in the lower sections of both valleys but no single town has shown any dominance in the region. St Jean-de-Maurienne is the biggest with a population of 11,000 while Modane despite being the traditional customs post and an important rail junction for nearly a century, has only about 6,000 inhabitants.

The Maurienne Valley runs round the southern edge of the Vanoise. It can be entered from the Combe de Savoie, as explained in Chapter 4, but from Grenoble this is a very long round-trip circling the Belledonne range to the north. It is more interesting to enter the Maurienne from the Romanche Valley by crossing the Col de la Croix de Fer. This is a part of one of the most dramatic and celebrated tours in the Alps, La Route des Grands Cols.

The Romanche Valley

The Lower Romanche

The River Romanche meets the plain at Vizille 10 miles (16km) south-east of Grenoble. The main road into the valley bypasses the town, but it is worth turning into the town centre if only to visit the castle. The centre of the town provides the entrance to the solid Château de Vizille, built between 1602 and 1622 by Lesdiguières as his country residence. From Vizille the famous "Route Napoléon" goes south towards the little town of Laffrey, the scene of Napoléon's famous return to power.

Besides its historical associations, Laffrey is nowadays important for watersports. On the Grand Lac de Laffrey it is possible to hire boats and sailboards as well as to swim. There are beaches around the top end of the lake. The two lakes further south, the Lac de Petichet and the Lac de Pierre-Châtel have fewer facilities, but all three provide very good fishing. Four miles (6km) beyond Pierre Châtel is the town of La Mure, a mining community, very well known now for its railway.

As the Route Napoléon continues towards Gap 25 miles (40 kin) to the south, it provides opportunities of approaching the Massif des Écrins from the west and gaining access at two points to the Parc National des Écrins. The road passes through La Salle-en-Beaumont. The 'Beau Mont' is the Obiou to the south-west, which is best viewed from Quet-en-Beaumont 3 miles (6km) further on. At the town of Corps, with its access to the Lac du Sautet, created by the construction of the Barrage du Sautet in 1935, there is the first possibility of going into the massif. The D212 to the left rises steeply towards a basilica, dedicated to Notre Dame de la Salette.

Shortly after the town of Corps a turn off the Route Napoléon towards the village of St Firmin leads into one of the longest valleys into the massif, the Valgaudemar. The destination of most travellers is La Chappelle-en-Valgaudemar, 10 miles (16km) further up the valley. Although the village holds no particular interest in itself, it is the base for a number of excursions into the surrounding mountains. There are walks in every direction, notably south along the river Navette, which tumbles down through the 'Marmites du Diable' and north towards the Réfuge de l'Olan, named after the peak which dominates the valley at this point. It is possible to drive beyond La Chappelle-en-Valgaudemar even higher to reach the Châlet-Hôtel de Gioberney which at 5,610ft (1,700m), is in wild rocky mountain country, on the edge of the 'Parc'. There is a most spectacular waterfall with the named in French 'La Voile de la Mariée' because as the wind lifts it, it gives the appearance of a bride's veil.

Another opportunity to approach the Massif des Écrins from the west is provided by following the course of the River Drac as it drops down from the mountains along the valley of the Champsaur 12 miles (18km) further south along the Route Napoléon.

The Lower Romanche Valley can only be reached by retracing one's path to Vizille. As the road makes its long and potentially dangerous descent into Vizille, the Lower Romanche Valley and the N91 can be seen to the right dramatically cutting into the mountains. Sadly there have been many fatal accidents at the bottom of the road as it turns sharp right towards Vizille, when overused brakes have burned out. After crossing the river, the N91 is reached. This main thoroughfare runs parallel to the river, often rising above it giving a

*Cross-country cycling at Alpe d'Huez. *C*

view of the extensive power stations and steel works that border it. For the first 12 miles (19km) the valley is most unattractive, although it is interesting to see how the factories are squeezed into the valley bottom. The industrial section finishes as the road crosses the river over the Pont de la Véna. The road turns right at Rochetaillée and is almost straight for the 5 miles (8km)

The Château de Vizille

The present imposing château was built on the site of an earlier castle and at first incorporated many of the older buildings that have now either been demolished or burned in one of the fires that ravaged the building in the nineteenth century. It was in one of these buildings, the Salle du Jeu de Paume, that the meeting of the Dauphiné Estates (Parliament) took place in July 1788. This meeting led to a resolution protesting at the suppression of the National Parliament and a general cry of 'No taxation without representation', and it began a movement throughout France that was to culminate in the French Revolution of 1789. For this reason Vizille prides itself on being the 'Cradle of the Revolution', and in the castle there is now a Musée National de la Révolution. The castle is entered from the Place du Château through an elaborate gateway with a statue of Lesdiguières on horseback in bas-relief above. Through the gateway the eye is taken by the very extensive park stretching away to the right. The castle is on the left and the entrance is reached up an elaborate *perron* or outside staircase. From the high entrance the extent of the park with its lakes, its trees and its wandering deer can be seen to full advantage.

into Le Bourg d'Oisans. The tortured rock layers that were compressed and twisted as the mountains were formed are very clear to see, especially on the western side. At Rochetaillée by the café there is a small road to the left that belies its importance as one of the setting-off points for the Route des Grands Cols, which is described later in this chapter.

L'Oisans – Central Romanche

Le Bourg d'Oisans is the tourist and activity centre for the Central Romanche Valley and the five valleys that join it. The town itself acts as a base from which to explore, but is not without interest itself. It has become the centre for studies of Alpine geology and minerals, and it prides itself on its scientific reputation as well as its position as a holiday centre. It tends to be busy throughout the summer, but this bustling activity adds to its charm. It has all the expected cafés and gift shops, but within two minutes of the centre traditional farms with haylofts can be found down side streets, reminding the visitor of its importance as the agricultural centre of the most fertile section of the Romanche Valley. Le Bourg d'Oisans has many facilities for sport, from rock-climbing to tennis, and there are frequent organised entertainments, usually free, such as firework displays, concerts and folk displays. It has become a national centre for rallies for four-wheel drive vehicles.

A museum has been opened in the Foyer Municipal to exhibit the wide range of minerals and fauna to be found in the surrounding mountains, the Musée des Minéraux et de la Faune.

One of the reasons for the importance of Le Bourg d'Oisans as a mineral centre is to be found rather surprisingly 6,560ft (2,000m) above the town near the resort of L'Alpe d'Huez. This resort is reached by an impressive series of twenty-one hairpin bends that climbs the mountain to the north and features in nearly every Tour de France. There is a museum in the village of Huez, La Maison du Patrimoine, that has a permanent exhibition about the silver mine, as well as temporary exhibits on other aspects of life in the villages of the Oisans.

L'Alpe d'Huez is one of the new all-year-round ski resorts with cable cars going up to the Pic Blanc at 10,912ft (3,327m), allowing summer skiing on the high glaciers. This facility gives the non-skiing visitor the opportunity to take the cable car to the first station for superb high-altitude walking, such as to the Lac Blanc or the Dôme des Petites Rousses, or to the upper station on the summit for the most comprehensive view of the Alps, from Mont Blanc in the north to the Barre des Écrins in the south. On a look-out point above the cable car station there is a plan to help to place all the various peaks that stretch away in every direction.

The Meeting at Laffrey

From Vizille, the N85 crosses the Romanche and goes south. This is the famous Route Napoléon. It follows in reverse direction the route that Napoléon took on his return from Elba in 1815. Five miles (8kms) south near the village of Laffrey, Napoléon met a small army sent out from Grenoble under the leadership of General Dellessart. This was the famous occasion, La Rencontre de Laffrey, when Napoléon strode forward on his own, pulled back his coat to expose the medal of the Légion d'Honneur above his heart and said 'Soldiers, I am your Emperor! If there's one amongst you who would kill his general, here I am.' This spot is marked by a statue of Napoléon on horseback. This used to stand in the centre of Grenoble until 1870 but was then transferred to its present site, which is well signposted. The area in front of the statue is now pleasant open parkland.

The Upper Romanche

The glacier that formed the Vénéon Valley was much fuller and more powerful than the Romanche Valley glacier. The latter was only a tributary that joined the main glacier as it moved down the Oisans basin. This is still evident today in the way that the N91 clings with great difficulty to the side of the very narrow Gorges de l'Infernat after the D530 turns off right into the Vénéon Valley. This turn is at the little village of Le Clapier, which means 'rabbit warren', a name associated with the terrain. Traffic is usually slow-moving here and demands patience. At various points it is possible to see the road a long way ahead, usually with a line of cars behind a heavy lorry struggling up the long incline on its way towards Italy. The gorge is deep and rather forbidding for 5 miles (8km) until after a tunnel the Barrage de Chambon is reached. This dam, built between 1927 and 1936, is one of the few in the Alps that relies for its strength just on its weight rather than any system of vaulting. It holds back the waters of the Lac de Chambon. For a good view of the lake, turn right immediately before it. There is room to park and a look-out point – also a welcoming café. The N91 crosses the dam before skirting the lake on the northern side. The entrance to a tunnel can be seen from the lookout point. Also on the other side of the dam the village of Mizoën can be seen high above the start of the lake. The road to the village makes an interesting detour, because it leads 5 miles (8km) up to two small Alpine villages, Clavans-en-Oisans and Besse. These villages with their narrow streets and their houses with roofs of stone slabs seem untouched by time, surrounded by mountains with views of the Grandes Rousses and the Meije.

From the Barrage du Chambon to La Grave along the Upper Romanche Valley (La Haute Romanche), the road runs very close to the River Romanche through the Combe de Malaval. On the left, streams coming down the hillsides end in dramatic waterfalls just beside the road. The first is the unfortunately named Cascade de la Pisseuse and just before La Grave there is a second, the Saut de la Pucelle, the Maiden's Leap. However by this time the eye is taken

Le Chemin de Fer de la Mure

In the area to the south of Grenoble known as the Marheysine, there is evidence of anthracite mines all around since many were active until very recently. In 1888 a small railway was built as part of the local rail network, but its main purpose was to take the coal north to the Drac Valley for transportation into Grenoble. This is now a tourist railway, 'Le Chemin de Fer de la Mure'. For 20 miles (32km) it skirts the edge of the mountains overlooking the Drac Valley. The line ends at St Georges-de-Commiers. The journey takes about 2 hours since the train goes slowly and has many stops for taking photographs, enjoying the scenery and admiring the feats of engineering. There is a very good little museum in the station at La Mure, as well as an underground mining museum at La Motte d'Aveillans 5 miles (8kms) north.

*The road above La Grave with the Meije in the background. *A*

more to the right to the hillsides on the opposite side of the river. The very lowest edges of the Glacier de la Girose can be seen at various points, apparently creeping down over the gullies in the hillside. At this point the valley widens out to reveal one of the most remarkable sights in the Alps, the little village of La Grave with the mountain of La Meije soaring above on the right. On a sunny day the mountain appears to glisten since the whole face seems to be made up of glaciers, the Glacier de la Meije in the centre, with the Glacier du Tabuchet beyond.

*Monument to the founder of the Tour de France by the Galibier Tunnel. *A*

La Grave is not quite in the valley bottom, it is on a rocky promontory on the opposite side, which gives it an even better position as a viewpoint. Just to the right, as the road enters the village is the cable car station with a large car park. The cable car ride is in two sections. First it crosses the valley in a huge sweep and rises to the plateau of Peyrou d'Amont at 7,872ft (2,400m). The second section goes on up to the Col des Ruillans at 10,532ft

(3,211m), although this station is called Le Râteau after the mountain on which it is situated.

Any point in La Grave acts as a good place from which to view La Meije, but there is a traditional site that affords particularly good views. This is the Oratoire du Chazelet. To reach it by road, it is necessary to drive through La Grave and turn right at the end of the tunnel. The turn is just as the tunnel ends and can be missed, so start indicating right half way through the tunnel. Climb up the hillside towards the village of Le Chazelet and park beyond the oratory which is on the left of the road and on a clear day provides stunning views of the Meije as well as a superb view back down the Romanche Valley

From La Grave to the Col du Lauteret, the road rises for 6 miles (9km) after passing through two tunnels. As the road rises, it is possible to see another glacier coming down from La Meije towards the east, the Glacier de l'Homme. The Col du Lauteret is the watershed between the Romanche that flows west and the Guisanne that drops down south-east to Briançon, where it joins the Durance. There has been a lot

Parc National des Écrins

From Le Bourg d'Oisans it is a short journey on the D530 to reach the valley that leads into the Massif des Écrins to the south. This is the Vénéon Valley that stretches for 15 miles (24km) to the little hamlet of La Bérarde. This is real mountain country. Although the valley is wide and welcoming at the start, it narrows and rises in steps. The road is often deep in the valley and does not allow many views of the peaks on either side. The villages of Venosc and Bourg d'Arud have attracted a lot of artisans. The lute-makers and other craftsmen in Venosc welcome visitors and are worth seeing, particularly on 11th and 12th August when there is a Fête Artisanal in the village. Further up the valley, St Christophe is the traditional home of many families of mountain guides. Nearby a memorial to Pierre Gaspard celebrates his climbing the Meije in 1877.

Most of those who reach La Bérarde, where there is a 5-star camp site, do so to go walking into the mountains above, which have at least ten Alpine huts open in the summer. The closest is the beautifully sited Réfuge du Carrelet, an easy hour's walk alongside the River Vénéon beyond La Bérarde. This is relatively straightforward, but to visit others, detailed maps and advice from the Bureau des Guides at Le Bourg d'Oisans or La Bérarde are essential. It is also quite easy and not too expensive to join a walk organised by the guides. This is perhaps the best way of getting the most from the Parc National des Écrins, the largest and most strictly controlled of all the French Parks. Dogs are not allowed even on a lead. Camping is forbidden, except for overnight bivouacing, and even this is not allowed within an hour's walking distance of the entrance to the park. An insight into the park can be gained by a visit to the Maison du Parc des Écrins in the Rue Gambetta at Le Bourg d'Oisans, which has helpful documentation and exhibitions of aspects of the very wide variety of flora and fauna, which include royal eagles.

The Col de Lauteret

The Col du Lauteret got its name from the presence of a temple *(Alta retum)* built by the Romans to placate the gods of the mountains. Known for this reason as the "Collis de altareto" up until the 12th century, it became subsequently the Col de L'Auteret and only recently acquired its present name. If possible, it is worth visiting the Col in July when the wild Alpine flowers are at their best. There is an Alpine garden at the Col, which is named after its founder Marcel Mirande and is run by the Botany Department of the University of Grenoble. The garden has over 3,000 flowers grouped according to their country of origin as well as relative altitude. It has achieved an international reputation for conserving and studying high-altitude flora. As such, its guide books are in English, as well as other languages.

of modernisation of the road to enable the Col to be kept open throughout the winter, since La Grave is supplied from Briançon. It also ensures that the road link between Grenoble and the Italian border is open all year round, except for occasional days of extreme weather.

The road joining the Col du Lauteret from the Maurienne Valley which has passed over the Col du Galibier is the final section of the Route des Grands Cols that began at Rochetaillée in the Lower Romanche.

La Route Des Grands Cols

If doing this 150 mile (240km) tour as an excursion from Grenoble, it is best to turn off the N91 at Rochetaillée and head north for the first pass, the Col de Glandon. Even if it is spread over several days and includes an exploration of the Maurienne, it is worth going round in this direction if only for the view south after crossing the Col du Galibier at the very end of the circuit, before dropping down to the Col du Lauteret.

From Romanche Valley to Maurienne

The valley of the River Eau d'Olle has two large artificial lakes. The first one, the Lac du Verney, is reached 2 miles (3kms) from Rochetaillée. Passing the second artificial lake, the Lac de Grand' Maison, which is the largest man-made lake in France, held back by the Barrage de Grand' Maison, the Col du Glandon is soon reached.

There is a direct road from the Col down to the Maurienne Valley, but the Route des Grands Cols bears round to the right and continues to climb until it reaches one of the most famous passes in the Alps, the Col de la Croix de Fer, at 6,783ft (2,068m). Beside the car park there is still an iron cross, although it is becoming rather battered in appearance. From this cross there is a very good view of the Grandes Rousses to the south-east. The three peaks that are particularly noticeable are the Aiguilles d'Arves. The café on the opposite side of the road is not very remarkable but does have one traditional local architectural feature. The side walls are built forward of the facade of the building, providing some measure of protection from crosswinds.

There are nearly always cars parked on the Col de la Croix de Fer, because it is a popular entry point for walkers and mountaineers who plan to explore the Massif des Grandes Rousses. The most popular climb from this point is to the top of the Pic de l'Étendard. Usually climbers set off from the Col in the afternoon and stay overnight at a mountain hut. The nearest, the Réfuge de l'Étendard, a rather untidy but welcoming huddle of buildings, is about a 2-hour walk away, but it is on a very clearly marked route and not too steep. It is a very good route for gaining an introduction to high-altitude mountain walking. The mountains above the Col de la Croix de Fer are celebrated for their rich variety of Alpine flowers, which are especially good in June and July. Marmots can be heard calling to each other in late summer as they prepare to hibernate and the cry of choucas (Alpine Choughs) can be heard echoing round the high valleys throughout the summer.

Beyond the Col de la Croix de Fer

St-Jean-de-Maurienne and the valley of the River Arc, which have been glimpsed on many occasions, are now clearly laid out below with the mountains of the Vanoise rising steeply behind. The Route des Grands Cols passes quickly along the valley bottom for 9 miles (14½km) before turning back south towards the Col du Galibier at St Michel-deMaunenne.

Pré de Madame Carle

It is possible to drive north deep into the mountains from Ailefroide to the Pré de Madame Carle. 'Pré' means meadow, but is a considerable misnomer since it is a stony area high in the mountains with very little grass around. This is the starting point for a 3-hour walk to the Glacier Blanc, with the Réfuge du Glacier Blanc at the end of the path. There are different versions of how the Pré Madame Carle got its name. The most likely and most prosaic is that the area was left to Madame Carle in her husband's will. He was Godefroy Carle, President of the Dauphiné and had been granted the land in 1505 by Louis XII. The most well known of the two legends is that Monsieur Carle, a knight returning from the Crusades, found that his wife had been unfaithful and conspired to have her killed on the spot by falling from her horse. A less well known version says that Madame Carle, a widow with several children, spent her life moving stones and cultivating the patch, turning it into a meadow and the site is named as a homage to her self-sacrifice. All versions are explained in the Information Centre which is sited next to the café and is open from 10.00 – 18.00 every day throughout July and August. The site can be reached by bus in the summer months from L'Argentière-la-Bessée in the Durance Valley.

St Michel-de-Maurienne to the Col du Lauteret

This 25-mile (40km) section of La Route des Grands Cols is one of the most famous high-altitude sections of road in the Alps. It rises to the Col du Galibier at 8,665ft (2,642m) before dropping down to the Col du Lauteret 5 miles (8km) later. The first part rises above St Michel, giving good views of the town and valley and after the hamlet of Les Grandes-Seignières enters the trees. There is a parking spot at the Col du Télégraphe, so that the views of the Arc Valley far below can be appreciated and even more so from the nearby Fort du Télégraphe.

*La Gargouille in Briançon's old town. *A*

*The main square in Gap. *A*

After the Col du Télégraphe, the road drops down to the village of Valloire. This is a thriving ski resort and there are numerous modern buildings around the centre, but like many high-altitude villages its history, of which it is very proud, dates back many centuries. The church is very richly decorated inside, the reredos decorated with gold leaf. On the left is a statue of St Pierre, the patron saint of Savoie, while on the right there is a statue of St Thècle, who was born in the village in the sixth century. She was an early pilgrim to the Holy Land, from where she returned with what were supposed to be three fingers of John the Baptist! They are now in the cathedral in St-Jean-de-Maurienne. If at all possible, it is worth visiting Valloire on the Feast of the Assumption, 15 August, when there is a very colourful procession and the ladies wear the beautiful local costume.

The countryside changes at Valloire. The trees no longer grow on the rocky hillsides, which are now bare and covered in scree. For 10 miles (16km) the road threads its way up to the Col du Galibier, before which there is a welcoming café.

The Col du Galibier is frequently included as part of the itinerary in the Tour de France and at the southern end of the tunnel there is a monument to Henri Desgranges (1865-1940), the creator of the Tour. It could be said to stand as a monument to the riders who pass this very severe test of stamina and strength. The tunnel was closed for a number of years for renovation, but has now been reopened, although cyclists are not allowed to use it!

The road drops down to the Col du Lauteret in long rather exposed sweeps contouring round the mountainside. As the lower Col is approached, it is possible to see straight down the long straight Guisane Valley in the direction of Briançon 16 miles (26km) away to the south-east. The Route des Grands Cols can be completed by turning

Parc du Queyras

The road to Guillestre is the start of the only road, which is open all year, into the Queyras region. The centre of the park, Château-Queyras, is 15 miles (24km) to the east and the highest village in Europe, St Véran 6,700 feet, (2,000m) is the same distance beyond. The whole area has the feel of being off the beaten track - a real attraction for its many visitors. In fact, it was suffering economically from this isolation and partly to counter this was made a Parc Naturel Régional in 1977. Wild life is now carefully preserved and craftsmen and women have been assist to return to the area. Every kind of sporting activity, from tennis to white water rafting, has been introduced to encourage visitors and there are detailed programmes of events to encourage people to get to know this fascinating mountain region. These range from tours of all the church sundials, a regional specialty with 300 days of sunshine a year, to guided walks in the mountains often staying overnight in huts as well as crossing into Italy.

towards La Grave and following the River Romanche for 23 miles (37km) back to Rochetaillée.

The Maurienne Valley

The valley of the Maurienne, named after the two patois words *'mau riau'* meaning 'wicked river', is 75 miles (120km) long. It is an important line of communication from France into Italy and for centuries was Savoie's only link with its capital on the other side of the Alps. It now has a road tunnel and a rail tunnel leading into Italy just south of Modane. The Lower (Basse) Maurienne leading from the Combe de Savoie to St Jean is very narrow and the valley bottom is taken up by the very busy motorway, the road, the railway and the river. Wherever possible, factories and power stations have been squeezed in as well. It is not an understatement to say that it is not very attractive. The only reasonable point of access to the upper hillsides is at La Chambre, where the road from the Col du Glandon comes down and meets the road from the Tarentaise that has crossed over the Col de la Madeleine to the north.

Central Maurienne (La Maurienne Centrale) stretches from St Jean to Modane, after which the valley begins a gradual transition as it becomes the Upper (Haute) Maurienne Valley. St Jean-de-Maurienne has always been known as the capital of the Maurienne. Its importance comes from its history - it was for over 1,000 years the seat of the Bishop of the Maurienne. This has left it with an impressive cathedral. At the entrance to the cathedral is the tomb of Humbert of the White Hands (Humbert aux Blanches Mains), the founder of the House of Savoie, and his monument put in place in 1826 by King Charles-Félix. Inside the cathedral, the pulpit and the eighty-two stalls carved of walnut are particularly fine, as is the superb alabaster ciborium on the left of the high altar. The cathedral was built on the site of an earlier church dating from the sixth century that now forms the crypt, which is sometimes open for visitors, as are the fine cloisters dating from 1452.

The road to St Michel-de-Maurienne gets narrow as the town is approached with huge cliffs on the right and steel and aluminium factories along the valley bottom. To explore the Upper Maurienne Valley, the road must be taken for another 10 miles (16km) to Modane. This town is developing as a frontier post after the opening of the Tunnel de Fréjus in

Réfuge de Napoléon

Opposite the main hotel on the Col de Lauteret is a rather squat and somewhat sombre looking building. This was originally a mountain refuge. It is named after Napoléon because he created a fund for building mountain refuges to reward the people of the Alps for their hospitality on his return from Elba. It can be seen from the date that this refuge was not built until many years after his defeat at Waterloo. The building is now used as an exhibition centre by the Parc National Des Écrins.

The Meije

The name of this dramatic looking mountain derives from its original name in the local patois. It was called "L'Oeille de la Meidi-jour" This is the same name as the modern "L'Aiguille du Midi", which overlooks Chamonix, but the locals in this area shortened the name of their mountain to "Meid-jour", which then became shortened to its present name of "Meije".

1980, France's longest road tunnel at 8 miles (12.8km).

Modane is the entrance to the Upper Maurienne Valley that stretches for 27 miles (43km) to the little village of Bonneval-sur-Arc. It is often explored by visitors crossing over in the opposite direction using the Col de l'Iseran from the Tarentaise Valley to the north. Throughout the Middle Ages it became a place of pilgrimage and rest for travellers who had successfully made the crossing from Italy. This accounts for the many religious artifacts in the region, as well as the tradition of manufacturing statues and other objects that grew up in villages such as Bessans.

To get the flavour of the Upper Maurienne Valley straightaway, turn left out of Modane along the D215 towards the village of Aussois. Initially the road passes iron foundries, factories and an electricity generating plant, and there are forts all around in the hills built to protect the road as it comes down from the Mont Cenis Pass. Three of these can be reached by turning right in the village of Aussois. From the next village of Sardières, a pleasant walk of half an hour through the trees leads to a remarkable natural phenomenon, Le Monolithe de Sardières. This isolated piece of rock standing some 295ft (80m) high, rises up above the trees and acts as a sort of milestone marking the start of the real Upper Maurienne Valley.

The village of Termignon is the southern gateway to the Parc National de la Vanoise. It is possible to drive very high into the park here. Termignon is an excellent starting point for short walking tours in the Vanoise, many of which begin in the little village of Bellecombe. It is possible in the summer to get a bus to the car park there to begin walking and there are good mountain huts within fairly easy walking distance.

At Lanslebourg, 5 miles (8km) east of Termignon, the N6 begins to climb the hillside on its way to the historic Col de Mont Cenis, used over the ages by kings and emperors with their armies crossing between France and Italy. At the Col there is a pyramid-shaped building incorporating a chapel, a museum and a Tourist Information Office. The most striking sight is the vast artificial lake kept in place by a huge earth dam at the southern end.

Returning down from the Col du Mont Cenis, the Upper Maurienne Valley stretches up to the right through a narrow gorge of La Madeleine and into the wider section, where the village of Bessans can be seen. This village is the folklore capital of the Upper Maurienne Valley, although it is now developing as a skiing and activity resort. The church

*The Castle at Vizille - the birthplace of the Revolution. *A*

and especially the Chapelle St Antoine are famous for their statues and wall paintings. In the nineteenth century local craftsmen started manufacturing little wooden devils, 'Les diables de Bessans', to commemorate the legend of a local man who reputedly sold his soul to the devil. The traditional ladies' costumes are quite unique, dark dresses combined with aprons and shawls of black and orange, and large wide head-dresses.

*Knives made by Opinel in St Jean de Maurienne. *H*

The villages beyond Bessans are unspoilt examples of typical mountain communities. At the head of the Arc Valley is Bonneval, which is best explored on foot. The houses are built of stone and their roofs are made of stone slabs in a variety of natural colours from light grey to brown. Bonneval is now a mountaineering centre.

The Briançonnais

Briançon is the highest town in Europe at 4,300ft (1,321 in). It is also an important crossroads. It was fortified by Vauban at the very beginning of the eighteenth century to protect the route to and from Italy over the Col de Montgenèvre. It is at the meeting point between the main French Alpine ranges and the Southern and Maritime Alps. It is near the source of the River Durance that flows south through the mountains to meet the Rhône south of Avignon.

The road from the Col du Lauteret passes along the wide Guisanne Valley and the line of hamlets that make up the ski resort of Serre-Chevalier. From the village of Chantemerle a cable car goes to the summit of the Serre Chevalier and there are others, for example from Briançon, which is 5 miles (8km) beyond Chantemerle.

The N91 conveniently skirts round the hillside and meets the N94 at a roundabout just above the old town, known as La Ville Haute, the High Town. It is best to park here on the Champ de Mars car park and enter the town through the Porte Pignerol. Very soon the main street, the Grande Rue, is reached. This is famous for its beautiful period houses and the water trough that runs down the middle, which is known locally as the Grande Gargouille. To the right of the main street is the Church of Notre Dame, also built by Vauban with an eye to defence. It has high walls, twin clock towers, one of which is a sundial, and hardly any windows. To the left of the old town is the Citadelle, which is approached through the Porte Dauphiné. The Citadelle was constructed in 1841 to replace the previous fortifications that had been demolished. The Tourist Office in the Grande Rue has details of organised visits to the old town and the Citadelle. The old town has a timeless quality and has changed little since it was first brought into Vauban's defensive system, but Briançon has developed greatly in the new lower town, known as Briançon-Ste Catherine. This can be reached on foot through the Porte Embrun at the lower end of the old town.

*You cannot get lost! *A*

Briançon, the old Roman town of *Brigantium,* has always been important strategically, but it also has a long history as a tourist centre. The air is clear and the town stands at the entrance to four valleys, the Guisance, the Durance, the Clarée and the Cerveyrette.

The N94 goes towards the east above the old town to the Col de Montgenèvre 8 miles (13km) away. There has been a ski resort at the pass since early in the century. The Clarée Valley bears off the Montgenèvre road 2 miles (3¹4km) outside Briançon and leads up to the village of Névache 10 miles (16km) beyond. The valley is soft and verdant with some delightful houses and churches, but the surrounding mountains are very high and rugged. Beyond Névache it is relatively isolated, and wildlife, especially the flowers, are undisturbed.

The Cerveyrette Valley to the south-east leads up to the very desolate Col de l'Izoard before the road continues into the Parc Naturel Régional du Queyras. This is normally approached from the south. Its name comes from the local dialect and means 'the large crag'. As the most isolated of all the National Parks, it is a haven for both flora and fauna. Certain butterflies such as the *Papillon Isabella* are found nowhere else in Europe.

From Briançon to Gap

The busy N94 goes south from Briançon and 60 miles (96km) later meets the Route Napoléon at Gap, after turning west at Embrun. It skirts the Massif des Écrins and provides access to the National Park first from a valley named La Vallouise, which is reached by turning right at L'Argentière-la-Bessée. This lovely valley was named after King Louis XI. In the early middle ages it was a base for the followers of an early religious reformer, Pierre Valdo. He was excommunicated and his followers were eventually defeated. One of those who tried to convert them was a Vincent Ferrier, after whom the village of Puy St-Vincent is named. There are also memorials in the valley to the followers of Pierre Valdo, the 'Vaudois'. The village of Ailefroide is the mountaineering centre of the valley and is the point of departure for the walk along the valley of the 'Celse Nière' to the 'Réfuge de Sélé' in the National Park. There are other access points and the many ways of enjoying the National Park are clearly explained in the many booklets produced by the National Park Authority and available throughout the area as well as at the Maison du Parc National des Écrins near the village of Vallouise.

The N94 follows the course of the river Durance south and 10 miles (16km) later the river Guil joins it from the left. The confluence of the two rivers is guarded by another Vauban construction. This is Mont-Dauphin, built in the eighteenth century as a fortified town, but never inhabited except as a military fort. It can be visited by turning left towards Eygliers. It is an interesting example of a military fortification and among the many exhibitions there is a good one about Vauban's work.

The whole region at one time was controlled on behalf of the Holy Roman Emperor by the local archbishops, whose see was centred on the town of Embrun. It is worth leaving the N94 and turning left into the town not only to see the Cathédrale Notre Dame-du-Réal, but to take advantage of the viewpoint from the gardens next to the Cathedral in the Place de L'Archevêché. The interior of the cathedral is considerably more interesting and impressive than its exterior might suggest. The alternating rows of dark and light stone attract the eye and the whole interior is lit by an impressive rose window. The organ, one of the oldest in France, but at present being restored, was donated by King Louis XI, who made a pilgrimage to the church. It is probable that the cathedral was named after this event, since Réal is a corruption of Royal. In the gardens outside there is a statue of a French poet and socialist politician, Clovis-Hugues, whose love of the town is described in the poem carved into the book which forms part of the statue. The gardens are on the edge of a vertical 250ft (75m) drop to the Durance valley. At the parapet there is an orientation table to help situate the many peaks which can be seen on the other side of the deep wide valley. There is considerable concern in the town that this viewpoint will be spoiled by a bypass being constructed directly below it.

Before leaving Embrun, it is worth taking a two minute walk to the Tour Brune. It has recently been renovayed and the ground floor provides information about the Parc National des Écrins and there are semi-permanent exhibitions.

It is evident that Embrun is a town devoted to tourists and many come to visit the Lac de Serre Ponçon. There are interesting trips into the mountains, such as the skiing area of Les Orres to the south of Embrun and the ancient abbey of Boscodon, set deep in the Forest of Boscodon to the south of the lake. However all interest seems to be centred on the lake and the many facilities which it provides. Many of these, such as boat rides, sailing, windsurfing and water skiing, can be found at Savines-Le-Lac, beside the bridge which carries the N94 for a quarter of a mile across the lake. The village was constructed in 1959 since the original was submerged by the rising waters. The lake, in the form of a crescent as the waters of the Durance rose up towards Embrun and the waters of the Ubaye rose up its valley south-east, is the largest man made lake in Europe. The original church of Savines, the Chapelle St Michel, has been rebuilt on a promontory in the Baie St Michel. It is now much photographed as it stands apparently isolated in the water.

The N94 moves away from the lake after passing above the Baie St Michel and 15 miles (24km) later reaches the town of Gap. There is an excellent museum, the Musée Departemental, on the left in the Parc de la Pepinière, just before the inner ring road. Beyond this junction there is, straight ahead, a statue of the Baron Ladoucette. He was a Préfet of the Département Des Hautes Alpes who is credited with modernising the towns and opening up communications at the beginning of the nineteenth century. Behind his statue is a very good car park from where it is easy to explore the centre of the town, which is largely pedestrianised.

Notre Dame de la Salette

In the church at Corps there is a monument on the right hand side, showing two children, Maximin and Mélanie, looking up at a statue of Our Lady. This is to commemorate an event which took place in 1846, when two shepherd children stated that they had seen a vision of the Virgin Mary. Just beyond the church at the southern end of the village there is a left turn to the spot where this took place, now called Notre Dame de la Salette. The road goes up to the enormous basilica which was built to commemorate the children's vision and welcomes great numbers of pilgrims, especially on the Feast of the Assumption (15th August).

Places to Visit: Hautes Alpes

Lower Romanche Valley

Lac de Laffrey

Lac de Laffrey
38220 Laffrey
☎ 04 76 73 16 37
Boats can be hired and fishing can be arranged.

Notre Dame de la Salette

38970 La Salette
☎ 04 76 30 00 11
www.lasalette.cef.fr
The church is permanently open during daylight hours to welcome pilgrims. The website has an English section which explains the various organizations which look after pilgrims and visitors.

Valgaudemar

Syndicat d'initiative
05800 La Chapelle en Valgaudemar
☎ 04 92 55 23 21
The tourist office is open from mid-Jun to mid-Sept 10.00–12.00 and 15.00–19.00 and it provides lots of information about activities in the valley.

Le Chalet Hotel du Gioberney

The Information office is open every day from mid-May to mid-Oct.

Vizille

Musée de La Révolution Française de Vizille W

38220, Vizille
☎ 04 76 68 07 35
Fax: 04 76 68 08 53
www.musee-revolution-francaise.fr
The park is free and is open every day except Tue 10.00–19.00 (20.00 from Jun to Aug). The museum is open every day except Tue 10.00–18.00 from Apr to Oct and 10.00–17.00 in Nov. Closed at other times.

Le Chemin de Fer de la Mure

La Gare W

38450 Saint Georges de Commiers
☎ 0 8 92 39 14 26
www.trainlamure.com
Throughout Jul and Aug a train leaves Georges-de-Commiers at the same time as a train leaves La Mure. These times are 9.45, 12.00, 14.30, 17.00. In May, Jun and Sept they are 9.45 and 14.30. In Apr and Oct two trains leave Georges de Commiers, at 9.45 and 14.30, but only one leaves La Mure at 17.00.

La Mine Image W

Les 4 Galeries
38770 La Motte d'Aveillans
☎ 04 76 30 68 74
www.mine-image.com
A visit to this mining museum,

set in a one-time mine, is usually incorporated with a train ride, but individual visitors are welcomed. It is open only at weekends and in the afternoon during Jan, Feb, Mar, Apr, May, Oct, Nov and Dec. From Jun to Sept there are guided tours on the hour from 10.00–17.00.

L'Oisans – Central Romanche

Le Bourg d'Oisans

Musée des Minéraux et de la faune des Alpes W

Place de l'église
38520 Bourg d'Oisans.
☎ 04 76 80 27 54
Open every day from Mon to Fri, 9.00–12.00 and 14.00–17.00.

Huez, La Maison du Patrimoine

Musée d'Huez et de l'Oisans

Route de la Poste
38750 Alpe d'Huez
☎ 04 76 11 21 74
www.musee.alpedhuez.com
Open every day except Sat 10.00–12.00 and 15.00–19.00 from Dec to Apr and in Jul and Aug.

The Upper Romanche

La Grave Cable Car

Open from mid-Jun to mid-Sept. During Jul and Aug a car leaves every five minutes 8.00–15.45. At other times every half-hour 10.00–15.45.

Jardin Botanique Alpin du Lauteret

Col du Lautaret
05480 VILLAR D'ARENE
☎ 04 92 24 41 62
www.web.ujf-grenoble.fr
The garden is open from early Jun to late Sept every day 10.00–18.00. The website has a good English section and the brochure accompanying a visit can be downloaded.

La Route des Grands Cols

Réfuge de l'Étendard

Réfuge gardé du Club Alpin Français

73 St Sorlin d'Arves
☎ of réfuge for booking: 04 79 59 74 96
There are a great number of mountain huts throughout the whole region but this is one which merits a visit because of its altitude and comparative ease of access.

Cont'd overleaf

Cont'd from previos page

W = Perfect for Wet days

Places to Visit: Hautes Alpes

St-Jean-de-Maurienne

Musée de l'Opinel W

25 rue Jean Jorès
73300 St Jean de Maurienne
☎ 04 79 64 04 78
www.opinel-musee.com
The museum is open throughout the year from 9.00–12.00 and 14.00–19.00 except on Sun and national holidays

The Maurienne Valley

Aussois

Maison d'Aussois

73000 Aussois
☎ 04 79 20 30 80
www.aussois.com
This office has details of every kind of activity from visiting the Forts de l'Esseillon to hiring a donkey. They will also arrange walks and climbs through the Bureau des Guides.

Col de Mont Cenis

Pyramide du Mont Cenis

Plan des Fontainettes
73480 Lanslebourg Mont Cenis
☎ 04 79 05 92 95
This museum, which concentrates on life as it was before the building of the dam, is open from mid-Jun to the end of Aug 10.00–12.30 and 14.00–18.00.

Bonneval

Office de Tourisme de Bonneval-sur-Arc

73480 Bonneval-sur-Arc
☎ 04 79 05 95 95
www.bonneval-sur-arc.com
The office and its English website give a lot of information about activities in this high mountain area.

The Briançonnais

Briançon

Office du Tourisme

1, place du Temple
05100 Briançon
☎ 04 92 21 08 50
www.briancon.com
The Tourist office which is open every day from 9.00–12.00 and 14.00–18.00 can arrange visits to the forts such as Fort des Salettes and Fort du Château as well as providing information about guided walks.

Maison du Parc national des Écrins

Place Médecin Général Blanchard

05100 Briançon
☎ 04 92 21 08 49
www.les-ecrins-parc-national.fr
There are a number of offices providing information about the national park. There is another very

good one at Vallouise as well as a small exhibition at Pré Madame Carle.

Parc Naturel Régional du Queyras

Maison du Parc
05350 Arvieux
☎ 04 92 46 88 20
www.pnr-queyras.fr
This office has a lot of information in English about activities in the Nationl Park and guided visits.

From Briançon to Gap

Mont-Dauphin **W**

Quartier des Artisans d'Art,
05600 MONT-DAUPHIN-FORT
☎ 04 92 45 17 80
Open from Jun to Sept 9.00–12.00 and 14.00–18.00. From Oct to Mar 14.00–17.00.

Savines-Le-Lac

La BD Pirates

05160 Savines-le-lac
☎ 06 86 01 24 49
www.savineslelac.com
Boat hire company. There are also excursions on the lake, lasting about an hour and a half. These begin beside the bridge which takes the N94 over the lake.

L'Abbaye de Boscodon

Abbaye de Boscodon
05200 CROTS
☎ 04 92 43 14 45
The Abbey church is open from 8.30–18.00 and is free of charge. A small charge is made for seeing the cloisters and the exhibition.

Musée Departemental, Gap **W**

6, avenue du Maréchal Foch
05000 Gap
☎ 04 92 51 01 58
The museum is open from July to Sept 10.00–12.00 and 14.00–18.00. from Sept to Jun it is only open in the afternoon and is closed all day on Tue.

Getting There

By Air

The most popular airport for visitors to the region is Geneva, but Satolas Airport near Lyon is a very quick way into the area, since it is just beside the A40 15 miles (24km) to the east of Lyon. The smaller airports of Grenoble St Geoirs and Chambéry are being developed by cheaper airlines to take an increasing share of tourist traffic. Chambéry Airport is used mainly in the winter months.

By Road

Modern motorways make access to this region very much easier. The motorways into the region from the west branch off the main north-south motorway, the A6. To get to the Jura, the A36 from Beaune goes direct to Besançon and even further east. The central section is served by the A40, which turns off the A6 at Macon. To reach the southern part of the area, it is best to take the A6 towards Lyon and then the A43 that threads its way to Chambéry and Annecy. This motorway crosses through the very centre of the region and gives the greatest degree of access, since it goes on to join the A40. The A48 is another useful means of access to the region, since it turns south off the A43 some 25 miles (40km) east of Lyon and goes direct to Grenoble.

The major roads into the region often follow the same sort of line as the motorways, but although cheaper and much more interesting tend to take longer. From the Paris area, the N5 goes via Dijon to the northern part, and the N6 via Lyon and Chambéry to the southern part. The N85 branches off the N6 and goes to Grenoble.

Within the region the road network is very good. There are inevitably some roads to avoid because of congestion — these are covered in the body of the guide, but overall the main roads give good access and although spectacular in places are relatively easy to use. It is worth mentioning that a car must be in good repair because the roads can be quite demanding on gears and brakes.

By Rail

The rail system into, and through, the region is very good. The trains leave Paris from the Gare de Lyon. Trains to the Jura nearly all pass through Dole and then either continue on into Switzerland through Frasne and Pontarlier in the centre or turn north to Besançon. The high speed trains, the TGV, reach Besançon in 2 hours 29 minutes or Pontarlier in 3 hours and 8 minutes. Normal express trains take 2 hours longer.

Haute Savole is reached via Macon and Culoz. The journey by TGV to Bellegarde takes 2 hours 58 minutes and Annecy 3 hours 31 minutes. Trains go direct to Savoie from the Gare de Lyon in Paris, and the whole length of the Tarentaise Valley is now electrified to take the TGV to Bourg-St-Maurice. The TGV time to Grenoble is 3 hours 10 minutes, but it is sometimes necessary to change at Lyon.

To transport the car, there are regular trains throughout the summer, which go direct to Briançon on certain nights. However no car transporters go direct from the Channel ports.

Within the region, the SNCF has a good network of local transport, often using buses as well as trains. These trains and buses provide an excellent method of exploring the region. For example the train from St Gervais up the Arve Valley is a particularly dramatic way of approaching Chamonix and seeing Mont Blanc.

Maps

There are many maps of the region, in a very varied format and different scale. The most well known tend to be the Michelin Local maps in a scale of 1: 150,000. The map numbers in this series needed to cover the area are as follows:

Doubs and Jura	321
Ain Savoie	328
Isère Savoie	333
Alpes de Provence Hautes Alpes	334

The Institut Géographique National, known as 'Cartes ign' publish maps in different scales. The Carte Régionale with a scale of 1: 250,000 is good for general touring. The map numbers for this region are as follows:

Franche Comté	R10
Rhône Alpes	R14
Provence-Alpes-Côte d'Azur	R18

Berlitz have just produced the start of a new series of motoring maps at 1: 200,000 scale. These include N°7 Rhône-Alps and N°11 Provence, Alps and French Riviera. They cover the area between the Mediterranean and north of Geneva.

Ign also do excellent maps at 1: 125,000 for exploring specific areas and if intending to go hiking the 1: 100,000 series is the most appropriate map. These are available in all good "librairies".

Climate

The climate of the eastern side of France is affected both by Atlantic and continental influences. Summer temperatures tend to be higher and winter temperatures tend to be lower than the average in France. It also means that late in the year between September and November the region is subject to very heavy rainfall. It is because the Atlantic is at its warmest and the westerly winds carry large amounts of water vapour. The mountains force the moisture-laden air upwards, and as it cools it turns to rain or snow. In most winters the Alpine region is covered with snow down to the lowest valleys. During spring and early summer the snowline recedes up the hillsides, uncovering pastures until it reaches the permanent snowline. As the rain clouds sweep eastwards across France, the first hills that they meet generally get the heaviest rainfall. For this reason the Pre-Alps and the Jura get heavier falls of rain than the areas further to the east. Deep into the mountains there are by comparison some very low figures. Not only is there a decrease in rainfall towards the east, there is less in the southern part of the region. The Jura is more subject to continental influences and as a result tends to get rain quite frequently in late August and September.

It is difficult to generalise about temperature in any mountainous area. The mountains can expose certain areas to wind and cold and prevent the sun from reaching them, while at the same time they can protect other areas from the wind and leave them to bask in the sunlight. The distinction between south-facing slopes (the adret) and the shady slopes (the ubac) has great significance throughout the region. It has affected the development of towns and the use of land, and obviously has a great effect on land prices, both for agriculture and house building.

Altitude causes great variation in temperature. When there was an observatory at the summit of Mont Blanc, the lowest temperature recorded was -9'F (-43'C). On average the temperature change is about 1 degree Celsius for every thousand feet of height, but this can be greatly affected by which way the mountain faces or how protected the site is. The Lac des Rousses in the Jura is frozen on average for 30 days a year, while 50 miles (80km) south beside the Lac du Bourget the village of Brison is so protected that olive trees are grown there. The average temperatures for January and July in Chamonix are 28'F (-6'C) and 63'F (17'C). Chamonix is situated at about 3,280ft (1,000m). Annecy is only a few miles away but at 1,410ft (430m) and in a very sheltered spot has figures of 34'F (1'C) and 63'F (19'C).

The altitude and the temperature dictate whether the moisture falls as rain or snow. Some years winters may be very mild and worry the ski operators, while other years the snow lies for a long time and to a great depth, causing damage from avalanches and flooding meltwater. Generally it will always fall as snow above 9,840ft (3,000m) adding to the neige éternelle, the permanent snow. But at lower levels there can be great differences because of altitude within very small areas. On the French shore of Lac Léman at Thonon there are only l0in (25cm) of snow a year, while the village of Tour near Mont Blanc 31 miles (50km) away recorded 33ft (10m) of snow every year for 37 consecutive years.

Accommodation

The region of the Jura and the Alps is very well equipped, with every sort of accommodation from hotels to holiday cottages. Before booking accommodation, the visitor to the area must have a fairly clear idea of what sort of stay he or she wants in the area, because the nature of the countryside can make travelling a slow business.

Every type of accommodation has its advantages and disadvantages, and there is such a variety that visitors will need to match their requirements with what is available. There are hotels of the highest quality throughout the region, some of the best being on the shores of Lac Léman or in traditional spa towns such as Aix-les-Bains. There are less grand hotels everywhere, many with good restaurants serving regional specialities. This can be a major advantage of staying in a slightly smaller hotel. Many of these smaller hotels call themselyes auberges, and some in the evenings act as canteens for French people who prefer to have their evening meal out. On these occasions the visitor has a great opportunity to experience local specialities as served in an everyday atmosphere. It can be quite as rewarding as more expensive and more fashionable establishments.

This region has a wider range of non-hotel accommodation than in any other part of France. The most well-known perhaps is the gîte or gîte rural. This can be translated roughly as a holiday home and would normally be rented for a minimum of a week. They are all carefully inspected and graded. A certain standard of accommodation and equipment is guaranteed. There are 6,100 of these scattered throughout the area, but they are so popular with people booking from year to year that it is essential to book a long time in advance. Their popularity suggests what good value they are. Contact addresses for gîtes as for all the other types of accommodation will be found in tourist office brochures and on their websites.

Many brochures mention gîtes d'étape and gîtes d'enfants. Both of these are more like hostels, but have usually been set up for a particular purpose. The gîtes d'étape, of which there are 140 in the region, are for stays of one or two nights, mainly for people doing a long-distance walk or pony trek. They have permanent wardens and are ideal for a short stop-over. Gîtes d'enfants are similar, but are for children who would stay for longer than a few days. They act as a base for groups of children on outdoor pursuit activities. The auberges de jeunesse are youth hostels, but generally take young adults and since many provide evening meals, staying in youth hostels is a very good way of visiting the region and meeting other young people of different nationalities.

One of the best ways of really getting to know an area is to stay with local families, who offer rooms with bed and breakfast. These are called chambres d'hôtes, and the families in this region offering this number well over 1000. This sort of accommodation can be even more interesting on a farm. More farmers see this as an added and welcome income.

There are campsites throughout the region, many of a very high standard. They can be found easily in a specialist camper's book. Some of them offer bungalows or mobile homes for rent by the week. But the area has quite a number of campsites attached to farms. These tend to be more personal and the farmers are encouraged to interest the campers in the surrounding area and the local produce. There are over 300 of these camping à la ferme, and they offer to someone really interested in the region more than the traditional campsite.

Finally, the subject of accommodation in the Alps would not be complete without mention of mountain huts. These are owned and run either by the Club Alpin Français (the CAF) or the National Parks. Some provide meals, but many only provide sleeping accommodation. This is normally in the form of bunkhouses. A few mountain huts, called réfuges in French, have surprisingly good facilities considering their altitude. Perhaps the most modern and best-equipped is the Réfuge Felix Faure in the Parc National de la Vanoise. This is a hard 2-hour walk from Pralognan, but worth the effort of getting there. A smaller and more accessible one is the Réfuge de l'Étendard, about 2 hours' quite easy walk from the Col de la Croix de Fer.

A word of warning. It is essential to book places in high altitude huts. Unless a place has been booked well in advance, avoid the mountain huts in the Mont Blanc massif, especially in summer. They tend to be very full and not very comfortable for this reason, and at the height of the season people often have to sleep outside!

There are addresses of websites for booking in the list below.

Cycling

As will be clear when driving, cycling is taken very seriously in France and cyclists are out on the highest passes following the Tour de France route. The Route des Grandes Alpes is becoming a popular run. Cyclists tend to be accepted more by French motorists and given a wider berth so it is safer. Because cycling is so popular, it is quite easy to hire road bikes in any small town. The tourist offices will have lists of companies which hire bikes.

There has been a great increase in the amount of off-road cycling (VTT) and an opening up of routes. Most cable cars allow bikes to be transported if there are high altitude off-road routes. This is a particularly popular activity in the Vercors region.

Fishing

There is good fly fishing in the rivers and a number of associations to assist, such as

FLY GUIDE ACTION

Jean-François Dussart

Guide de pêche
70 Chemin de la Gare
73100 Mouxy
Guide Alpes Pêche organise courses throughout the region but mainly on the River Doubs. They can be contacted on www.alpes-peche.com

Fishing is allowed in all the lakes, but the precise rules for fishing in each lake need to be obtained from tourist offices or fishing clubs. There are a number of accredited guides who cover the area and their details can be obtained from Organisation de Séjours Pêche Personnalisés

Le Village
38480 St Albin de Vaulserre
www.rhonealpespeche.com

Golf

Golf has increased in popularity in France and there are an increasing number of golf courses throughout this region, some in quite unlikely places, considering the terrain. The classic courses are near the traditional tourist centres, such as Annecy, Aix-les-Bains and Évian, but whichever course is chosen there will be a warm welcome.

Golf Club d'Aix les Bains
95, avenue du Golf
73100 Aix les Bains
www.golf-aixlesbains.com

Golf Club du Lac d'Annecy
www.golf-lacannecy.com

Évian Masters Golf Club
Royal Parc Évian
Rive Sud du lac de Geneve
74500 Évian
☎ 04 50 75 46 66

These are the classic courses, but there are many local ones such as the beautiful 18 hole course at Corrençon in the Vercors which can be contacted be contacted at

Golf International de Grenoble
Route de Montavie
38320 Bresson
☎ 04.76.73.65.00
www.golfgrenoble.nexenservices.com

Hot Air Ballooning

There are a number of resorts where it is possible to take a flight in a Hot Air Balloon, called a Montgolfière after its French inventor, but one of the world capitals of Hot Air Ballooning is near Megève in the little village of Praz-sur-Arly. The contact address for information on this is:

Alpes Montgolfière

776 Route du plan de l'Aar,
74210 Praz sur Arly
☎ 04 50 55 50 60
www.alpes-montgolfiere.fr

Other useful addresses:

Haut-Doubs Montgolfiere

Grange des Houillettes
25300 Pontarlier
☎ 03 81 69 68 44
www.haut-doubs-montgolfiere.com

Espace Montgolfières

25, avenue Jean Moulin
39000 Lons le Saunier
☎ 03 84 47 66 61
www.espace-montgolfieres.com

Ballon Libre Haut-Jura

14, rue Pasteur
39200 Saint-Claude
☎ 03.84.45.07.80
www.aventurier.fr

Hang Gliding

Hang gliding in all its forms is carried out throughout the region, as can be clearly seen. On a sunny day the skies are full of hang gliders, using every kind of craft from the rigid deltaplanes to the single parachutes, called parapentes in French and in September the skies above the Grésivaudan near Grenoble are filled with the participants in the annual Coupe Icare. It is possible for the inexperienced to hire accompanied rides. They are advertised as "tandem" or "biplace". The local tourist office will always have the names of companies that offer these rides, but some useful addresses with English websites are:

Summits Professional Training

Le Mummery
27, allée du Savoy
74400 Chamonix Mont-Blanc
☎ 04 50 53 50 14
www.summits.fr

Sport 2000 - Les Volatiles

196 Avenue des Jeux olympiques
73620 Les Saisies
☎ 04 79 38 95 54
www.les-volatiles.com

Aeroslide

30 Allée de la Nublière
74210 DOUSSARD
☎ 04 50 44 32 14
www.aeroslide.com

Écrins Vol Libre

Chalet Bulle d'Air - Le Chateau
05260 Ancelle
☎ 04.92.50.80.86
www.aventurier.fr

Poupet Vol Libre

39110 Saint-Thiebaud
☎ 03 84 73 04 56
www.poupetvollibre.com

Découv'Air

32 rue du Comté de Montbéliard
25660 MONTFAUCON
☎ 06 23 18 35 42
www.decouv-air.com

Tout Doubs Parapente

56 bis rue Henri Baigue
25000 Besançon
☎ 03 81 80 38 90
www.parateam.com

Kayak and Canoe

This is another sport which is widely practised in the region from the Doubs in the Jura to the Durance south of Briançon. Local tourist offices will have full information about what is going on in their area. One of the most internationally renowned centres is the Tarentaise Valley and a good address for information about this area is:

Coureurs de Rivières

Vulmix
Bourg St Maurice/Les Arcs
73700 France
☎ 04 79 04 11 22
www.coureurs-rivieres.com

For general information about canoeing and kayaking the website of canoe-rhonealpes is excellent in that it has maps showing every river in the region. They can be contacted at:

Comité Régional Rhône-Alpes Canoë-Kayak

16 place Jean-Jacques Rousseau
38304 BOURGOIN-JALLIEU
☎ 04 74 19 16 12
www.canoe-rhonealpes.com

White Water Rafting

This is a popular sport on many Alpine rivers and is quite safe if done with reputable companies. Some addresses which might be useful are:

Adventures Payraud

1871 chemin des peupliers
74190 Passy
☎ 04 50 93 63 63
www.sportsdeco.net

A7Aventures

Bioge
74200 La Vernaz
☎ O4 50 72 15 12
www.7aventures.com

Franceraft Zone de Loisirs,

73210 Centron
☎ 04 79 55 63 55
www.rafting-savoie.com

Websites

Where possible above, websites have been indicated with postal addresses under the different headings. The websites below will prove to be of value for general enquiries.

For the Franche Comte Region (Chapter 1)

www.interfrance.com/en/fc/franche-comte.html

For the Doubs Region (Chapter 2)

www.doubs.com For the Jura Region (Chapter 3)
www.jura-france.net

For the Prealpine Region (Chapter 4) an excellent site, but with no English,

www.123savoie.com

For Haute Savoie (Chapter 5). This is covered by 123savoie, but also see

www.savoiehautesavoie.com

For Savoie (Chapter 6) the most comprehensive site for links to smaller sites is

www.savoie.rhone-alpes-tourisme.com

For Grenoble (Chapter 7)

www.grenoble-isere-tourisme.com

For the Chartreuse and Vercors Regions (Chapter 8)

www.chartreuse-tourisme.com
www.vercors.com

For the Isere Region (Chapter 9)

www.isere-tourisme.com
www.ot-briancon.fr

For finding out about Mountain Huts and booking beds

www.chamonix.net/english/accommodation/caf_huts.htm
www.clubalpin-chamonix.com
www.clubalpinannecy.com
www.queyras.com
www.les-ecrins-parc-national.fr
www.vanoise.com/indexgb.htm

Index

M

N

O

P

Q

R

S

T

V

Y

Published in the UK by
Landmark Publishing Ltd,
Ashbourne Hall, Cokayne Ave, Ashbourne, Derbyshire DE6 1EJ England
☎: (01335) 347349 Fax: (01335) 347303
e-mail: landmark@clara.net
website: www.landmarkpublishing.co.uk

1st Edition
ISBN 13: 978-1-84306-312-4
ISBN 1-84306-312-3

British Library Cataloguing in Publication Data: a catalogue record for this book is available from the British Library.

Print: Cromwell Press, Trowbridge
Design: Michelle Hunt
Cartography: James Allsopp

Front cover: In Chanonix, looking down the Rue du Docteur Paccard towards the Aiguille du Midi . *B
Back cover, top: Cable cars crossing the Isére. *A
Back cover, middle: Château de Menthon. *A
Back cover, bottom: Chartreuse - Cross country sking. *C

DISCLAIMER
While every care has been taken to ensure that the information in this book is as accurate as possible at the time of publication, the publishers and author accept no responsibility for any loss, injury or inconvenience sustained by anyone using this book.